BAR YARNS AND MANIC-DEPRESSIVE MIXTAPES

BAR YARNS AND MANIC-DEPRESSIVE MIXTAPES

JIM WALSH ON MUSIC FROM MINNEAPOLIS TO THE OUTER LIMITS

Jim Walsh

University of Minnesota Press

Minneapolis

London

Published by the University of Minnesota Press
111 Third Avenue South, Suite 290
Minneapolis, MN 55401-2520
http://www.upress.umn.edu

Printed in the United States of America on acid-free paper

The University of Minnesota is an equal-opportunity educator and employer.

22 21 20 19 18 17 16   10 9 8 7 6 5 4 3 2 1

Library of Congress Cataloging-in-Publication Data
Names: Walsh, Jim.
Title: Bar yarns and manic-depressive mixtapes : Jim Walsh on music from Minneapolis to the Outer Limits / Jim Walsh.
Description: Minneapolis : University of Minnesota Press, [2016] | Includes bibliographical references and index.
Identifiers: LCCN 2016035700 (print) | ISBN 978-1-5179-0181-3 (hc) | ISBN 978-1-5179-0007-6 (pb)
Subjects: LCSH: Walsh, Jim—Anecdotes. | Music journalists—United States—Anecdotes. | Popular music—United States—Anecdotes. | Minneapolis (Minn.)—Anecdotes.
Classification: LCC ML423.W27 A5 2016 (print) | DDC 781.64092 [B]—dc23
LC record available at https://lccn.loc.gov/2016035700

CONTENTS

The sway of alcohol over mankind is unquestionably due to its power to stimulate the mystical faculties of human nature, usually crushed to earth by the cold facts and dry criticisms of the sober hour.

—William James, nineteenth-century philosopher and mystic

INTRODUCTION
GOING UNDERGROUND

My earliest memory of scribbling in a notebook while listening to music is New Year's Eve, 1974.

I was fourteen and then as now not a big fan of mean girls and boys, so that night I intentionally stayed away from the junior high parties and was happy to have my big brother Jay's bedroom all to myself. He was at work as a busboy and waiter at Anchor Inn, now Bunny's in St. Louis Park, where our Uncle Tommy tended bar for many years.

I can still see the view from Jay's window that accompanied so much of my marathon listening sessions those long-ago dreamy nights: a basketball hoop and our driveway, that still swishless nylon net alit by the Fifty-first and South Colfax–Aldrich alley lamp, and all those Minnesota stars as I hit the outer limits with Rod Stewart, Elton John, the Rolling Stones, the Monkees, America, Joni Mitchell, Bob Dylan, John Denver, James Taylor, Simon and Garfunkel, Bread, Cat Stevens. . . .

Jay had great taste, smart ears, a luscious glow-in-the-dark turntable, a killer stereo system, and all the good records, and he almost always indulged my hanging out in his room at all hours of the day and night, locking myself in his little vinyl church as I would at a time when my Catholic school education was fast being eclipsed (and augmented) by the real-time fire and mysticism I was mainlining via rock 'n' roll and singer/songwriters.

That last night of 1974 as I plowed through my eighth grade favorites, in a bed heaped with shimmering black vinyl records laying out of their jackets and all across the bed and floor, I listened intently into the wee hours of 1975 and wrote about how the music made me feel, where I was in my life, how it helped give me perspective on all those as-yet out-of-reach adult ideas of love, desire, and the big mysteries of life. I quoted lyrics and doodled and wrote down questions and observations until 4 A.M.

Summerteeth

NO MATTER HOW MUCH they liked or disliked Cameron Crowe's *Almost Famous* as a whole, the scene that most affected everyone I've talked to is the one where the older sister leaves home. Before she does, she tells Crowe's fifteen-year-old character, "Someday you'll be cool. Look under your bed."

When he does, he finds a treasure trove of albums. He flips through the jackets with a mixture of wide-eyed wonder and golden-boy guilt, before coming to The Who's *Tommy*. He pulls it from the stack and finds a note stuck to it that reads, "Light a candle and listen to this, and you will see your future."

For anyone who was raised on vinyl, that moment will carry a certain amount of nostalgic significance. And although it doesn't always happen with so much ceremony, the ritual of older sisters or brothers handing down records to their younger siblings is as time-honored a custom in rock fandom as first beers, first concerts, first crushes.

In the film and in real life, Crowe's sister splits, and he doesn't see her again for several years. I suppose because his character becomes a rock critic, many people have asked me about that scene and about how I first got hooked on music. My answer is, I like the ending to my story better: my older brother Jay gave me full access to his record collection, but he stuck around, and we became best friends through music.

The night I saw *Almost Famous,* that scene took me back to Jay's bedroom, where I spent so much of my adolescence. I can still feel the curve of his sunken mattress under me, the snug fit of the headphones, the stereo receiver glowing in the dark, the lingering smell of incense. I can still see the sticker from Joni Mitchell's *Blue* affixed to one wall, across the way from a poster of Steve McQueen on his motorcycle ready to jump the fence at the end of *The Great Escape.*

I'm four years younger than Jay, which seems like nothing today.

But when you're fourteen and your big brother is eighteen, it feels like an unconquerable chasm between geekdom and cool. For so long, we were living under the same roof, following the same rules. Then, suddenly, he was out in the world, driving, working, going to high school and then college, exploring, experimenting.

And bringing home lots of really cool records.

When he was at work, I'd lock myself in his room, get under the blankets, put out the lights, and put on the headphones. My own record collection was growing, I was figuring out what I liked and what I didn't, but his was big and heavy and mysterious. And since they were his records, whenever I alternated from mine to his, I learned something about him and got an inkling about what he was going through. Which was important, because our main mode of communication in those years was grunting at each other. I was a tagalong, he was checked out. But with music, we slowly found a common language that spread to our younger brother, Terry, and our three sisters. I've occasionally wondered what all our lives would be like had Jay never filled that big milk carton box next to his bed with records.

Some nights, I'd fall asleep in his room with the headphones on, only to wake up to the sound of him banging on the door and yelling my name. My rose-colored glasses have probably dimmed this memory, but I can't ever remember his being truly mad at me for putting him out of his own room. He probably cut me some slack— not because we were having heart-to-hearts about music (those would come later), but because I think he knew that I was getting the same thing out of it that he was. Maybe he even suspected it was something we could share.

Something we still share. Over the years we've been to countless bar shows and concerts together, and even though we don't go out as much as we used to, the bond is there. Different songs remind me of him, stuff we did, conversations we've had, and they stick in my head like parts of the songs themselves. Then there's newer music, the introduction to which always starts with one of us going, "Hey, have you heard that new . . . ?"

One of our latest loves is Wilco. God, we love Wilco. We love Wilco in the same way we've loved The Clash, the New York Dolls, the Stones, the Replacements, Ike Reilly, the Faces, and dozens more. We love them because they have roots that go all the way back to that bedroom but that are planted firmly in our adult homes. We love them because their latest, *Summerteeth,* is a terrific rock 'n' roll record, and what that means, all that that means to us, is that it is a record about love and liberation, which at its core is what all the best rock 'n' roll is always about.

We love "We're Just Friends," which celebrates the confusing power of platonic love, and "She's a Jar," which could only have been written by a married man with kids, who knows by heart the Springsteen lyric, "God have mercy on the man who doubts what he's sure of." We love Wilco because their songs tell the truth, and the truth that "Pieholden Suite" holds is that even when they try their best, sometimes good men hurt the ones they love.

And we love them because when I called Wilco's Jeff Tweedy to talk about all this the other day, he said, "I mostly got turned on to records by my older brother Steve. I'm the baby in my family by ten years, so my sisters and brothers all had good, real records that they left behind when they moved out and went to college.

"They had the weirdest collection for people not really into music. Like, my introduction to the Rolling Stones was *Between the Buttons.* And there was a lot of art-rock stuff, like all the Tangerine Dream records. I was listening to all these dope-smokin' college records when I was ten years old.

"Later on, I remember I was starting to succumb to peer pressure a little bit. I was filling out a Columbia Records Club form at the kitchen table one night, and my brother was home from college. He saw me filling out 'Styx' and 'Kansas,' and he ripped it out of my hands and said he'd go buy me some good records, and I don't think I ever turned back from there."

(November 11, 2000, St. Paul Pioneer Press)

Rereading this now I realize what a lucky man I have been and am, and how lo, these many years later I love my brothers fiercely and could write an entire book about that alone. But early on, the circular nature of listening to music and writing made the very act of it feel spiritual, so I kept doing it, and I still have that New Year's Eve 1974 notebook and most every other scrap of paper I've ever written on, stored here in my basement, which sits a few blocks away from the South Minneapolis home I grew up in. Welcome:

Boxes of writings, published and unpublished, lay at my feet. Records, cassettes, CDs, posters and photos of heroes and friends, strangers and acquaintances, keep me company. Come along? Pull up a chair and dig in with me for a while . . . .

I was born on February 2, 1959, the day of Buddy Holly's last concert at the Surf Ballroom in Clear Lake, Iowa, and while it has been said that February 3 is the day the music died, I was just getting started. I've been writing to the sound of music for forty-five years, and here it must be said that the roots of this book are in the love story that happened between my sunny and smart parents, Ann and Jerry Walsh, who met at the Prom Ballroom in St. Paul and who danced to the optimistic postwar big-band sounds of the day to the tune of six kids and many stories.

Fly Me to the Moon

THE BEST LOVE STORY I KNOW started in the Irish-Catholic ghetto of South Minneapolis on August 28, 1948, and rounds the bend this weekend at a resort in Deerwood, Minnesota, where its makers will somewhat reluctantly celebrate their fiftieth wedding anniversary.

The guests of honor don't want any fuss, but they don't have a choice, because what their friends and family and six kids and their spouses have come to know is that marriage is a song that goes bump in the night, and that all sorts of good people with good dreams die and/or change. So if you get the chance to step back and wonder at something this durable, this thriving, you seize it with champagne and wisecracks and everything you've got.

And if you can, you write it down for anyone who might happen upon it, because it's a love story worth telling—about soul mates/opposites attracting and drifting and staying together—and because it pretty much explains why I am the way I am, and why I still think love is the answer to most any question you've got.

My parents met at the now-demolished Prom Ballroom on University Avenue in St. Paul. She was seventeen, he was nineteen. They were with different dates that night, listening to Gene Krupa's big band, and they hit it off immediately. She liked his blue eyes and easy smile and his love of music and the fact that he didn't drink. He liked her blue eyes and easy smile and her quick wit and the fact that she didn't drink.

"We got along famously," he said many years later, but at the time a friend told him, "Hey, bubby, she's hot for you, but you'll never get to first base with her."

They dated for three years, then he went off to fight for his country in Korea. For two years they carried pictures of each other and wrote love letters. When he came home, they got married and he got a job and they started a family: four kids in three and a half years, then two more for good measure.

"Those were some really tough times, but as somebody said, I'd go back and do it all over again," she said. "When you have a bunch of little kids, it's intense. But never in our minds was there a question that there was any different way to live or any choice to be made, because we'd made our choice. It wasn't as if you couldn't do anything differently, but it was a commitment. A commitment of love."

They were good Catholics. They went to church every Sunday with the kids in tow, filling up one pew at Annunciation, the big neighborhood church that his parents and all their friends and their kids' schoolmates went to. They did the Stations of the Cross and the angelus and the rosary and the one that goes "Remember, man, that you are dust, and to dust you shall return."

But something nagged at him. The answers he was getting were too easy, and his questions were getting more complicated. During his lunch breaks from work, he started going to the bookstore and began devouring what decades later would be known as alternative spirituality—Buddhism, mysticism, Vernon Howard, J. Krishnamurti, Edgar Cayce. He stopped going to church, and one by one their kids followed.

She kept going. By herself. She too soon tired of the stuffy neighborhood church and found another family, in the old and young and black and white community at St. Leonard's of Port Maurice, a tiny church in the heart of Minneapolis. She still goes. Every Sunday. She does readings and sings songs and prays and feels the love of God and humanity. She has been known to walk out of the service if something the pastor says riles her, usually something she perceives as sexist or antiwoman. She is unwavering in her belief that there is a God, a creator of all things beautiful. She is a lioness of faith.

"I don't believe in God," he said. "I go back to the quote 'A hundred monks, a hundred different ideas of what or who God is.' I don't believe there's a creator. It's very hard to explain, but I believe that we are the creators of ourselves. We are it. It's an ongoing process—never started, and it will never end. We are the creators, and we have to figure out ourselves what that is."

"Dad's a spiritual person," she said. "He's seeking God in his way, and I am in my way. We respect each other."

"We've both come to realize that it's very personal," he said. "Every individual goes on their own search. And when you're lowered in that box into the ground, you're alone, and you'd better have it figured out for yourself."

They live in a modest house in West Bloomington, surrounded by books and baubles of long-term love and pictures of their children and grandchildren. But it is, as they laugh, "a house divided." He is a staunch Republican. She is a bleeding-heart liberal. He is a bullheaded conservative. She is a fierce feminist. He monitors the Drudge Report and Rush Limbaugh and Eckhart Tolle and the Belfast Cowboys and margaritas. She monitors public radio and Tommy Mischke and *Jeopardy!* and the Belfast Cowboys and white wine. Her glass is half-full, his is half-empty. She loves big groups of people. He loves solitude. She likes to travel. He likes the Travel Channel. She golfs, and he runs. They read everything that comes into the house and argue about it—columnists, news stories, facts, figures, minutiae. Nothing is taboo; nothing gets swept under the carpet.

"It's a very flavorful part of our marriage," he said. "I often think of guys who go home to their wives who go, 'Yes, dear,' and they agree on everything. I don't know. It's so strange. We argue. And we *argue*. Not about religion, mostly about politics. And we swear we're not going to do it, but then the next day's paper comes."

On New Year's Day, I set up a video camera and sat them down at their dining room table to ask them about their lives. She wore a *Pioneer Press* sweatshirt; he wore a blue sweater. She sat with her hands folded in front of her and laughed at everything he said. He played with a Hershey's Kiss that was sitting on the table and joked that I wanted to get them on tape because I think they're going to die soon.

He's a smart son of a gun. Years from now I will look at that tape, as I did the other night, and I'll cue it up to the part where he tears up talking about his definition of love ("Coming in that driveway and seeing her in the kitchen window"), and I will remember the night a couple of months ago, when I went over to their house to watch *Punch-Drunk Love* with him, and, just as I was going into the kitchen to get something to drink, I saw him kiss her good night. I turned away because it felt private and sacred, and it will give me a shot in the arm and something to shoot for.

"I can remember times being very sad that that newness is gone, because it's so precious," she said. "Now there's such a peacefulness. It doesn't compare with the newness. They're both wonderful. The middle times were much harder, because we were so busy and there were so many people to care for. And to have this at the end of the road—to be alone together . . ."

". . . it's fun," he said, twirling the Hershey's Kiss like a top.

(August 27, 2003, City Pages)

From them I get the gift of writing from a hopeful heart and a manic-depressive music-loving head and soul. Along with my Irish DNA and all the storytelling and musical roots that suggests, those two beautiful people planted the creative seed in me, and I've intended to honor their love story with my work and my life, and even though I've fallen short of emulating their perfectly instructive marriage, I love my life and I love being their son, and all the words and songs I've ever been touched by in some fashion begin and end with them.

And so I dedicate this book to my parents and my kids, Henry and Helen, and to you, whoever, wherever, and whenever you are; to whom it may concern and to whoever is still listening to the sound of a single voice in a single sitting on this very strange planet, thank you for reading, and please consider this an invitation to my heart, that big one pumping hard here on my sleeve.

I'm the most romantic person I know—about life in general, my hometown, and its music and people—and I intend for this collection to stand as something of a love letter to my family—members adoptive, biological, found, musical, and otherwise—and to all the musicians, readers, and listeners from around these parts, whom it often feels like I was born to write about and for, like it was dumb luck or destiny that I landed here at this time and place with a mission to chronicle as much as I could of what went down, and to fulfill that most elemental definition and function of the word *scribe*.

I was here when all this amazing music happened in this little prairie town, and for a few decades and with no end in sight I wrote it all down as fast and as well as I could.

But before I did, so did my dad.

Chickery Chick

AS THE PROM AND GRADUATION RITES of spring get played out in all their youthful glory, Jerry Walsh is here to remind us that not much and quite a bit has changed since he was a high school senior in 1945.

Jerry Walsh is my dad. I'm feeling sentimental and very close to him these days because he turned eighty-four this month and his memory's not what it used to be. At the same time, a few weeks ago I started rifling through his file cabinet in the basement of our parents' house in West Bloomington. I found a bunch of cool stuff, including his dog tags from the Korean War, papers from his days as an employment counselor and furniture salesman, and letters and birthday cards from all six of his kids, but nothing as cool as the batch of columns he wrote as a senior in high school, which I never knew existed until this week.

Turns out my dad was a helluva writer. While working for the DeLaSalle student newspaper the *Islander* (the first paper I wrote for), he won a writing contest to pen the "High School Huddle" column for the *Minneapolis Daily Times*. It appeared regularly throughout 1945, often on the same page as up-and-coming writers Sid Hartman, Dick Cullum, and Walter Winchell. He wrote about music, babysitting his kid sister, the war, and his generation.

To read his words all these years later has been inspiring. A few "Huddle" highlights:

> *By this time Salk's [corner drug store on South Lyndale and Diamond Lake Road, now a Starbucks] is filled to capacity with almost every kid in South Minneapolis. The air is filled with flying soda straw wrappers. In one corner a crowd of girls have captured the movie magazines and are gazing rapturously at the profiles of Van Johnson or Dana Andrews. The back booth is taken up by a crowd of boys*

singing 'Chickery Chick,' with George Konop, the hottest man on the drums next to Gene Krupa, giving them a rhythm accompaniment on the paper napkin holder.

On Friday nights after the show, basketball game, or club meetings the kids usually drop in on the Catholic Youth Center (CYC) dances for cokes and weekly gossip. On a typical night after club meeting we begin to drift toward 2120 Park Avenue, all set for a riotous evening, and maybe even trip the light fantastic with that certain someone. While we are about two blocks away the sound of a hot band reaches our ears and some overzealous young lad screams, 'Boy, oh, boy! Listen to those cats kick,' and from then on it's every man for himself. The schools usually represented throughout the crowd are De La Salle, St. Anthony, St. Margaret's, St. Thomas, and Holy Angels. Every week we try to find out who the VLKS and Checkerooz are, and what the names mean, but St. Anthony girls are faithful to their clubs, and the answers yield little information.

Putting out a high school paper seems to be really more fun than work. The thrill of seeing your own story in print is almost indescribable. After writing a few stories you begin to think that maybe you're good enough to apply for a reporting job on a citywide newspaper. But after you try to write a story in the same style as some foreign correspondent, or a columnist like Walter Winchell, it dawns on you that these writers have a little more talent than you thought.

Excelsior [Amusement Park] has opened with a smash! Kids and everybody and his grandma seem to be hitting for Lake Minnetonka. Speaking of lakes, Thomas Beach at Lake Calhoun is the scene of many a cat session as the gals lie there getting a creamy tan to go with their white formals (meow).

Today the teenagers go mad over boogie riffs and basses, and their parents sit back and say, 'Oh, it's just a fad. It will vanish in a couple of years.' But will it? Those who attended the Hazel Scott concert at the auditorium will remember sitting patiently and politely while Miss Scott played some of the classics. Then, in the second part of the program, as she started playing the famous New Orleans walking bass, the crowd gave one joyous moan, and from then on the joint was jumpin'. Who were these people who went crazy over Miss Scott's bass rhythms? Was it just another gang of bobby soxers? NO! It was some of their parents, the people who said they didn't like boogie. What I'm trying to say is that when little Johnny Jones comes home from a hard day at school and sits down to listen to some hot trumpet solos, or deep-throated piano rhythms, his mother should leave him be, even if he does play the same record 392 times. Little Johnny is just in one of his musical moods. So in due respect to parents, we ask them to please let us have our jam sessions, record sessions, and music magazines in peace.

(May 25, 2016, Southwest Journal)

Dad didn't publish much of his writing after that, but, inspired by him and music, I took up the torch. I'm honored to put together this collection for the publishing house of my alma mater, the University of Minnesota, culled from my days and nights covering the music beat in the Twin Cities and beyond, and the truth is I'm jazzed about it. Writing is my job, my vocation, what I was born to do, though in recent years I've had to question as much because my chosen profession of journalism has experienced a seismic shift. Through it all, I've kept working and writing. I've kept my spirits up as best I could, living and learning and gleaning wisdom and loving and supporting my kids and writing stories and songs and making community and taking life seriously and making mistakes and music, and with this book I feel like I have a rare chance to look back fondly and with profound gratitude.

We Could Be Heroes Just for One Day

"SHUT THE DOOR FOR A SECOND," said my dad, sitting in the family room watching TV. I was in fourth grade. I did as told and settled into a chair next to him. He had a philosophy-spirituality book on his lap, like always. Our eyes stayed on the TV.

"Your brother told me you were telling him about how babies are made," he said, softly. "I just had a talk with him and explained it, and I realized that you and I have never talked about it. I wondered if you had any questions."

I thought I was pretty up to speed on the birds and bees, and told him as much, but soon realized I had no clue at all when he forged ahead with what exactly went on with a man and woman. I was in over my head and grossed out. I wanted to ditch the awkward heart-to-heart and go outside and play. I was good. But first I thought I should ask the old man a question to make sure he knew he'd done his job.

"Why do people do it, Dad?"

He never missed a beat.

"Because it feels good," he said, and I went out to play.

Ten years later I found myself on the dance floor of a Richfield hotel, freaking out freely and effeminately at a bunch of Incarnation Grade School friends' summer high school musical party. The music on the turntable was Elton John, the Rolling Stones, Ohio Players, Queen, T. Rex, P-Funk, and David Bowie. For a couple of transcendent hours I moved my hips and feet accordingly, ran my fingers through my hair, licked my lips, and felt the soul release of teenage kicks and androgyny. The night was young.

Until. Out of the corner of my libido I felt someone watching me. When I popped out of my pop reverie to check, I saw three drunk Richfield rednecks glaring at me from the sidelines. They muttered and pointed, and it was clear they didn't appreciate me or my Rod

Stewart or Iggy Pop, so I recruited Pat Wollack and Johnny Rath, a couple of my huge basketball/guitar player pals, to escort me to the parking lot. I got in my car and raced out of there, the drunks followed, but I lost them and got home safely.

I hadn't thought about that kid or that moment until this time last year. I was in the dressing room at Blacklist Vintage, and my friend, the shop's owner, Vanessa Messersmith, asked me through the curtain, "How does it look?"

It was snug. A jump suit that left little to the imagination, way too tight and far too revealing for my comfort level, but as I stood there looking in the mirror I had a flashback to that kid, that fear, and those rednecks, and decided on the spot—with Vanessa's encouragement—to wear it on First Avenue's big stage the next night at the annual Rock for Pussy David Bowie tribute.

So I did. Just before I took the stage, I went into the backstage dressing room's bathroom and changed. Vanessa gave me some mirror shades, Mary Lucia sprinkled me with some glitter fairy dust, David Campbell gave me an affirmative whoop, as did John Eller, who whipped the band into action. I slapped my butt cheeks for the crowd, stripper-style, then we launched into Bowie's "Heroes," an anthem about peaceniks, misfits, and outsiders finding solace in each other in a time of war.

Last weekend, as Minnesota lawmakers declared war on all of us who have ever felt, loved, or been gay, I found myself on the train tracks of Northeast Minneapolis in the middle of the afternoon. I jumped off the tracks when I saw a train approaching, then turned to watch it speed past.

It was filled with people of all ages and races. The faces blurred into a tapestry of tired smiles, a reaction to the smiles and peace signs I flashed their way. A few kids returned the peace signs, and in the second-to-last car sat a plump young lady. Our eyes met, from about fifty yards away.

The train bulleted along, and in an instant we both knew that the instant was about to be gone. So I blew her a kiss.

She blew it back, we waved quick good-byes and broke into huge grins. My heart swelled, and I'm certain hers did, too; we both felt it.

"Did you see that?" I said to my buddy, who hadn't. The girl on the train and I were the only ones on the planet who had experienced it, but it was as real a love connection as they come.

Which was somewhat comforting, a subtle reminder in these times of scarlet letters, sexual suspects, and same-sex lynchings: no matter what laws go on the books, no matter how hateful the ignorance, people will find good love and good sex with whomever or whatever they please.

Because it feels good.

Now go outside and play.

(May 30, 2011, Southwest Journal)

Nye's: The Long Good-bye

THE TUESDAY BEFORE THANKSGIVING, my friend Tom Willford shimmied on the dance floor in the back room of Nye's Polonaise Room, as my brother Terry and his ace band St. Dominic's Trio once again entertained the Tuesday night troops with their heart-and-soul–shaking rock 'n' roll, and, as they have every Tuesday for going on six years, kissed, put to bed, and once and for all tucked in the tired Minnesota trope that "nothing good ever happens after 10 o'clock."

To the contrary, as the clock above the band and bathrooms neared midnight, Tom was rocking out to a guest appearance by my old friend Ike Reilly, the Libertyville, Illinois, punk rocker who landed with most of his band at Nye's after having just blown the roof off another Northeast Minneapolis institution, Grumpy's, and who was ramping up to do similar damage to First Avenue the following night.

As Reilly-Walsh guided St. Dom's through a mash-up of "Highway 61 Revisited/Walkin' the Dog," and as Ike's howling blues harp mated with Tim Martin's banshee trumpet solo to a rapt couple dozen that included Ike's teenage son Kevin and several Tuesday regulars and out-of-towners, I made my way down the length of the bar to put my arm around Tom, who explained his obvious and supremely in-the-moment euphoria with, "You gotta enjoy it while you can, Jimmy, because you never know when it's going to end."

Happy Thanksgiving: little did Tom or I know that as we spoke and danced, plans were being made to close Nye's, and, barring an unforeseen metro planning miracle, by this time next year the sixty-five-year-old Minneapolis nightclub will be dust and/or condos. (I tried visiting it last night, but it was closed and cold and dark, and when I peeked in the windows, hell if the napkins, menus, band posters, and other ephemera didn't already look like something out of a Ken Burns doc waiting to happen.)

But before it goes the way of all great long-lost bars, love letters like this one are bound to make the rounds, and for good reason: every town should be so lucky to have a bar like Nye's, a locally owned nightclub and pioneer in the land of ten million organic foodies and craft brewers that should be celebrated for seven decades of bringing people together via songs, stories, neon lights, and Naugahyde booths. Snobs regularly call Nye's a "dive bar," but if you love the human aquarium and Minneapolis history, it's hallowed ground—as holy as the plot that houses the church sitting behind it, Our Lady of Lourdes.

Anyone who's spent any time at Nye's can name meaningful nights there. Luckily, I celebrated birthdays and DeLaSalle High School reunions there, surrounded by friends and family, and fell in love with the joint on Wednesday nights with Molly Maher and Her Disbelievers and the Erik Koskinen Band, who for almost a decade turned the joint into a real-deal honky-tonk. I've also done my time at the piano bar, most recently Tuesday nights with big-hearted maestro John Eller, who generously fills the room with slurred standards and glammy pop-rock singalong magic.

I've commemorated the entire spectrum of the human experience there, including births, jobs, loves, deaths, divorces, and holidays, many of which have been deliciously augmented by homemade baked goods from Tuesday regulars Kim, Maggie, and Kayla. Dive bar? Maybe. But also a home away from home.

My brother broke the news to me about Nye's rumored closing over Thanksgiving dinner. I told him I didn't buy it, because a world without Nye's is unbelievable and unthinkable and uncivilized, and because I didn't and don't want to believe it, but *C'est la vie,* and Tom's right: knowing everything we know about this thing called life, there's no time like the present to celebrate the present.

(December 2, 2014, Southwest Journal)

ONE

SPIRIT IN THE NIGHT

I grabbed the paper bag with the record store logo and the words *Positively Fourth Street* scrawled across the side, tucked it under my arm, and headed out into the night. I was eighteen years old.

It was the summer of 1977, the summer between high school and college, the summer of my aching bursting bleeding Irish American liberal poet's heart, the summer punk rock broke, and all I wanted to do, all I was doing, was write in my journal, play pickup basketball, work at my job as a dietary aide and kosher cook at Mount Sinai Hospital in downtown Minneapolis, hit Oarfolkjokeopus Records for my thrice-a-week fix, and listen to as many records as was humanly possible.

This night, this bag, meant everything from Elvis Costello's just-released *My Aim Is True* and The Clash's *The Clash* to Springsteen's *Born To Run*, Bob Dylan's *Blood on the Tracks*, Patti Smith's *Horses*, the Sex Pistols' *Who Killed Bambi?*, Harry Nilsson's *A Little Schmilsson in the Night*, Jackson Browne's *Late for the Sky*, David Bowie's *Station to Station*, the Ramones' *Rocket to Russia*, Al Green's *Greatest Hits*, Elton John's *Goodbye Yellow Brick Road*, various assorted Stones, P-Funk, and Yardbirds, and a local folk compilation called *Live at the Extemp*.

The bag was slightly soggy from my sweaty boy-man hands, so the bottom gave out a little when I perched it on the passenger seat of my car. I'd bought a silver-and-black 1970 Thunderbird with suicide doors from a buddy for $500 that sported satin pillows and Playboy bunny decals in back, an eight-track tape player in front, and a transmission that gave out after a couple of months. It was a vainglorious first ride, but that summer it was also a boy-howdy alternative to the family station wagon I'd been borrowing and a freedom of '77 acknowledgment that, as Ike Reilly would sing a few decades later, "cars and girls and drinks and songs make this world go around."

I was ready . . . for something. I'd spent my high school years listening to, and gleaning existential guidance from, songs. Their connection to me was a mystical one that worried my mom and bonded me with my brothers and sisters, and more than anything I loved listening to the cacophony of voices harmonizing in debate at my family's dinner table, and to music, music, music. I'd just graduated from DeLaSalle, the (then) liberal Catholic high school founded by the Christian Brothers on the banks of the Mississippi River, where classes such as "Jesus" and "World Religion" were mandatory, and *Jesus Christ, Superstar* and *Godspell* were part of the zeitgeist. Love and the smiley face were all around.

But from every iota of black wax magic pulsing inside the record store bag I knew there was another world—of danger, sex, camaraderie, mystery, and romance—and inside me, reluctant me, simmered dreams of being something, doing something connected to all these older magicians and songsmiths, and of living a life of purpose I'd heard about from the priests and nuns and music I'd been immersed in since I was a kid.

The summer of '77, like most Minnesota summers, was a tropical playground dipped in blankets of humidity and set by lakes, creeks, rivers, and miasmic forests of lush weeds and foliage that nest blood-sucking mosquitoes and louder-than-bombs crickets. Jimmy Carter was president, *Star Wars* was three weeks old, Anita Bryant was antigay crusading, the Son of Sam was terrorizing New York City, Elvis Presley was about to die next to his toilet in Graceland, and desire was pouring out of the adrenal glands of South Minneapolis's contribution to the largest graduating high school class in the history of the United States.

We went to DeLaSalle, Washburn, Regina, Central, Southwest, Benilde, Holy Angels, and Roosevelt, and for us, post–high school teenage kicks meant working jobs at the SuperAmerica, Red Barn, or Mount Sinai Hospital, killing time before college, and running wild and driving free through the wide-open streets and prairies of the Midwest, where bike paths, dirt roads, cornfields, and a certain untested and unrequited innocence showed the way. I was getting the itch to sing in a band, while at the same time, some of my friends were performing in the high school summer play at Incarnation Grade School, the same grade school my mom attended and in the biggest Catholic parish in the city at the time.

I liked going to the after-parties, hosted as they were by a lively bunch of naughty beer-drinking and cigarette-smoking kids, so after a warm-up cruise around Lake Harriet, I headed over to the closing-night party held at one of the actress's parent-free house. When I arrived, record bag in hand, I quickly discovered that my girlfriend was giving me the cold shoulder because I chose not to attend the play that night.

I held the bag of records by my side. I entertained no great scheme to commandeer the turntable. I listened to the show reviews and gossip. I quickly decided it wasn't conducive to a guest deejay, so while the beer and conversation flowed, I made myself invisible. After a few minutes of wallflowering, I ducked out. I walked down Fifty-sixth Street, my mind and heart empty, until I came to Penn Avenue and Armatage Park, whose four baseball fields were lit up and calling to me like a landing runway. I walked down the grassy hill to the spot where all four center fields converged, dropped to my knees, and lay down on my back.

Stars, moon, fireflies, silence.

The bag rested on my chest.

My friends were all having fun.

I stared up into the night sky and said out loud, "What the hell is wrong with me?"

We're Going to Be Friends

WE USED TO CALL 'EM KEGGERS. Someone would get a keg of malt liquor and a tap and a bunch of plastic cups, and everyone would end up down by the Mississippi River bluffs or behind Nicollet Island by nine or ten o'clock as the sun went down and the mosquitoes got up. Summer 1977.

That's the last time I went to a kegger. By then, the Ramones were a fixation, I'd danced with my friend Liz Healy to the Suicide Commandos doing the Tubes' "White Punks on Dope" at Regina High School, and the following year The Clash would come to the St. Paul Civic Center and blow things wide open.

But before all that, there were keggers. Sweet, innocent, I-wonder-if-she'll-show-up keggers.

I went to only a few in high school, and what I remember most is the music. Guys would prop up their car stereo speakers on their Chevettes and Thunderbirds and their parents' station wagons and send out their teenage mating calls into the thick river darkness in the guises of David Bowie, Marvin Gaye, Queen, the Stones, Al Green, Alice Cooper, Earth, Wind, & Fire, Elton John, Rod Stewart, The Who.

They were all in the background, the way they are in *Dazed and Confused,* the great kegger film named after the great song by Led Zeppelin, and also remindful of the White Stripes, who, no matter what some backlash-spamming killjoy may have told you, are nothing if not the best kegger band going at the moment.

By that, I mean that the Detroit duo of Jack and Meg White sounds blues-newsy great up close and far away. They smell like sticky bug spray and heavy pollen and heady hops and grains. They've got a lovely take-me-or-leave-me-alone attitude; they sound like they've been living in their own Houses of the Holy for the past few years; they do reportedly unforgettable live shows; and they fly under the masses' radar just enough so as to retain their souls.

Plus, they wear red-and-white uniforms, like volunteer candy strip ers at the punk-rock nursing home; their sound is spare, heavy, loud, primal, and supremely sexual. The Whites' third album, *White Blood Cells,* is a muddy riverbank with a hot swimming hole at the center: "Fell in Love with a Girl" is a rocker for the ages; "Little Room," a paean to the creative spirit and thinking small; "Hotel Yorba" is a back porch shuffle that actually shuffles; "The Union Forever" is a self-challenge that springboards off a warmed-over "House of the Rising Sun."

But instead of Eric Burdon's aged coming-of-age-with-whores story, Jack yowls his antifame credo into the chasm of a perplexed material world: "Well, I'm sorry but I'm not interested in gold mines, oil wells, shipping, or real estate, what would I liked to have been? Everything you hate."

The way he spits it reminds me of another band, another time. The night before the Civic Center concert, The Clash hung out at the Longhorn in downtown Minneapolis, where the Buzzcocks and Gang of Four were playing. When the Buzzcocks finished, I walked out of the club with my Commandos dance partner Liz, whom I went to grade school with, and Pat Downey, whom I went to high school with.

Out of nowhere, The Clash's Mick Jones walked up to us. I stuck out my hand and said, "Hey, man, we've been waiting for this [Clash show] all summer." Jones kept his hands in his pockets and coolly Brit-barked, "What's your names?"

"Jim, Pat, Liz," said we, three nineteen-year-old Midwestern kids with band buttons on our shirts and our whole lives in front of us. After a few more seconds of deadpan chitchat, Jones split.

Liz and I were thrilled, but not Downey. As the guitarist's slight frame disappeared up Fifth Street toward his hotel, Downey cursed, threw his fist in the air, and yelled, "I'm gonna replace you someday!"

When I saw Downey the next night at the concert, he'd shaved his head. He pogoed off into the crowd, moved to New York not long after that, and I haven't talked to him since. Liz was hit and killed by a car on the corner of Lake and Hennepin the next summer, and the White Stripes' "We're Going to Be Friends," among many others, makes me think of her.

My twenty-fifth high school reunion is at the end of this month. I hope to see Downey there, with an update. The White Stripes are at First Avenue on Saturday. I hope to see you there, with a tap. Summer 2002.

(July 11, 2002, St. Paul Pioneer Press)

Baptism by Bruce

WHY WAS I COMPELLED, at the end of September, to trek to Philadelphia for two of Bruce Springsteen's six shows with the reunited E Street Band? And why does the thought of his appearance at Target Center this week quicken my pulse like no other rock show has this year?

For the answers, we need to go back to a warm summer night in 1978. That was the first time I saw Springsteen in concert—at the old Metropolitan Sports Center in Bloomington with seven thousand other loonies who could tell you who they were with and what various flights of fancy their lives have taken as a result of that night.

Me, I was nineteen years old. That night, I remember Springsteen—scrawny, badass, animated like no rocker I'd seen before or since—jumping into the crowd during "Spirit in the Night," and my brother Jay and I ending up in front at the end, pogoing and pounding on his motorcycle boots during "Rosalita." I remember him singing a lyric that sent tremors through my nervous system, a lyric that I have come to regard as not only the quintessential Springsteen missive, but the lyrical embodiment of rock 'n' roll itself. More on that later.

After the show, at a house in South Minneapolis, a bunch of my fellow Catholic school grads were partying after a high school play. I found my friend/kindred music spirit Paul Kaiser and dragged him out to the front steps.

"Man, I saw something tonight . . . ," I stammered. I quoted the lyric, then just shook my head and looked at my feet. I was embarrassed; it was too personal. He laughed, "Bruce Springsteen, huh? You can't explain it, can you?"

It was true: I had never witnessed anything so raw or so exuberant, and I couldn't articulate what it had done to me. So I split from the party, walked home to my folks' house, got in bed, and started writing—and, thanks a lot to Springsteen, haven't stopped since.

What I was trying to do that night was hold it in my hands, to capture bliss in a bottle. I was nineteen, I was nothing. My dreams were just that. I ached to see things, to be something, anything. I wanted to know if love was wild, I wanted to know if love was real.

A lot has happened since then. I grew up. Found love. And— and this is a big *and*—that stammering fool at that party went on to make his livelihood out of trying to explain the unexplainable. All of which has made me a lot tougher to impress than the twenty-year-old kid who blew an entire hospital paycheck on a customized E Street Band jacket with *Jimmy the Saint* stitched above the heart.

So, frankly, on the flight out to Philadelphia last month, I was a little worried. Because, while I knew it wouldn't—couldn't—be the same as the four- and five-hour spiritual trips the E Street Band regularly provided me with in the '70s and '80s, I didn't want to come away from another sterile '90s arena show, or some lame nostalgia trip, feeling dead inside.

So this was something of a test, I decided, as the lights dimmed at the First Union Center in Philadelphia.

Unlike the start of most concerts, where shadowy figures dart on stage under the cloak of darkness, the E Street Band came out one by one, under a soft golden light, waving and grinning like old friends showing up to a potluck dinner. It was the first time I'd seen them together in eleven years: pianist Roy Bittan; drummer Max Weinberg; keyboardist Danny Federici; guitarist Nils Lofgren; guitarist Steve Van Zandt; Bruce's wife, singer/guitarist Patti Scialfa; saxophonist Clarence Clemons; and Springsteen.

That's when I fell into the dunk tank of nostalgia and decided to enjoy the water. Largely because, while most rock stars' music makes you think about their lives, Springsteen's music demands that you think about your own. So when Weinberg locomotive-thrashed his hi-hat cymbal and Springsteen whispered the opening line to "Candy's Room," the hair on the back of my neck stood up.

The next song, "Adam Raised a Cain"—a cauldron of father–son tension—was followed by "The Ties That Bind," and I realized that the last time I'd heard either one in concert I was the son, and that now my job is to provide my kids with that heat, with something to butt up against.

By the third song, "Prove It All Night," I was a puddle. It took me back to something I hadn't thought of in years, when my band mates and I, armed with spray paint one night after practice, climbed some railroad boxcars and a rusty tower to deface a billboard on Hiawatha Avenue with "Prove It All Night!" and "Bruce Springsteen and The E Street Band Rule!"

And so on. During "Jungleland," after Springsteen howled, "Kids flash guitars just like switchblades, hustlin' for the record machine, the hungry and the hunted explode into rock 'n' roll bands," Van Zandt ripped off a thunderbolt lead. For that ten seconds, he became Johnny Rey, Kevin Martinson, Bob Stinson, Dave Alvin, Terry Eason, Slim Dunlap, Robert Wilkinson, Ernie Batson, John Freeman, and every other guitar player in every dive I've watched spill their guts over the past two decades.

When did I know that the test was over? That I had passed? That would have been during "Cadillac Ranch," when I found myself hopping from foot to foot like a drunken Muppet, and lolling my head like a bobblehead doll that had just regained his innocence and lost his critical faculties.

The next night, Springsteen encored with "Thunder Road." It was the last time he would sing it as a fortysomething (he turned fifty September 23). So when he sang, "You're scared, and you're thinking that maybe you ain't that young anymore," he backed away from the microphone and, sincerely taken aback by the moment, laughed.

The next lyric is the one that got me stammering some twenty years ago, but he didn't even sing it. He let the crowd do it, and the sound of all those voices raised to the Pennsylvania heavens got me thinking about how this whole country has been made to feel old of late, by an entertainment industry that pushes teenybopdom like bubblecrack, by the malling of neighborhoods, by a culture that worships technology and materialism over community and spirituality.

As a result, in the past year, I've had people aged twenty-five, thirty, forty, and fifty tell me that they feel old. One is my forty-eight-year-old brother-in-law, Neal, who attended the first show with me. He had never been to a Springsteen concert but afterward said, "All my favorite acid-rock bands came back this summer, but seeing them just made me feel old. This made me feel young."

And why not? In this, the Age of Irony, Springsteen is thoroughly unironic, and romantic. The musical landscape has shifted dramatically since the E Street Band was last on the road, and seemingly overnight, *rock 'n' roll* has taken on the same dirty-word obsolescence as *feminism.*

Yet there is Springsteen, an unabashed, unapologetic rock 'n' roll disciple. The blond-wood Telecaster still smokes, his wrist is still wicked quick, he still mugs mightily and mighty goofily, he still talks between songs (though, sadly, not as much as before), and still jumps off the risers. Pretty spry for an old guy.

My dad, who turned seventy-one this year and still can't believe it, had a favorite saying when we were growing up: "I still feel like I'm sixteen." Now I know that he wasn't talking about arrested development. He was saying that the more life that happens, the less you know about the meaning of life. Instead, the mystery just deepens.

When I was sixteen, I thought I'd have more figured out by now. But the thing nobody tells you is that you never do figure it out, completely. Sure, you can attain a certain level of personal peace and happiness, but the hunger you were born with shifts, the dreams change, the search for wild love remains insatiable.

That's why it's impossible for me to call Springsteen's music a relic. Those songs are ageless, and those two shows in Philadelphia reminded me in no uncertain terms that when it comes to live performers, no one—no one—comes close. Nobody has ever knocked me out, picked me back up, given me a shot in the arm, broken my heart, and resuscitated it, all in the span of the same three hours, the way he has, and did.

When I was younger, Springsteen's music provided me with a road map to manhood and gave me permission to be both saint and sinner. Now, songs such as "Badlands" still make me "want to go out tonight and find out what I got," but they elicit less of an ache because I know that nothing compares to the art of real life and that music can be found in the mundane.

To wit: the Sunday after I got back from Philadelphia, my son, Henry, and I went to House of Mercy Baptist Church in Lowertown St. Paul. Some local musicians were staging a tribute to the Louvin Brothers, a country-gospel group from the '50s and early '60s that has influenced Springsteen and many others.

By the time seventy-two-year-old Charlie Louvin himself came on, four-year-old Henry was pretty restless. On our third trip to the drinking fountain, Henry stopped in his tracks at the back of the church. His mouth dropped open. He was staring outside.

"I just love the city lights," he said, genuinely wonderstruck. "C'mon, Dad." We went outside and sat down on the cool, hard steps. He snuggled up next to me to get warm and started caressing the stubble on my chin, the way he does when he's especially affectionate.

We were quiet, and we sat that way until he put his arm around me and said, "Let's just sit here for a while and look at the city lights, and then we'll go back in and hear the music. Okay?" Good idea, I said, before my throat lumped shut.

I was forty, I was nothing. Inside the church, a once-in-a-lifetime show was taking place, but Henry and I stayed on the steps. Because at that moment, we—or at least I—could hear the music just fine. It had drifted from the Philadelphia heavens and was now echoing off the buildings of downtown St. Paul. It was a choir.

It was me at nineteen, feeling scared. It was my brother-in-law at forty-eight, feeling old. It was my dad at seventy-one, feeling sixteen. It was my son at four, feeling awed. It was everyone who has been made to feel out-of-touch, unhip, or hopeless. We were all there.

Maybe you were, too, singing along to a familiar lyric:

"Show a little faith, there's magic in the night."

(October 31, 1999, St. Paul Pioneer Press)

Taken by a Photograph

I'M SITTING HERE WAITING for an inspirational e-mail to arrive, one I've been waiting on for a few days, but before I tell you about it, if you've got a few minutes, I'd like to tell you a story.

I was in third grade when my parents bought the big house on Colfax Avenue in South Minneapolis. It was great, because for the first time in our lives my two brothers and three sisters and I weren't all crammed into the same big bedroom. The other cool thing was that in the basement there was a bomb shelter.

A lot of homeowners built them in the '60s, I guess. Ours was this huge dark tunnel made of sheet metal, concrete, and sand. It came ever-ready for Armageddon, complete with bottled water stored in hollows on the floor and a wind machine hooked up to the chimney, the thinking being that if the blitz came and the house was buried in rubble, well, all you'd have to do is crank the arm of the wind machine and gasp easy until help arrived.

After the novelty of playing Time Tunnel and Hiding from the Nazis wore off, we stopped going down to the bomb shelter. One night at dinner, my dad, who probably figured the days of needing personal air-raid shelters were long gone, said he'd build us a rec room and buy us a foosball table if we tore out the bomb shelter.

Which is what we did the summer I was fifteen. Me, my brothers, my sisters, the whole neighborhood. The Denmans. The Kalinowskis. The O'Rourkes. We cranked wrenches and pounded hammers and wore Dad's handkerchiefs and Mom's scarves over our mouths so we wouldn't breathe in the dust from the piles of sand we bucket-brigaded out the back door. For most of July and August, we dug, lifted, carted, sweated, crawled on our bellies, and pretended we were Charles Bronson in *The Great Escape*.

When we finished, Dad kept his part of the bargain. In short order, he built us this hideous Brady-Bunch-dropping-LSD playroom, with red-orange shag carpeting, wood paneling that we covered with posters (Elton John, Renaldo and Clara, Simon & Garfunkel, Jimi Hendrix), and a foosball table. We ran speaker wire down from the family stereo upstairs, and night after night we played foos, cranked the Ramones, Stones, Nils Lofgren, Springsteen, Bowie, Patti Smith, Marvin Gaye, Dylan, and Al Green, and, after everyone had gone home, I'd go back down to the foosball room alone and talk to Jackson Browne.

In my head, I mean. He was onto something, something about solitude and salvation that dovetailed with the liberal Catholic education I was getting in high school during the day. At night, I'd stack up his records on the turntable, grab a Dew from the fridge, descend the gun-metal-gray basement steps, turn out the lights, lie down, and listen to *Saturate before Using, For Everyman, The Pretender, Late for the Sky, Late for the Sky,* and *Late for the Sky.*

I'll spare you the sentimental goo, but suffice it to say it was everything that every boy-or-girl-in-a-bedroom memoir ever says about the mystical connection people have with music: along with many others' his songs gave me hope, gave me peace, made me look within, made me want to rock, find love, have adventures.

So much so that I also wanted to someday explain to him what he meant to me, which I now realize is impossible, as impossible as it is for me to explain to you what he meant to me, as impossible as it was for me to bring myself to say "Thank you" to him the other night.

It was November 12, at the soon-to-be-demolished Guthrie Theater in Minneapolis. He had just performed at a benefit concert for Minnesota's Gyuto monks. After I filed my review, I got invited to the after-show reception, which is the sort of thing I rarely go in for, but this one wasn't too bad: Jessica Lange, Sam Shepard, Richard Ford, Greg Brown, and other beautiful people whose work I admire were there, and I couldn't have cared less.

I moved to the back of the room, nodded at a critic from the other paper, leaned against a pillar, and saw him standing there. He was talking to a couple of guys around my age who were holding pens and CDs and wearing the unmistakable frozen rapt-nervous look of the Big Fan. Most of the other people in the room looked like fat cats who go to these things regularly, buying material for the check-in portion of the next morning's conference call to corporate headquarters.

One woman I met that night and will love forever said, "Sorry I don't know any of your music. You're not the Brown who sings, 'Uh! I feel good!' are you?"

Chuckles. Ice cubes. Chitchat. No.

Someone offered me a beer. "No, thanks, I'm cool," I said, but I was so far from cool my ears were starting to sweat.

I kept glancing over at him. There he (expletive) is, my inner teen whispered. Remember him? Remember me? He was there. He helped us. Remember all that stuff about life and death and the journey and the mystery and the search for the perfect love? Go tell him. Try. Tell him how it turned out for us. Thank him, you jaded old (expletive), or I will never talk to you again.

Just as I was about to bolt, along came Russell and Chris, the wise-guy ministers from House of Mercy church, who had crashed the party. One of their friends—the woman I met and will love forever for here comes why—had a camera. Once he got a whiff of my past affection and present condition, Russell's mission, God bless him, was to get me to get my picture taken with Jackson.

After three or four false starts, I finally took a breath, walked over to him, brushed his arm, and said, "Brother, can we have a photo?" He said, "Sure," and put down his plastic glass of red wine.

I think I shook his hand. A weird calm came over me and cut out my tongue.

Russell, nothing-to-lose Russell, barged in and threw me a rope and introduced us. Russell poked his finger in my heart and told him, "The first record review this guy ever wrote was about you in his high school paper," which is true, about *The Pretender* in 1976.

He thanked me for writing about him. I looked at my shoes almost the whole time and mustered, "Man, I've been listening to you forever. I've been writing about you forever."

I did not tell him about the times I almost met him or how many times I've seen him sing. I did not talk about all the wanderlust and heartache he incubated in me, or how hard I have fought to keep at bay the loneliness he wallowed in and warned me about. I did not tell him I don't listen to him very much anymore, that his search led me to other searchers and songs, or that my wife and son recently laughed at me when they gave me the fortune-cookie fortune I now have taped up on my computer.

It says, "Stop searching. Happiness is inside of you."

Two photos were snapped. Russell made them happen. He choreographed a shot of the three of us together, then one of just me and Jackson. We stood at attention, put our arms around each other, and I was delighted to not be shaking.

As we stood waiting for the camera to warm up, ever so slightly, I patted him on the back. He did the same thing. My inner teen said, "How 'bout that? Jackson Browne just patted us on the back."

The shutter clicked. I started to say "Thanks," but the emptiness of it caught in my throat and dissolved like a soggy lozenge. I patted him again on the small of his back as a red-and-yellow-robed monk the size of the brother on *Everybody Loves Raymond* cut in on me.

We never said good-bye. I was on Cloud Nine.

I thanked Russell and Chris and walked out of the place and was so giddy I shouted across the parking lot to Richard Ford about how much I liked his novel *The Sportswriter*. When I got home, I dug out *Late for the Sky* and played it into the night.

The e mail? I just got it. It's a photo of me and an old friend. I'm the one on the right, with the lucky-to-be-alive-I-wonder-what-happens-next smirk.

(December 2, 2000, St. Paul Pioneer Press)

For a Dancer

PETER LAMB WAS NINETEEN YEARS OLD when he was killed, the year I graduated from high school. I never knew him very well, but I'll never forget him.

He was tall, dark, handsome, and, best of all, a nice guy. My girlfriend, Kurse, was in love with him. Everyone was, I guess. He was tough and talented and quietly witty, with a queasy smile and a little bit of devil in him. His girlfriend, Judy, was a sweetheart, too.

One night, Peter and Judy were coming off an icy exit ramp in Minneapolis, and his car skidded out of control. Judy got out with a few scratches and bruises. Peter died at the scene.

Not long after, Kurse and I went to a party. I could never figure out what to say to her those days, so I did a lot of stammering and listening. I brought some records to the party, and when we had a moment alone, I told her I had a song I wanted her to hear.

I put the record on the stereo, dusted off the vinyl, and cued up "For a Dancer" by Jackson Browne, a solemn ballad built on a featherbed of piano, organ, violin, and Browne's healing voice.

I knew about it because the album belonged to my older brother, Jay, whom I've always imagined found solace in "For a Dancer" when a friend of his died in a swimming accident around the same time.

I played it for Kurse twice that night. I sat on a folding chair by the stereo; she sat on the floor, rocking in a fetal position, clutching a glass of wine, smoking a cigarette, staring straight ahead. Her eyes were puffy slits. I drove her home, kissed her goodnight, and let her borrow the album.

We broke up a couple of years later, but we've stayed in touch. We're both married with children now, and I called her up recently to compare notes. We went out to lunch, and it was great, talking old times. Which is what we did Monday afternoon, when I called her to talk about Peter Lamb.

She said her family was just talking about Peter on Mother's Day. She said she's given "For a Dancer" to countless friends and acquaintances who've lost someone, including several families she met as a nurse in the pediatrics unit at the University of Minnesota Hospital.

"I couldn't believe it when I first heard it," she said. "It was like someone was writing the words in my mind. You were so enraged and bitter and sad, but that song is still a tribute to the life they did lead.

"I played it and played it and played it. It was so comforting. And it was perfect for Peter, because you considered him a dancer. He danced through life."

She said she knows the lyrics, including the last verse, for which a buoyant gospel chorus joins in. Me, too. I can still type it by heart: "Don't let the uncertainty turn you around, go on and make a joyful sound."

After all these years, the reason I still come back to "For a Dancer"—which Browne recorded in 1974, two years before his wife, Phyllis, committed suicide—is that instead of trying to offer answers, it seeks to sow seeds of hope at a time of hopelessness. It appears on Browne's third album, *Late for the Sky,* which I recently dug up for Brianna, a teenage friend of mine. She'd never heard "For a Dancer," but one of her friends died of cancer last winter, and I figured she could use it right about now.

I have a feeling she's not the only one.

(May 17, 2000, St. Paul Pioneer Press)

TWO
ON THE ROAD TO FIND OUT

No Direction Home

THE MINNESOTA DEPARTMENT OF MOTOR VEHICLES issued yours truly a driver's license a couple of months after my sixteenth birthday. I'd survived all the parallel parking drills and other tests, but there was one more hurdle to be hurdled.

It came not from the state but from my mother. "You can only use the car," she said to me the day after I got back from the testing center, "if you promise to not play the radio."

By then, Ann Walsh realized that her fourth-born was gone on music, that it took me places that not even my driver's license and my late Grandma Walsh's hand-me-down '66 Impala (dubbed the White Bomb by all it was handed down to) could. She knew she had a dreamer on her hands, and she feared that the combination of a fast White Bomb and faster beats would conspire to wrap my dreaming adolescent ass around a tree.

The No Radio mandate didn't stick, of course. I told her not to worry, assured her that I'd be careful, and lit out. Besides, whatta-yagonnado, Ma? Within weeks, I was tooling around the lakes with the radio blaring. Within months, I had installed a cassette deck and cheap bulky stereo speakers that make the boom cars of today sound like drive-in theater cans.

A couple of decades later, not much has changed. And now that the Labor Day weekend is upon us, when more Minnesotans hit the roads than at any other time of the year, and when thousands more will embark on fall color tours and cabin-closing missions in the coming weekends, this is a good day to roll down the windows, crank up the volume, and celebrate the unique joys of listening to music in the car.

And it just so happens that such a celebration provides me with a rare opportunity to confess one of my deepest, darkest secrets. In fact, there are only a handful of people—my closest loved ones excluded—who've heard the story I'm getting up the nerve to tell you. Yes, it is time to come clean. It is time to admit that Ann Walsh's instincts, though it took some twenty years for them to come true, were right on the money.

What she feared, lo those many years ago, was that her son would be seduced by the most sonically perfect music-listening environment there is. In the car, music feels better, deeper, weirder, more intense. Music can transform even the most ordinary vehicles into chapels of reflection and introspection.

And the endless parade of roadside sights, billboards, and bumper stickers that accompany it can make for one big, beautiful, endless haiku.

Adopt a highway. Chewin' out a rhythm on my bubble gum. Deer crossing next five miles. I was born in a crossfire hurricane. KFC all you can eat buffet.

I'll try to find you left of the dial. Betty's Pies. I hope you had the time of your life. Food Gas Lodging Next Exit.

Where were you when we were getting high? Ask me about my grandchildren. Mean People Suck. Love and mercy: that's what you need tonight.

Car wheels on a gravel road. Way Station closed. May the wind take your troubles away. Live Bait. Impeach Clinton Now. Everybody knows this is nowhere. Everybody plays the fool. Everybody hurts, sometime.

What my mother suspected is that for some of us, music in the car is as close as we'll get to flying on the ground. For hours at a time, we become Peter Pan or Michael Jordan, soaring. Songs and scenery reach a perfect synchronicity, as if God, that greatest of all music video producers, planned the sound track for whatever it is that's coming through the windshield.

Outside, water towers and telephone poles fly by, the blacktop is cut by white and yellow lines and unmowed highway dividers. The road is framed by cornfields, brush, birch trees, barbed-wire fences, pine trees, firs, radio towers, silos. Inside, the chapel is lousy with the smell of junk food, air conditioning, cow pies, the occasional dead skunk, and the sound of harmonicas, fiddles, what-have-you, and magic.

Speed Limit 70 Minimum 40. When we come to the place where the road and the sky collide. New Brighton, A Minnesota Star City. We will not be lovers. Fines double in work zones. Packers power. New cruiser cup only at Taco Bell. I wanna be your man. I wanna be your dog. I feel like I'm livin' in the wasteland of the free.

Anyway, the confession.

A few summers ago, I set out in my car to drive up north to do a story on former Soul Asylum drummer Grant Young, who owns a resort not far from the Canadian border.

I got on 35W and started driving. It was a brilliant summer morning. I had a cup of coffee in me and was working on a second. The sun was baking my free arm, and I had a bag full of tapes and CDs on the passenger seat. Couldn't have been giddier.

The truth is, I'd been waiting for this drive for some time, since I had recently become a father for the first time, and my quality listening time had dwindled. Which is what I've heard plenty of new parents say, but music in the car has always been my favorite thing—for the solitude, and the singular state of consciousness it holds. Or unconsciousness, as it were.

An hour passed. Two. Three. I was flying with Peter and Michael, thumbs-upping truckers, drumming on the steering wheel, singing at the top of my lungs, jotting down psycho notes.

She was an American girl. Oh Sandy, the aurora is rising behind us. Roadwork begins July 13. These are the breaks. I Brake for Animals. I love Wisconsin. Start seeing motorcycles.

How does it feel, to be on your own, with no direction home? We like the cars, the cars that go boom, we're Bunny and Tigre, and Welcome to Iowa.

At first, I didn't believe it. But as the realization that I had driven four hours the wrong way sunk in, the first sound I heard was my mother's voice.

I turned the radio off and drove in silence for a mile or so to the first exit.

I had a quick lunch, got on north 35, and reached into the bag. I had twelve more hours of driving in front of me.

That is not the confession. This is: I was happy about it.

(September 4, 1998, St. Paul Pioneer Press)

Side of the Road

I'VE LISTENED TO Lucinda Williams's "Side of the Road" hundreds of times, but the one I remember most came in early June 1989. That evening, I was driving my 1980 K Car through rural Georgia as the big red sun was going down. I had just graduated from college, four years after my semi–punk-rock band had split up, and I was on my way from my hometown in Minneapolis, Minnesota, to Jacksonville, Florida, to do a summer internship at the *Florida Times-Union*. I had no air conditioning, the windows down, and the Georgia night cooling me off. Spraying out of the tape deck was Lucinda's 1988 self-titled masterpiece.

It's a terrific road record, full of flights of fancy and highway imagery, and the sort of crunchy snare drums, moaning violins, bluesy acoustic, electric, and slide guitars, and top-o'-the-lungs sing-alongs that can get you through the worst white-line fever. For most of that late afternoon, Lucinda's voice and characters kept me company like a therapy group laying bare our deepest unsaid desires. Every one of them, from the obsessed lover in "I Just Wanted to See You So Bad," to the restless waitress, Sylvia, in "Night's Too Long," to the yearning soul who just wants a few "Passionate Kisses" in this cold cold world, hit the ether with the same shared inflection of wanderlust.

They spend their lives itching and searching for a sense of place, which describes me now and then but mostly then. I don't think I admitted as much when I lit out for Florida that summer, but the fact is, I was driving to find myself. I wanted to be a writer, and I wanted to leave my beloved Minneapolis to see another part of the country, to live away from my family, and to see what it would be like to wake up every day without my wife next to me.

So two days into my trek, when Lucinda crackled out of the dashboard with the first verse to "Side of the Road" in that too-cool-to-be-forgotten drawl, it's no exaggeration to say that she was, as Neko Case puts it, "singing my life back to me."

Lucinda's father, like mine, was a writer. I've talked to her about the writing apprenticeship she received from her father, the renowned poet and professor Miller Williams, and about how as a young girl critics, novelists, and poets surrounded her. What a way to grow up! What a path to artistry! And what Midwestern kid with wild dreams of the writerly life wouldn't be seduced by thoughts of Southern nights filled with intellectual discourse and midnight bohemia?

Some of my earliest memories are of drifting off to sleep with my brothers and sisters, all of us upstairs in the same second-floor bedroom, and hearing the far-off sound of Dad banging away on his typewriter. He was writing. About what, I still wonder. I was six or seven, but even at that age I could imagine manila envelopes and pitch letters. Most of all I remember the *pfft-pfft* sound of typewriter keys hitting billowed paper, and something about it made me sad. Something told me that the life my dad had made for himself wasn't enough, that he wanted the world to know he was something more than my dad. A sound like that lodges in a son's brain. So does the sound of it stopping.

Other than letters and his own diary, I'm pretty sure my dad never wrote much after those days, and now that I'm a parent I know why: if you're doing it right—if you're wrestling with them and bathing them and listening to them and telling them stories and helping with their homework and just being there—the way he did it, which is why it's the way I do it, then kids take it out of you. Not the urge to write, which never goes away, but the time and energy to write, to the point where, at the end of the day, you want to collapse in a heap, not sit down and plumb your subconscious.

I'm not saying my dad gave up—far from it. One thing he did to feed his soul is bring records into our house, and books. His mind never stopped asking questions, he never stopped asking us questions, and he never stopped reading. Our basement was filled with books, and my dad's study was overflowing with biographies, philosophy books, get-rich-quick paperbacks, and novels. We all read while growing up, and we plumbed my dad's office and the basement for titles. And if I'm being entirely honest with myself, I think I wanted to be a writer because I wanted to communicate my love for him, to one day be a book on Dad's shelf.

But before that can happen, a writer must suffer, and the *Times-Union* internship meant that I'd be away from my wife, Jean, for almost four months. We'd been together for ten years, and in retrospect, since it had been so long since I'd lived on my own, I think it was a test for us, a crossroads. Sure, I needed some practical newspaper experience. But along with that, I wanted to see what it felt like to be alone. Now here I was, tooling east down I-90, and aching along to "Side of the Road," which unfolds verse by verse (no chorus), like a potboiler of the heart that wonders, "Were they happy and content, were there children, and a man and a wife? Did she love him and take her hair down at night?"

Here's where it gets a little surreal. At that moment, a grass field flanked my sunburned left arm, and out the passenger-side window, near the side of the road, sat a tiny farmhouse. As Lucinda's last lyric segued into the violin solo and the farmhouse raced past the bug-corpse-strewn windshield, the corner of my eye caught the soft orange glow of a second-story window and the silhouette of a man and woman. For the next hundred miles, until I pulled into a motel for the night, I drove and wondered about them, and me, and Jean. I wondered about what would happen to us, and to every couple we knew, because at the very least "Side of the Road" demands such reflection. It pits independence against commitment, and dreams a dream of independence within commitment.

The neat ending to the story is that I did the internship, Jean and I missed each other, and at the end of the summer she flew down and drove back home with me, "Side of the Road" playing more than a few times along the way, even though Jean is not a Lucinda fan. We've been together ever since, we've got two kids, and it's a wonderful life, I must say, but there's a but: Lucinda was in town recently. I hear she has a new boyfriend, and a small part of me was jealous. I wondered if she takes her hair down at night and wondered how it feels to jump from lover to lover the way I've never done.

Have I found myself? The short answer is, "No." I played "Side of the Road" the other night, and hearing it again made me realize that for the most part I'm still that kid-man in that car. It also made me realize that, like Lucinda, that wanderlust, the push to follow that unbroken line to a place where the wild things grow, is still there to some degree. This I think I get from my parents, who are still alive, still in love, and still reading.

Sometimes they read what I write. After doing so a couple of years ago, Dad told me he was proud of me, which is something we don't do so much in my family. So when he did, we both skated over it as if he'd just told me about a good trifecta he'd hit at the racetrack. In fact, he might not even remember saying it. But I do. A sound like that lodges in a son's heart like a song.

(Spring 2001, Music.com magazine)

All Down the Line

I'M EXCITED TO HEAR the Rolling Stones at TCF Bank Stadium this week, but not as excited as I was when I drove two days straight to Florida with my big brother Jay to see them forty years ago this summer. Since then, me and the Stones and the times have changed and, not to make too big of a gentrification deal out of it, but it occurs to me that two of the hallowed grounds that were instrumental in introducing impressionable young me to the rebellious power of freedom, decadence, sex, drugs, and rock 'n' roll are now a Patina and a Starbucks.

In the early '70s for just a couple of years, the corner that now houses the Patina on Fiftieth and Bryant Avenue South in Minneapolis belonged to Humble Sounds, one of the first independent record stores in indie-record-store-happy Minneapolis. It was a few blocks from my house, and I used most of the money I got from babysitting and working as a cashier and cook at the Red Barn on Twenty-fourth and Nicollet to buy records there, and I can still smell the incense that was burning when my fifteen-year-old virgin Catholic boy hands picked up and fingered for the first time Andy Warhol's working zipper on the jeans-bulging cover of *Sticky Fingers*.

I liked it, and I liked rock 'n' roll, and Humble Sounds was the place where I bought the Stones' *Metamorphosis* and *It's Only Rock & Roll*, and many more records before it shuttered in 1974.

At the same time, the corner that now houses the Starbucks at South Lyndale and West Diamond Lake Road was Salk's Rexall Drug, and that was where I was standing, at the newsstand by the soda fountain, when I picked up the June 19, 1975, issue of *Rolling Stone* magazine. Inside beckoned a beige full-page ad for the Rolling Stones Tour of America 1975 and its fantastically sinister metallic eagle logo, and this, at the bottom of the page: "The Rolling Stones. The Greatest

Rock & Roll Band in the World—August 2, 1975. Gator Bowl. Jacksonville, Florida."

I was in. I was sixteen years old. I'd just gotten my driver's license, I spent a lot of time driving around listening to cassette tapes, and the Rolling Stones were the most important thing in my safe little life. I'd had it bad since seeing the quadraphonic concert film *Ladies and Gentlemen, The Rolling Stones* twice at the Skyway Theater in downtown Minneapolis the previous summer, and as I started making my way through the first ravages of adolescence, Mick Jagger's sashes and Keith Richards's wicked cool, and all those dark and dirty songs about wine, women, and Satan bewitched my teenage imagination like nothing else.

Punk rock was still a couple of years away from changing my life forever, and at the moment the Stones were the height of subversion for me. "Gimme danger," like Iggy Pop sang on "Raw Power" from around the same time; I bought the mag, rushed home, and showed it to Jay, and two months later we blasted down to Florida in a beat-up 1966 Impala that our grandmother gifted us and that we'd dubbed the White Bomb.

We'd seen the Stones a few weeks earlier on that tour: my first time, June 9, 1975, at the St. Paul Civic Center, where an elaborate lotus-shaped stage with mechanized petals and a giant inflatable penis ushered in "Honky Tonk Women." I was floored, we were hungry for more, and we were met with surprisingly little parental resistance when we hatched our pilgrimage plans.

We followed the ad's Money Orders Only instructions and bought general admission tickets at $11 each (top end for the Stones' current Zip Code tour tix at TCF: $450), which came a few weeks later in the mail, and a couple of days before the show we launched out on our 1,500-mile trek, a couple of knuckleheads on the road to find out.

Upon hitting the highway, we had an unsaid pact: Stones, and Stones only, on the car cassette tape deck. *Exile on Main Street* got us through most of Wisconsin. At 5 A.M. outside Chicago, we stopped to stretch our legs and play Frisbee to "Brown Sugar." We blasted *Hot Rocks, Let It Bleed,* and *It's Only Rock & Roll* through Indiana, Ohio, Tennessee, and, in a raging thunderstorm, into Georgia.

After twenty hours on the road and a blissful rest in an Atlanta motel, we hit the Jacksonville city limits and took in its tangle of bridges and low-income projects. The sight of hot and poor African American families lolling in the afternoon sun on porches provided a poignant reminder that we were two white middle-class Midwestern kids who had come a long way to hear "four white blokes from England playing American music," as Charlie Watts would describe the band to *60 Minutes* interviewer Ed Bradley a few decades later.

It was the first day of August 1975. Gerald Ford was president, disco was sweeping the country, and the Jacksonville Express was preparing for a World Football League game against the Memphis Southmen starring Larry Csonka, Jim Kiick, and Paul Warfield. It was the summer of the Stones in Jacksonville, but it was also the summer of *Jaws,* and in the seventh week of its run, the megablockbuster had created shark hysteria. Swimmers were staying away from the Florida beaches in droves.

We checked into a crappy little Travelodge, watched some college football and a Black Oak Arkansas concert on the tinny motel TV. The next day we woke with the sun, found the Gator Bowl, and parked about half a mile away from the stadium, and about twenty feet from a fire hydrant.

Outside the stadium we bought T-shirts proclaiming, "The Rolling Stones—The Greatest Rock and Roll Band in the World—Aug 2, 1975; Gator Bowl, Jacksonville, Florida." Inside, the Gator Bowl grass was already filled with flesh, so we parked ourselves twenty rows up in the stands. It was ten o'clock in the morning, ninety-two degrees, no shade. All around us, hundreds of our 75,000 fellow '70s rock freaks were passing out from the heat.

It was the freewheeling days of general admission and festival seating, and four years before eleven people would be trampled to death at a Who concert in Cincinnati and change rock concert security and safety laws forever.

The show started just after 1 P.M. After sets by the Atlanta Rhythm Section, Rufus, and the J. Geils Band, and just before the Stones hit the stage, a small thundercloud settled over the Gator Bowl, cooling the drained and delirious crowd. The taped between-band music gave way to another sound: Aaron Copland's "Fanfare for the Common Man," which reviewers had been saying trumpeted the Stones' entrance like they were Roman gods, sent down from above to provide real-deal '70s bacchanalia to the likes of sixteen-year-old me. Yum.

As the horns faded and the five Stones (including guest keyboardist Billy Preston) took the stage, Richards played the seductive opening riff to "Honky Tonk Women" until Jagger appeared from behind a huge speaker, clad in a two-piece silk outfit with flared pants tied at the ankles, red shoes, and a purple cape. He slowly danced his way to the edge of the stage, pressed his lips to the mike, and moaned, "I met a gin-soaked barroom queen in Memphis . . ."

From there, we got what we drove all those miles for: "Rip This Joint," "Love in Vain," "All Down the Line," "Time Is on My Side," "Jumping Jack Flash," "Fool to Cry," "You Can't Always Get What You Want," "Brown Sugar," "Sweet Virginia," and more. Richards, in the midst of his decade-long heroin addiction, looked sicker than usual. His skin was pale, cheeks gaunt, eyes pretty vacant. He stumbled his way through guitar parts and backup vocal chores, and Mick was forced to sing the whole of "Happy," Keith's lone lead vocal of the set.

Midway through, Jagger straddled a fire hose, doused the throng, and a half-hour later closed with an ornery "Midnight Rambler." Sunburned, dehydrated, happy, and exhausted, we returned to our parking spot only to find the White Bomb had been towed or stolen. We reported it to the Jacksonville cops, who put an APB out on it, and while we got it back a couple of days later, upon our return voyage home that news hadn't yet reached a Wisconsin cop, who stopped us at 3 A.M., pointed his gun at my head, put me up against the hood of the White Bomb, and slapped the handcuffs on.

We were not car thieves, we ultimately convinced the cops; we were Minnesota kids on our way back from seeing our favorite band, and now we were cold and tired and out of money and almost out of gas. The cops felt bad. They escorted us to a nearby La Crosse gas station, where we pumped in our last two bucks. They offered to lend us gas money, which we politely refused, and hours later as the sun was peeking over the St. Paul skyline, we were in the home stretch. We had no brakes, we were running on empty, and because we were using a rag as an oil cap (I'd left the real one on top of the car at a SuperAmerica in St. Louis), the Bomb wouldn't go faster than twenty-five miles an hour.

We limped down the shoulder of I-94 and coasted down 35W to the exit ramp into South Minneapolis. We somehow avoided stoplights, pedestrians, and other, healthier cars. Jay eased the Bomb through back streets, pulled into our parents' driveway, and crashed into the family fence, creating a dent that would stay that way for another couple of decades. In our sweaty Stones shrouds we climbed from the Bomb to bear hugs from our parents and sister. We were home, and we were finally sick of the Stones for the time being.

In the forty summers since, I and the times and the Stones are completely different animals, perhaps best illustrated by the juxtaposition of the announcement of that 1975 tour via a performance of "Brown Sugar" on a flatbed truck rolling through Manhattan with the uninspired video announcing the current Zip Code tour, which looks like an ad for a cell phone service. What's more, only a handful of photos exist from that Gator Bowl concert, but it's a safe bet that the TCF Bank concert will be yet another one of the most photographed events in the history of the world.

"Don't tell anyone, but I don't own any albums by the Rolling Stones. They're just so archetypal, so very rock and roll—and that, I find, can be a difficult thing to admire," wrote the *New Yorker*'s Anwen Crawford last week in her essay "The World Needs Female Rock Critics," and part of me appreciates the forward-pushing anti-establishmentarianism. I get it; the sea change is on and the white male is toast, but it says here that music transcends all sorts of human categorizing and any purported music lover whose collection willfully rejects, say, *Aftermath* or *Beggar's Banquet* is difficult to admire. I, too, once threw plenty of the dinosaur rock babies out with the bathwater when punk rock came along and ultimately made my way back, but I never stopped listening to the Rolling Stones.

One of the more memorable bits of Walker Art Center's current International Pop exhibit is a film that includes British news reports of Jagger being arrested on marijuana charges in the early '60s. The newsreel captures him amid staid British society with an omnipresent grin and dancing in handcuffs. It's easy to forget, but that clip is a reminder, in a world rife with 24/7 rebellion and bad boys and girls, that the Stones once stood smartly for youth, art, and personal freedoms that heroically challenged the powers that be.

It's also worth remembering that they helped invent rock 'n' roll, and that they were once simply a gang of scruffy British kids trying to get their little band heard but were rejected by 283 unimpressed Minnesota kids at the Stones' first area appearance at Big Reggie's Danceland in Excelsior on Lake Minnetonka on June 12, 1964. "Nobody liked them; I had never heard them or heard of them," Butch Maness, bass player for the Stones' opening band that night, Mike Waggoner and the Bops, told author Rick Shefchik for Shefchik's wonderful book *Everybody's Heard about the Bird: The True Story of 1960s Rock 'n' Roll in Minnesota*. Maness went on:

> They hadn't made their big boom here yet. When we played, everybody got up and danced. When they played, everybody sat down and had a Coke. When we were changing spots, I tried to get a conversation with [bassist Bill Wyman]. He mumbled a couple of words and went off stage. They wouldn't talk to us. They realized we were a better band than them. We were. They came out with their weird stuff and the kids didn't like it. . . . The last set, the kids kind of ignored them. I don't remember if they booed them. I don't think they played the complete last set. I think they got pissed off and quit. We did the first, they did one, we did another set, and they did the last one. The ironic part about that is a year later, they're millionaires, and we're starting to play their music and still getting five hundred bucks a night. Where's the fairness? We were just as good a band or better, talent-wise.

These days the Stones are as corporate as corporate rock gets, but at the heart of it all remains Richards, who in interviews constantly returns to the enduring romance of rock bands, and the idea that "a band isn't a band in the proper sense of the word if it doesn't play in front of people. A band starts to play in front of people. That's how a band always starts. It doesn't start to make records or money or anything else, it starts to play on a stage in front of people."

Me, I wouldn't drive 1,500 miles to see the Stones again, but I'm glad I did, and at the moment I'm left wondering exactly how much "The Greatest Rock & Roll Band in the World" means to me now. I've sung their songs with my bands and with friends in bars. I have friends who will be ditching their kids' high school graduation parties and heading to Dinkytown Wednesday night to partake in the semi-debauchery. My twenty-year-old son's favorite song is "Paint It Black." When I told my sixteen-year-old daughter I'd driven to Florida when I was her age to see the Rolling Stones, she wasn't sure who they were, but she asked me if I'd let her do the same thing.

Not a chance, I told her. But I did get her tickets to see Babes in Toyland.

(June 2, 2015, Minnpost.com)

Legalize It

ONE OF THE FIRST TIMES I smoked marijuana was with Peter Tosh.
It was July 10, 1978, and the cofounder of the Wailers and his
band were opening for the Rolling Stones at the St. Paul Civic Center. During "Legalize It," the title track off Tosh's 1976 solo album
and the first mainstream-produced record to champion the medicinal
and spiritual benefits of weed, the thirty-four-year-old native of West-
moreland, Jamaica, pulled out a spliff the size of a baguette and lifted
it to the heavens. Cheers.

I was nineteen years old, a few months older than my son is now.
Mick Jagger had just been onstage, doing his bony-assed chicken
dance while guest dueting with Tosh on their hopped-up version of
the Temptations' "(Walk and) Don't Look Back," so by sheer star
power the then-mostly-unknown reggae legend had the twenty thousand rock kids in the palms of his blunt-loving hands.

Sporting a floppy red, yellow, and green Rasta tam, Tosh stepped
to the lip of the stage as the sensual reggae churned behind him, lit
up the joint, and took a massive hit. Bedlam. As he exhaled, he squat-
ted, leaned down, and in communion handed the big bat down to
my brother Jay, with whom I'd camped outside the Civic Center for
most of the day and survived a few hours of classic '70s arena-seating
pounding to land our spot in the front row, dead center under Jagger
and Tosh's microphone.

With our brother Terry a couple rows in back of us and ASIA
security guard Jesse Ventura holding the line in front of us, Jay lifted
the joint into the air, took a hit, and passed it to me. I repeated the
ritual, to roars of approval from the throng, and passed it off into the
pulsing night.

I thought about all this, and about my own history with smoking
weed, as pot became legal in Colorado January 1 and as other states—
twenty and counting—prepare to enact similar laws soon. I read,

listened, and watched as pundits both vilified and championed pot, and heard theory after theory posited—from pot makes you dumb to pot makes you smart; pot makes you more creative; pot is good; pot is bad; pot makes you less ambitious; pot is fun; pot is boring; pot makes you paranoid; pot is great for depression, anxiety, music, sex, food; pot makes you schizophrenic; pot is a gateway drug; et cetera.

What I know about so-called stoners comes from life experience, not punditry or politics, and to generalize, they are some of the kindest, most open-hearted and open-minded people you'd ever care to hang with.

What else I know is that we are not truly a free people if smoking weed is considered a crime—not when guns, alcohol, and tobacco are legal—and that if the powers that be who are still patting themselves on the back for legalizing gay marriage and building a taxpayers-funded football stadium for out-of-state billionaires can't do this work of the people, then Minnesota is hardly the progressive state it likes to bill itself as.

In Minnesota, the land of ten thousand brew pubs, the government sanctions all sorts of potentially dangerous activities, from airlines to fast food to violent entertainment, but its heretofore staunch stance against medical and recreational marijuana suggests a lumbering body in bed with the prohibitionists of yore and a pharmaceutical industry that doesn't want a populace regularly achieving a consciousness that questions authority, examines ways of being and living, and dares to demand the same liberty and freedoms afforded citizens of other states.

No, I'm not about to join NORML or become a champion of weed smokers' rights, but I will say that I know for a fact that many of your neighbors smoke weed, and that one of the last times I smoked was in December inside the Lakewood Cemetery chapel, after a friend lit up at the conclusion of an especially poignant funeral, and on Christmas Eve in front of another buddy's fireplace, when he offered me a hit of his liquid marijuana–spiked e-cig. In both instances, we were criminals and scofflaws, a designation the Minnesota Legislature should take seriously when it reconvenes February 25.

"Dad, how can they do that?" was my son's response a couple of years ago, on our way home from First Avenue, where he and his girlfriend took in a concert by the Los Angeles hip-hop crew Odd Future, who blatantly smoked bags of weed onstage.

The best I could do was explain Minnesota law, tell him that the times are changing, warn him again about the effects of weed on the developing teenage brain, and recount for him my night in St. Paul with Tosh, whose largely unheard forty-year-old message should be ringing out far and wide across Minnesota starting right now.

(January 13, 2014, Southwest Journal)

Merry Christmas to the Thief
Who Stole My CD Player

TO THE PERSON WHO STOLE the Discman CD player out of my car last weekend, there are a few things you should know about it, vis-à-vis operating instructions and such.

The volume control is that little round wheel with ridges on the left. It doesn't get very loud, but if you turn up your radio on the dash, you should be all right. There's no bass or treble control, so you're on your own with that, too.

You didn't take the converter wires that connect it to the tape deck and cigarette lighter, so you might want to grab some of those if you want to play CDs in the car. If you plan on just using it with your headphones, you'll need some batteries. Two double-A batteries will get you about twenty-five hours; after that it starts to skip and fade.

Let's see, what else? Oh, yeah, the player has magic powers.

It can take you places. Highways, byways, yellow brick roads, forks in the road, paths least taken, ditches, dirty boulevards, happy trails, wild goose chases, flights of fancy, space odysseys, lunar landscapes. It can get you lost and found, sometimes in the same trip. It can make places you've been to hundreds of times seem foreign and places you're visiting for the first time feel familiar.

At full power, it can conjure people you miss or dead people whose music makes you feel close to them. If the night is right and the windshield's doing its stained-glass-window thing and you've slipped in whatever's your pleasure—punk, funk, blues, gospel, classical, classic rock, hip-hop, big band, klezmer, jazz, country, spoken word, comedy, folk, indie rock, reggae, zydeco, bluegrass, world music, children's music, Christmas music, all of which and more have been spun in the shimmering silver cylinder you now hold in your hands—it's like the dead are riding shotgun.

That's true with the living, too. It can allow you to be with people you love but who are far away and people you love but whom you can't really be with. It also can get you closer *to* people you love who are sometimes sitting right next to you or giggling in the back seat.

They never advertise this sort of valuable information with the new CD players, so it's a good thing you picked up a used one. Hard to imagine how they'd pitch it. Already broken in! Not another one like it in the world! Natural aphrodisiac! Wards off the blues! Accentuates the positive! Guaranteed to make you feel cool, fearless, tough, sexy, and tender, even if you're totally lame!

I'm the original owner. I know what this baby can do. It's a time machine, a magnificent conversationalist, and it will give you as much as you give it. I had it for a long time. It made me some good friends, some amazing acquaintances, and even a few enemies, but who's counting, right?

You know what I liked most about it? Whenever I turned it on and looked out at the faces of people in cars next to me or walking down the street, it always made me feel connected to them and to something bigger.

That's about it. I can't think of anything else. I made a bigger deal out of this than I meant to. All I really wanted to do is tell you how to work the damn thing. But it's all good. It's all yours.

So is the CD that was in it when you took it. If you've got kids, they're going to love it, especially the song with the sitar—I think it's No. 10—the one with the name we could never remember so we called it the George song. We used to sing along to it every day. Not anymore.

Merry Christmas, stranger.

(December 8, 2001, St. Paul Pioneer Press)

THREE
MIX #1
CRUSH ON YOU

Singing in My Sleep

THE CASSETTE TAPE was first introduced in Europe in 1963, but didn't gain widespread use in North America until the early '70s. Since then, the cassette has been both savior and scourge to a music industry paranoid about home-taping, but it has allowed the rest of us to bypass the usual means of music distribution and send straight-to-the-aorta messages of love to loved ones and/or wannabe loved ones.

Or, as Dan Wilson sings on Semisonic's new single "Singing in My Sleep," "Got your tape and it changed my mind, heard your voice in between the lines . . . . Now I'm falling in love too fast, with you and the songs you chose."

Or even more simply, "This is my rock 'n' roll love letter to you"—as the Bay City Rollers sing to me on a tape a friend recently made me.

Call them whatever you want—love letters, mixtapes, compilation tapes—but anyone with a record collection, a tape deck, and a passion for mixed emotions and subliminal messages has made them at one time or another. Unlike albums, or radio formats, or *Time–Life* compilation boxed sets, mixtapes are spiked with bizarre choices cobbled together at the tapehead's whim/inspiration. Little-heard nuggets play next to big radio hits, and long-forgotten songs from the past fade into undiscovered album cuts from the present.

Over the years, I've made and received countless such tapes. Most of the ones I've made have been fashioned for family and friends. But the ones I've received and played to death—the ones I know by heart as well as any carefully sequenced album—have come from friends, relatives, readers, strangers. As I type this sentence, an old mixtape is in the deck, Bob Dylan croaking "Lenny Bruce." Next to the deck is a cardboard box stuffed with tapes.

The artwork varies: some are colorful, painstaking works of art; others are just the basics—black felt-tip pen, artist, title, over and out. Some combine the two, with song titles and dabs of watercolors. Some don't even bother with a cover or a track listing. Some have themes— Christmas songs, lust songs, breakup songs, anniversary songs, birthday songs. Some have titles: "Can You Handle It?" "Sound Track to Nothing," "Soul Music," "My Sucky Old Tape," "Stuff I Thought You'd Like," "Party Tape" (several of these).

All have one thing in common: they are fiercely antiformat, very DIY, and decidedly free-form. Cabaret Voltaire segues naturally into Leonard Cohen into Nick Lowe into Tupac Shakur into the Undertones into Rose Royce into Boss Hog into a klezmer band into a Hawaiian slack-key guitar master into " 'Til There Was You" (from *The Music Man*) into Mark Eitzel into Black Flag into "Somewhere over the Rainbow" into Chet Baker into the Hudson Brothers into GG Allin into live bootlegs into cruddily recorded songs or spoken words from the tape-makers themselves.

On paper, it looks scattershot. But the beauty of the mixtape is that no matter how eclectic the mix, in the end it all makes perfect sense—to the listener, perhaps, but mostly to the maker. To every mixtape, there is a context, a reason for putting "American Pie" next to "I'm So Bored with the U.S.A.," or for pairing "Whistle While You Work" with "Theme from *Bridge on the River Kwai*."

Tapeheads make their tapes for friends, lovers, exes, themselves. They are sent as tools for seduction, musical education, seduction, grieving, joy, seduction, and fun. And now, someone has finally gotten around to penning a musical tribute to the compilation tape as courting device.

"Singing in My Sleep" is that song. And if it enjoys the same sort of success the Minneapolis-based power trio's current hit, "Closing Time," has, songwriter Dan Wilson's tale of a couple of tapeheads' burgeoning romance will shine a light on a peculiar passion that music lovers have been practicing for years—though the mixtape coming-out party isn't being hosted by Semisonic alone.

On his new album, Aussie songwriter Paul Kelly sings, "You made a special tape for me . . . I put it on today, then I had to turn it off, from Junior Brown to Dr. Dre, and You Am I along the way."

To be sure, there is a unique sensuality, an uncommon intimacy that comes from the mixtape ritual. A love letter has lines that can be read between, but a batch of songs has lyrics and musical viscera that suggest what the tapemaker feels about you, knows about you, suspects about you. And every song says, "I thought about you."

As Wilson sings, "I've been living in your cassette, it's the modern equivalent, singing up to a Capulet, on a balcony in your mind."

Indeed, the poets from inside the cassettes often express ambiguous messages or other feelings that we can't quite get at during the light of day, and that chance to play deejay of the heart is the biggest allure to making/receiving compilation tapes—but not really. The mixtape is a tossed-off postcard with an audience of one, so any overbearing sense of critical thought goes out the window. The world is not listening. There is no one to impress but you. And the recipient. And God. Which is why sequencing is so important.

During some late-night taping jags, I've been guilty of getting tired, and as a way of simply finishing a tape, I'll slap on a song that doesn't feel right. In record-company and rock-critic jargon, such tracks are called "filler." But with mixtapes, filler is okay—even charming, in its own way—because there are no rules to making mixtapes. Unless, of course, you're Rob Fleming, the obsessive record-shop owner/deejay/music geek from Nick Hornby's riotous *High Fidelity*. Early in the novel, Rob tries to seduce his girlfriend, Laura, with what else? As Hornby/Fleming says:

> I spent hours putting that cassette together. To me, making a tape is like writing a letter—there's a lot of erasing and rethinking and starting again, and I wanted it to be a good one, because . . . to be

honest, because I hadn't met anyone as promising as Laura since I'd started the DJ-ing, and meeting promising women was partly what the DJ-ing was supposed to be about.

A good compilation tape, like breaking up, is hard to do. You've got to kick off with a corker, to hold the attention (I started with "Got to Get You off My Mind," but then realized that might not get any further than track one, side one if I delivered what she wanted straightaway, so I buried it in the middle of side two), and then you've got to up it a notch, or cool it a notch, and you can't have white music and black music together, unless the white music sounds like black music, and you can't have two tracks by the same artist side by side, unless you've done the whole thing in pairs, and . . . oh, there are loads of rules.

The most important of which is: the fewer rules, the better. The only rule I've developed is not a rule but a habit. I always end up making tapes late at night, when concentration is at its most delirious.

The only other rule is for the tape recipient and is a hard and fast one: mind your manners. Have some decorum. We work hard on these things, and to get a simple "Thanks" or "Yeah, I got it—where'd you get that one live thing?" is not enough. We want more. Truth be told, we want reviews. Where were you when you played it? Did you get what I was trying to say?

Of course, if you wanted to, you could make every tapehead's ultimate fantasy come true—make a reciprocal tape. One that taps into our innermost shared feelings. Maybe even answers the first tape, song for song. Ideally, the artwork would be fashioned out of crayon and Sharpie, and the tape called something like, "The Greatest Mixtape Ever Made—First in an Ongoing Series."

(August 4, 1998, St. Paul Pioneer Press)

Short Man's Room

LAST JANUARY, a friend mailed me an advance cassette of Joe Henry's new album *Short Man's Room*. I had it in the car deck while driving over to the nursing home to visit my uncle, a hard-bitten sixty-six-year-old Irishman whose love for booze had gotten the best of him yet again. Almost killed him, in fact.

Mind you, the visit wasn't entirely my idea. My uncle and I had never really been close; I'd helped him move a couple of times and we saw each other on holidays, but that was about it. I was happy to go see him, but it was mostly on my mom's request that I was taking time out from my busy schedule for this morning's mercy call.

When I got to the nursing home, I wasn't positive he knew who I was, so I made a point of mentioning my name a couple of times. I pushed his wheelchair into the visitor's room, and we made small talk about the upcoming Super Bowl. All the while, a mentally challenged kid banged his cane on the side of my uncle's wheelchair. Feisty as ever, he finally whirled around and barked at the kid, "If you do that one more time, I'm gonna kick your ass." Never mind that my uncle had just got done telling me he could barely walk to the toilet. It was funny—almost as funny as his scorn for the other patients, who whiled away their days cutting out newspaper coupons.

After a half-hour, we said our good-byes and I told him I'd try to visit him again that week, which I never did. I got into the car, popped *Short Man's Room* back in, and cued up the title song, which had been running through my head the whole visit. Set to an almost Victorian shuffle/waltz, an old-timer recounts his life and times and doles out wisdom to a young buck who's visiting the duffer's hearth. I rewound and fast-forwarded one verse over and over until I got back to my job, my deadlines, my important stuff. Somewhere between Lake Street and Franklin Avenue, "Short Man's Room" became mine. And my uncle's.

Like all great music, *Short Man's Room* speaks—make that "whispers"—to a listener's deepest dreams and diaries. The parable of the dried-up uncle is my Joe Henry story, and I've got a million of 'em. But you've got yours, too, or will soon enough, if you give *Short Man's Room* sufficient headphone time, or even if you just let it waft through the rooms of your home while making the bed or making love. But be warned: there are no videos to babysit your imagination, no current events for your knees to jerk to—just the three bare essentials of beautiful moods, words, and music.

Indeed, Henry's songs leave plenty of room for personal application. The disc includes a lyric sheet, but it's not much help. Because he uses "smoke signals instead of telegrams" in telling his tales, the listener, singer, and song are all equal players in determining where, as Henry sings in "King's Highway," a story will unwind.

"I think any kind of art works that way," he says from his home in Los Angeles.

> You send it off in one direction, and where it goes and how it affects people—that's kind of the idea of it. It takes on a life of its own, and where it goes . . . you kind of wish it well and hope it doesn't double back on you.
>
> If you painted an abstract portrait of someone that you never knew, just because that's a character you conjured, and someone saw it and it looked just like their mother to them—it's gonna hit them in a very different way than you ever anticipated. But you're not gonna tell that person that that response isn't a genuine response. I would never tell anybody that a song isn't what they think it's about. If that's how it hits you, then that's what it's about.

Which isn't to say that the eleven songs on *Short Man's Room* or Henry's previous three albums—1986's *Talk of Heaven* (Profile), 1989's *Murder of Crows* (A&M), and 1990's *Shuffletown* (A&M)—are works of fiction. The singer says his songs are just that—his songs—but in the same breath he says he's unwilling to box them in:

> I'm not a video artist, and that's not by accident. I have no real

interest in tying the songs to any sort of image. It's just like Orson Welles doing *War of the Worlds* over the radio. Everybody has their own idea of what their own demons would be if they were ever confronted with them, and you could cut everyone's imagination off at the knees if you show them what your demon looks like. But if you can set it up in such a way that their mind goes to work, then people are always going to fill in the blanks with something that's potent for them.

As a master of understatement toiling in an overblown music industry, Henry's career has been spotty at best thus far. A native of North Carolina who lived in Georgia and Ohio as a youth, he was never a part of music scenes in his later homes of Michigan or New York. Likewise, though his craft is folk-based, he's never been part of the folk fest circuit, and he's developed an innate skepticism for joining any such clubs. As a result, there's no label sound for Henry to live up to, no scene causes to further, no eager passengers waiting at the bandwagon station. Just him. An island, a scene unto himself.

"I would imagine [trying to live up to a certain sound] would be very limiting," he says. "Everybody I grew up listening to were loners in what they did. You know, the obvious people—Bob Dylan, Van Morrison, Tom Waits—singer/songwriters who were working when I was just starting to learn. I've always been kind of infatuated with people who just had a very singular vision, whether it was Bob Dylan or Lightnin' Hopkins."

Even his name conjures something intrinsically lonesome, adrift on a sea of generic Americana: Joe, as in DiMaggio, Jackson, Friday. Henry, as in Aaron, Huggins, Ford. But Henry is no best-kept secret. He is, along with the likes of Paul Kelly, Freedy Johnston, and Jules Shear, yet another pioneering singer/songwriter in danger of not being heard. Because his only gimmick is his songs, Henry is much like the protagonist of John Irving's *A Prayer for Owen Meany*, in which a modern-day Christ makes his second coming on a much smaller scale: he can't save the world this time, so he'll just do what he can, just touch a few souls.

Truly, Henry epitomizes the dawning of a new underground in American music, an underground that's slowly coming to the conclusion that less is more. Nowadays, music that can be seen on television is about as personally relevant and rewarding as the Mall of America, and Henry is living proof of the two music businesses emerging at the end of the twentieth century. One is about music. The other is about entertainment. It's the difference between art and recreation: the Entry or Uptown versus Mississippi Live. Ironically, the great divide is best illustrated by Henry at one end and his sister-in-law, Madonna, at the other:

> People ask me about my sister-in-law all the time, and I'm not trying to be coy when I say, "She and I are not in the same business." You know, we're just not. I don't think she recognizes us in the same business, either. She knows this is what I do—in fact, when I played a show in New York last week, she came to the show, much to my astonishment. Not to put her down, because she's obviously really good at what she does, but my personal feeling about what she does is that her persona is her career, and records and videos are commercials for her persona.

Because he realizes his music is "just not going to mean that much to that many people," Henry isn't holding his breath for either critical acceptance or a Madonna-sized public profile. But he admits to wanting more:

> Hey, I'm like anybody else—I'd like to own a house someday. You know, I'd like for Levon [his ten-month-old son] to have everything he oughta have. I'd like for Melanie [his wife, whom he met in high school] to not have to work if she didn't want to. So as an independent businessperson trying to do this, I certainly find that there're days where I'm really frustrated and I'm going, "Why is there this hump I can't get over?" Then there're other days when you just kind of sober up and say, "That's got nothing to do with anything."
>
> You know, I doubt [poet, satirist, and religious writer] Thomas Merton worried about whether or not anybody cared. There's a great quote from Thomas Merton that I used to have inside my notebook for a while, and I think this works whether you're a

spiritual person or not. He said, and I'm paraphrasing: "If you write for God, you will enlighten a lot of people and you will be fulfilled; if you write for other people, you may make a splash in the world and be known for some time and then you'll fade away like everybody else does. And if you write for yourself, after ten minutes, you will look at what you yourself have written and you'll be so disgusted that you'll wish you were dead."

And I challenge myself with that all the time. At the point where I'm most frustrated, I think that's mostly vanity. You do your work because that's what you do. You either get satisfaction out of doing it or you don't. If I find myself worrying about whether [critic] Dave Marsh likes it, then that thought has a brother, which is trying to write a song that Dave Marsh likes. And then you're finished.

Such idealism went and got Henry dropped from A&M Records almost before *Shuffletown* was released in 1990. Despite the lip-serviced hosannas he heard from the label's creative staff at a prerelease meeting, the head of marketing spoke the awful truth.

After the meeting was over, he walks over to me and says, "I just have to ask you: Why would you make a record like this?" He was just kind of mystified why I would intentionally set out to do something that was, in his mind, so worthless, such a dead end. And right then, after all those months of being patted on the back, I just knew. The light came on. I went home and told Melanie, you know, "We're finished here. We shouldn't even be doing this."

A&M's loss was the North Carolina–based Mammoth Records' gain. Henry recorded *Short Man's Room* live to eight-track over a five-day period at local producer/engineer Brian Paulson's makeshift studio in the offices of Rykodisc in Minneapolis's Warehouse District. The songs are fleshed out beautifully by the Jayhawks and violinist Mike Russell, with guest spots by Soul Asylum guitarist Danny Murphy and banjo player Dave Boquist. It was an after-hours project, and it sounds like it. "The first time we were in there," Henry recalls, "it was like me and [Jayhawks singers/guitarists Gary Louris and Mark Olson] sitting in a line of three secretaries' desks. I was sitting at a little desk with a plastic rose and a picture of somebody's family staring at me."

The office building sessions were originally meant to be demos, but Henry liked the feel of the recordings, and after consulting with manager Dave Ayers, he decided to turn the project over to Mammoth. The result is a classic American folk-rock record, the sparse but by no means slapdash *Short Man's Room*. There are only minimal overdubs, but plenty of natural ambience. Put your ear to the ground at the beginning of "King's Highway" and you can hear somebody drop a pair of keys as Louris and Henry smack their lips in anticipation of telling a tale of nonchalant murder. On another label, another studio, those sounds would have been punched out, cleaned up. For Henry, who does production work with T-Bone Burnett in Los Angeles, the experience was freeing.

"This might sound obvious, but after a while a lot of studio work stops being about music and starts being like math," he says. "I just happen to really believe that if you know what you're trying to get onto tape is a feeling of five guys in a room playing, you know, maybe . . . the first place to start is to get five guys into a big room and play."

What a concept.

"Yeah, well—keep it under your hat. I'm trying to get a copyright on it."

A timeless travel through myriad characters and moods, *Short Man's Room* feels like it was made by a very old soul, a Rip Van Winkle with an acoustic guitar and dobro who's oblivious to the speed of today's society and its musical trends. While rap, metal, and punk push their respective envelopes, Henry's sound is a fading, yellowing postcard that could be used as somebody's favorite bookmark. Something, someone has been reincarnated in this haunting *Room,* and at times it sounds like the singer is not a singer but a medium.

It's a celebration of regulars ("Last One Out," "Short Man's Room") and youth ("Good Fortune," "Stations," "The Diving Bell"). And true to its themes of life, death, and everything in between, Henry dedicates the record to his son and the memory of a late friend. Fittingly, *Short Man's Room*'s finale is the exquisite "One Shoe On," a first-person account about a guy dying. A guy dying happy. Which brings me back to my Joe Henry story.

This past Father's Day, a bunch of us got together for a barbeque. My uncle, whose kid isn't much interested in Father's Day anymore, stopped by for burgers and brats. He's been out of the nursing home for months now; he's living on his own in an apartment and thinking about selling his car so he can take a trip. Maybe to Vegas, because he thinks the casinos here are a rip-off. My dad calls him Lazarus.

On the porch, three generations stuff their faces with potato salad and key lime pie; the talk is of *Batman Returns,* the streaking Twins, and Ross Perot. My uncle says he's kicked the bottle once and for all but interjects drinking war stories that elicit nervous hiccups of laughter. Out on the lawn, my two-year-old nephew's running in circles by himself, catching the natural buzz of dizziness. His tipsy smile bouncing off the bright June sun makes it look like he'll live forever. Somewhere, a Joe Henry song is coming to a close.

(July 8, 1992, City Pages)

After the Dance

MUSIC AND MEMORY PART XXII (in reference to *Al Green's Greatest Hits* and Marvin Gaye's *After the Dance*): four summers ago, I went to my twenty-year high school reunion. It's tempting to say that it provided me with a moment of sweet revenge, but I'd be lying if I did. What it did provide me with, though, is a pretty great high school reunion story.

I attended DeLaSalle, the Catholic high school in downtown Minneapolis, in the late '70s. During my sophomore year, I fell in love with the school's brightest light, whom I'll call Mary. She was from North Minneapolis, a cheerleader, but never mind the stereotype. She cheered because she had this insatiable lust for life; she loved everything about her huge family, her school, her community. I was fifteen. I was whipped.

I was a good kid, with good friends. I played baseball (we never won a game, but we had a blast) and wrote for the school newspaper (some of the guys called me "poet" for a couple of weeks, which I dug), and, as Janis Ian and Kurt Cobain and other sideliners throughout history have noted, that profile doesn't usually win the head cheerleader.

Because our graduating class was small (eighty people or so), cliques weren't the crushing caste system I've heard about in bigger schools. I wasn't a star athlete or anything, but I talked to Mary about her boyfriends on the phone every other night for almost two years. I can still feel the clammy receiver, the cauliflower ear. She cried a lot. I comforted her. I hugged her. I can still smell her perfume. I can still feel her head on my shoulder from the night we sat together on a bus ride coming home from a basketball game in Rochester. She played "Feelings" on her tape deck over and over. You know, "Whoa, whoa, whoa, feelings, feelings of love." For another guy.

She turned me on to Marvin Gaye and Al Green, and the combination of all those songs about dancing and getting it on and her rainbow smile, school spirit, wronged heart, and great body did a number on me. It kept me up nights writing about her and listening to music.

Yes, Mary broke my heart. I was just as much to blame, though, because I think I knew the score even then, but I didn't know how to let go. I went to her basketball and volleyball games (she introduced me to her mom as "my No. 1 fan," and writing this makes me blush as hard as when it happened), wrote her cards and letters, got to know her family, and she was just too nice/flattered/young to tell me to get lost, that I had no chance with her. So I put on a brave face and learned the meaning of the word *platonic*.

Our senior year, I got up the guts to ask her to prom. For the first time since I'd known her, she wasn't dating anyone. I asked her in the winter, months before the dance. She said no. Sweetly, but no.

"Things tend to happen on prom night . . . ," she giggled, which I didn't understand. But after talking with my pals, I later figured out that she was talking about sex, which I was quite a ways away from having, much less thinking about having, on prom night.

Mary, the homecoming queen, ended up going to prom with the homecoming king/football star, whom she started dating just before prom, and just after two basketball stars. That was the beginning of the end of my obsession with Mary. By the time she wrote, "I love you madly" and "We were made for each other" and "Nothing could keep me away from your gorgeous bod" in her full-page farewell to me in my senior yearbook (God knows what I wrote in hers), I was over her.

After graduation, we ran into each other a few times, and each time was less painful. She got married and had kids, and so did I, but a first love that hits the way Mary hit me doesn't go away so neatly. Probably because you don't want it to.

A couple of months before our twenty-year reunion, she called to ask if I could help out. I begged off as being too busy but said I'd put together a questionnaire for everyone to answer: What have you been doing? Are you married, divorced, have a boyfriend/girlfriend? Do you have kids? Whom do you wish you had dated in high school? That sort of thing.

The night of the reunion, I sat down at a table and checked out the questionnaires, which Mary had laminated and bound into a photo album. Three or four of my buddies were standing behind me, watching as I flipped the pages, waiting for my reaction. When I got to Mary's page, there was my name under the "wish-you-had-dated" question in that still girly-girl-after-all-these-years penmanship.

As I looked up to see her face, my pals—all of whom knew that she had broken my heart, and felt for me, because at one point, even though I didn't really care, it kind of seemed like the whole school thought I was a sucker—hooted and howled and patted me on the back.

She fixed her big brown eyes on mine, as if she had been waiting for this moment for a while, and said, "I blew it." She said it twice.

Nobody hooted or howled after that. Maybe she was drunk, or kidding, but that's not how I remember it. I didn't talk to her about it then, or ever, mostly because I didn't feel the same way, so I didn't know what to say. Nor can I presume why, exactly, she came to feel the way she did.

What I do know is that it was just like her to do something like that. Kind. Generous. Flirtatious. Part of me wanted to thank her for acknowledging the purity of that love, that time. The other part wanted to hold her, comfort her, call her.

Which brings me back to Al Green. At the bookstore the other day, he was singing about Mary over the speakers, and just like that, there I was, running full speed down the Hennepin Avenue Bridge on a cold winter night in 1976, past the Grain Belt Beer sign, trying to get away from Mary—who that day had found yet another new boyfriend who wasn't me—and on with my life.

Oh, and one more thing: Andrea Swensson, will you go to prom with Andy Uzendoski? I don't know anything about him other than the beautiful letter he wrote me and the beautiful music he loves, but if that's any indication, you could do a lot worse. He asked me to ask you for him, so consider this your Jumbotron.

And Andrea? Whatever your decision, please, for the sake of soft boys everywhere, be gentle.

(May 6, 2001, St. Paul Pioneer Press)

All about Chemistry

ANDREA SWENSSON SAID YES.

There is no bigger headline in your Pulitzer Prize–winning, down-sizing newspaper today, so clip and savor, baby.

You may remember Andrea from a column a couple of weeks ago, in which the pop music columnist reminisced about his would-be prom date "Mary'" from many years ago and concluded with these sentences:

"Andrea Swensson, will you go to prom with Andy Uzendoski? I don't know anything about him other than the beautiful letter he wrote me and the beautiful music he loves, but if that's any indication, you could do a lot worse. He asked me to ask you for him, so consider this your Jumbotron."

Well, Andrea Swensson said yes. She e-mailed the columnist to say so, told him all about what she loves about Andy and that they'll be attending the Eastview High prom in Apple Valley together May 26.

Andrea Swensson said yes. Maybe on prom night she and Andy will talk about music, or his drumming, or her gift for writing, or the Ginkgo Coffeehouse, where they discovered each other at a Dan Israel gig, and how his song "Overloaded" changed their lives.

Maybe they'll talk about Semisonic, whose new record, *All about Chemistry,* has become the sound track to their friendship, or Joe Henry, Bruce Springsteen, Mason Jennings, Miles Davis, Jeff Buckley, the Jayhawks, John Prine, or Tim Easton, all of whom Andy adores.

Maybe they'll talk about the e-mails they sent the columnist in the past couple of weeks, like the one in which Andy called Andrea "the greatest girl I've ever met." Or like this one from Andrea:

I am so happy. I don't know the ending to this story yet . . . but for now, I am going to prom with someone who understands Dan Israel, who understands your interpretations of music, who truly understands me like no one else has. And that is definitely more than I could ever ask for.

A combination of music and your articles have made two lonely people very, very happy. Thank you for helping two totally clueless teenagers find each other. Thank you for putting into words what other people only feel when they listen to music, and thank you for the little bits of advice that manage to seep into your articles every day that help to get through this confusing and wondrous experience called adolescence.

This is a job? I get paid for this? Did you hear?

Andrea Swensson said yes. Maybe next Saturday she and Andy will go to the dance, and their friends will give them grief because they read all that mushy stuff about them in the newspaper. Then again, maybe they won't. Maybe their friends will say yes to someone, something, too. Maybe we all will.

Maybe Andrea and Andy will kiss. Maybe they'll stay up all prom night listening to music. Maybe they'll stay up all prom night listening to each other. Maybe they'll be happy.

Maybe they'll get married someday, like the columnist's kid sister will tomorrow, glorious tomorrow, Joey Ramone's birthday. Gabba-gabba-hey!

Maybe a lot of things, but one thing is certain: it was a brutal winter. People who usually seize the day found themselves waiting for the other shoe to drop. They didn't feel like themselves, and they hibernated with their pain. They worried about their parents, their kids, their mortality, their lovers, their mental health. They thought about old friends, and new friends, some of whom they don't talk to anymore, and every time they heard a singer sing, "Do you ever think about me?" they thought about them and wondered what the hell was wrong with them.

Then Andrea Swensson said yes, and everything changed. The world shifted on its axis. Did you feel it? It happened on May 6, but the ripple is just making its way to us now. Birds are biting, fish are singing, glands are glanding, girls are grabbing sailors and kissing them on the street like it's V-J Day, and the cold gray of Snoopyville has turned this burg into one great big free David Hockney painting.

Andrea Swensson said yes. As in: John climbing Yoko's ladder, Marv Albert's orgasmic catchphrase, the "Roundabout" guys, and "She loves you, yeah, yeah, yeah!"

As in: Sí, oui, yep, sure, alrighty, well all right, right on, word up, okay, okey-dokey, affirmative, you betcha, right back atcha, absobleep-inglutely, Roger Wilco, uh-huh, amen.

As in: Not no.

Andrea Swensson said yes. And ever since, cars, coffee shops, and hearts have been filled with that song that goes, "It's a beautiful day," which we all now know those Irish cats wrote for us, for this moment, for this "end of the Ice Age," as the cartoonist/dentist Peter Kohlsaat so perfectly put it the other night at the Turf Club.

Andrea Swensson said yes. Aftershock: strangers holding doors for each other, ogling each other, flirting with each other, cutting out the middlegod. Instead of saying things like, "Jesus loves you," they're saying, "I love you." The sun is out. Hope springs eternal. Love is in the air.

The hometown baseball team is on the cover of a national sports magazine with the headline, "Do you believe in miracles?" The columnist's kid sister and her man are reading this right now, and they are saying, "I do."

The meteorologist will chalk up all these good spirits and the fact that everyone feels so much better than they did a month ago to the warm weather. The poet will say that it's the annual rite of renewal we've come to know as "spring." Who are they kidding?

Andrea Swensson said yes.

(May 18, 2001, St. Paul Pioneer Press)

I Saw the Light

IT WAS ONE OF THOSE MOMENTS that only happen in the movies. Honestly, the *A Star Is Born* scenario still sends shivers down the spine of this witness to the electrocution. Last December at the Cabooze, an all-star lineup of local music gunslingers gathered to pay tribute to the late, great Hank Williams. As gigs go, it was as close to nirvana as any night club critter could ever hope for: superb music, packed house, good holiday cheer, and a guy walking around in a black leather jacket with a serious painting of Hank on its back.

Then it happened. Near night's end, an unknown, unassuming woman took the stage and moved tentatively to the mike. A palpable wave of uneasiness swept over the Hank faithful both on- and offstage, guitarist Bob Dunlap and bassist Nick Ciola started up the band, and the mystery woman (one Janie Miller, it was discovered later, a singer from Golden Valley who performs a Patsy Cline tribute show) belted out the first verse of "Your Cheatin' Heart." The stunned crowd fell silent for a second, caught its collective breath, then exploded.

"That was probably the biggest high I've ever had, by far," the twenty-seven-year-old Miller says. "I had done a show that night at the Canyon. And [Proton Productions' Kevin Daly, Miller's agent] got me down there, and I was like, 'This is crazy. I don't know what I'm doing.' I didn't know any of those guys onstage. But when I let out the first few words, everyone went crazy, and my bottom lip was shaking because my adrenaline started pumping so hard. I couldn't believe it."

Miller first became infatuated with Cline in 1986, when she saw *Sweet Dreams,* the Patsy biopic starring Jessica Lange. After a couple of short-lived singing jobs in Minneapolis, she traveled west "in search of life" and to follow her dreams of becoming a singer. She hooked up with a couple of guys who were in the business of staging tributes to —but of course—Burl Ives and Marty Robbins, and the trio traveled around the Northwest performing at Elks and Eagles lodges for a year.

Motherhood gladly interrupted Miller's singing career for a spell, but now that she's back in Minneapolis, she's formed a full band and will be playing out soon. And while she believes her Cline tribute show is always improving, she also realizes that the magic she helped create back in December will be hard to duplicate. "Those kinds of things are once-in-a-lifetime spontaneous moments that might never happen again," she says. As anyone who was there can tell you.

(February 19, 1992, "Crawling from the Wreckage" column, City Pages)

Times Like This

"FUCKIN' A, SLIM!" shouted the man at Palmer's Bar last Thursday around midnight, and then he shouted it again.

"Fuckin' A, Slim!" Never mind the light of day, the man's coarse bravo was the perfect exclamation point to the song that Bob "Slim" Dunlap had just played at Palmer's, that decades-old West Bank survivor whose charms are nicely summed up in an online bar review: "This is the only bar in Minnesota where immigrants, punks, college kids, old hippies, homeless people, crack heads, and gangstas share the same space without it being a presidential ad campaign."

That much was true this night, as Slim's son and Palmer's employee Louie Dunlap manned the door and premises, and the sons and daughters of the hippie-punks gathered around the open fire in the outdoor back patio to warm themselves with smokes and spirits on a chilly spring night. Inside the bar, there were shots of hard liquor and soft sweater girls, tipsy bikers and bombed bombshells, three-dollar cover, a guitar case festooned with a Dylan sticker that read "It's Not Dark Yet . . . But It's Getting There," and local music photographer Jenn Barnett, crawling around the front of the stage to capture the moment that Slim captured with his classic tune "Times Like This."

Alas, the times, they don't require much more reiteration, but let it be said that many members of the rowdy bar audience wore scarlet letters of the recently and longtime unemployed; the down-and-out part- and no-timers; the nicked-up-but-getting-along family men and women in need of a respite from the Great Worry. On instinct, they crawled out of their own various great depressions to gather at the pub and find calm at the center of the storm that is "Times Like This," the title track to Slim's 1995 CD, which, as so much music does these days, sounds prescient, wise, warm, important.

To be sure, while much American culture is about escape, "Times Like This" is about the now, as in times like this. It's an us-against-the-world love song, sung to a sweetheart in the midst of a hard stretch, and fifteen years after he recorded it, Slim inspired bowed heads and counted blessings and a couple of "fuckin' a's" when he sang, "It's times like this that we learn what we really miss."

"Creativity is about constraint," said Twitter founder Biz Stone in a recent interview, and the kid is dead on. Slim Dunlap is the epitome of constraint. He plays what he wants when he wants, and because of that and so many other reasons, he is nothing short of a gunslinger— showing up at bars only occasionally, and when he does, shooting out the lights with a bluesman's salt-of-the-earth style. As the entry on him in the Trouser Press Record Guide concludes, "More, please."

(April 9, 2009, Downtown Journal)

Partners in Crime

"WHEN WE GET TOGETHER, we have this chemistry that happens."

Of all the clichés that fill the rock interview cliché book, the one above may be the most tired of all. And even though every band that's ever set foot on a stage has uttered it, *chemistry* is the only word for what happens when everything comes together, and the sum of the parts becomes greater than the whole.

Bob "Slim" Dunlap knows something about band chemistry. He was in the Replacements, one of the greatest chemistry sets rock science ever concocted. But perhaps Dunlap knows about band chemistry even more so today. In an era of hired guns and revolving lineups, watching the three-year-old Slim Dunlap Band is to bear witness to musicians who obviously love being with each other.

"All the bands I've ever been in have never been able to go on the road and play night after night after night like this one," says bassist Johnny Hazlett, a friend of Dunlap's for more than twenty-five years. "Which definitely makes it tight. And we all get along great."

The latest test of that rapport came earlier this week, when the band was driving nonstop from California. (One of the last stops on their three-week tour found them playing a gig at San Francisco's Paradise Club, which was attended by Hootie & the Blowfish singer/guitarist Darius Rucker.) On the way back to Minnesota, Hazlett got sick to his stomach in the van—the sort of predicament that only a rock band, or a good marriage, can survive. And laugh about later.

"If I wasn't playing with Bob, I really doubt I'd be playing with anybody," says Hazlett. "I don't like to be in a band just for the sake of it. I like to be around the people I like to be around. I don't know how to describe it. We're all kind of goofy—inside jokers. And we're all kind of hooked into the same thing."

That same thing they do is evident whenever they play, and it's even steeped in Dunlap's tremendous sophomore album, *Times Like This*, even though the band members' contributions to the Dunlap-produced and -played work were minimal. *Times Like This* is a slice of a life spent in rock 'n' roll. And while some of Dunlap's ruminations are obviously deeply personal, the emotions are transferable to the relationships forged within the band.

The title track is a throat-lumper about a marriage in hard times that could be the sequel to "Partners in Crime" from Dunlap's solo debut, *The Old New Me*. What's more, it could be a reminder to himself and his bandmates to forget their relative obscurity and seize the day. "Girlfriend" finds a big brother consoling a little brother (bandmate?) about the kid's dateless fate. From the chiming pop of "Cozy" and "Radio Hook Word Hit" to the ironic folk-blues of "Hate This Town" and everything in between, *Times Like This* is all over the map stylistically and philosophically—not unlike Dunlap himself.

"Driving around the country with him, you hear a million stories," says guitarist Jimmy Thompson. "You don't have to bring a book or magazine: you just sit and listen to Slim. You've got to take the stories with a grain of salt, though. They seem to change a little from time to time."

"Bob knows the answer to every single question on every single subject you could ever imagine," laughs Hazlett. "If you want to know anything, bring it up when you're playing cards with him, and Bob'll have the answers. He's the most eccentric guy I've ever met. And the most lovable."

In their day, the Replacements gained a reputation for flying by the seats of their pants. A similar without-a-net approach is also at the core of Dunlap's band, which has developed a practice of learning songs in the dressing room right before going onstage. Even the most loyal followers of the group don't know what's going to happen on any given night.

"I sure don't," laughs Hazlett. "At first, it was real frightening for me, especially because I'm just not that great a musician. I was kind of terrified, but I've got Thomps to lean on. If he can yell out the notes, and Bob usually picks simple songs. But I kind of like it now. That's another thing about Bob: he doesn't like to over-rehearse. And that keeps it more fresh."

"It's exciting," says Thompson. "You never know what's coming. He never has a set list, and we rarely rehearse. You have to be ready for anything, and I like that aspect of it. A lot of people's shows will be so well-thought-out and rehearsed that it's already stale before you hear it."

Such experimentation can create magical moments, which ultimately leads to the trotting out of another rock interview cliché: camaraderie.

"It's true, though. He certainly fosters that," says twenty-seven-year-old drummer Brian Lilja, who was recruited by Dunlap from now-defunct local rockers the Draghounds. "The first time I practiced with him, I was nervous as all get out. But within ten minutes, I just felt like it was fun, and nothing but fun, and I didn't worry about anything else.

"He really looks at it from the standpoint of the four of us. He's not caught up in anything other than playing. He's not caught up in the machinery of making records or any of that, so none of that pressure gets to us. It's so cool that he chooses friends to play with him rather than some hot-shot players."

Though Dunlap is the band's focal point, Lilja is its soul. He is a spectacular drummer, and his infectious smile-grimace routinely spreads to his bandmates and spills out into the bar. Asked to put that feeling into words, Lilja stammers, then thinks out loud: "Just totally the feeling of the best place to be at that time. There's nothing that I'd rather be doing than being there. I smile at Jimmy, and I smile at Johnny, and I smile at Bob. It's so great to make eye contact with 'em. You just feel like you're saying thank you."

For what?

"Thank you for letting me play with you. And thank you for letting this happen between the four of us."

(November 8, 1996, St. Paul Pioneer Press)

FOUR
BAR YARNS

From the Land of Sky-Blue Waters

"THE THINGS PEOPLE WANT TO DO with the Hamm's Bear are unbelievable," says the Hamm's Bear, sitting in a booth at Grumpy's in northeast Minneapolis. "Off the charts. It gets weirder every time."

The Hamm's Bear is full of himself. He's been bragging to me all night about how much action he gets. He's been talking about how he can walk into any place in town and instantly be the life of the party. Right, I say. Prove it. I mean, let's face it: the Hamm's Bear's heyday was a few decades ago, and he sure as hell is no Crunch or Goldy Gopher, two state mascots the Hamm's Bear scorns.

"I want to fight them all," says the Hamm's Bear, who occasionally speaks in the first person. "I'd like to kill that Vikings guy, that Hagar the Horrible, because he wears bear skin. The Hamm's Bear doesn't play basketball or football. He's a hockey guy, because he likes winter and ice and blood, but his main sport is drinking. The Hamm's Bear challenges what's-his-face from the Timberwolves"—Crunch—"to a drink-off."

Anyway, to prove the powers of his animal attraction, the Hamm's Bear takes me across the street to the Twenty-second Avenue Station, a neighborhood strip club better known as the Double Deuce. "The Hamm's Bear is getting ready to hibernate," says the Hamm's Bear, looking down past his large snout at the street as he gingerly steps off the curb. "It's going to be a long goddamn cold winter. The Hamm's Bear needs to see some box."

The Hamm's Bear has been to the Double Deuce only once before. That moment now lives in bar infamy: the night people threw money at the stage and begged the strippers to dance with the Hamm's Bear. As a result, when the door to the joint opens this night and the patrons see the Hamm's Bear bumbling in, every face in the place lights up. "He's baaaack! He's baack!" they sing, working-class smiles creaking through hardened-for-winter mugs.

Straightaway, Double Deuce owner Glenn Peterson regales the Hamm's Bear with stories of his lifelong Hamm's fixation and his prized possession, a neon Hamm's sign he stores at his cabin for safe-keeping. The Hamm's Bear nods and says nothing: the Hamm's Bear has heard it before.

"On my table up north right now, I have the Hamm's salt-and-pepper shakers, I have the original neon sign—it was given to me as a gift," says Peterson. He's excitedly speaking into the Hamm's Bear's snout and making eye contact with the Hamm's Bear's permanently jovial eyes. "I buy Hamm's in the thirty-pack all the time. I can't go to my cabin without a thirty-pack of Hamm's, because all of my friends up there, this is what they drink.

"This guy I know who lives on Island Lake, 240 miles north, where I have a cabin, he has a basement full of nothing but Hamm's memorabilia. He has no idea how much this stuff is worth. Everybody up there drinks Hamm's. This is the north country, and they still drink it, and sell it, and love it."

The man inside the Hamm's Bear is one Corey Shovein, a thirty-five-year-old salesman for the local Hohensteins beer distributor. As a self-described "beer geek," Shovein knows his Hamm's history by heart. The Hamm's brewery was started in Milwaukee in 1865 at a time when regional brewers ruled. Campbell–Mithun Advertising of Minneapolis created the campaign that featured the Hamm's Bear and the jingle "from the land of sky-blue waters." The Ojibwe artist Patrick DesJarlait came up with the Hamm's Bear.

In the year 2000, the St. Paul *Pioneer Press* named the Hamm's Bear as a runner-up on its list of "150 Most Influential Minnesotans of the Past 150 Years." But his once-ubiquitous image is nowhere to be found these days: the same forces that assassinated Joe Camel, for marketing to children, hit the Hamm's Bear with a ricochet.

"The song was catchy, the imagery was catchy, and even though you don't see him anymore, it shows how formidable the advertising was," says Shovein. "People still know who the Hamm's Bear is. People ask to have it in parades and all that kind of crap. But it's hotter than the gates of hell in this thing, so the Hamm's Bear prefers winter."

In the past three years that Shovein has been donning the costume, the Hamm's Bear has been asked to engage in every sexual situation imaginable. The Hamm's Bear has been propositioned, punched, and partied with. He has found himself in corporate boardrooms, private parties, and athletic events. And he has brusquely knocked over kids who are too young to appreciate the Hamm's Bear legacy.

"I put it on whenever anyone asks," says Shovein, a married father of two toddlers. "It can be a little addicting. I generally lug around a Polaroid, and we do a dollar a photo and give that money to charity or give the money to the servers. It turns into a melee. Honestly, people just line up to get a hold of the Hamm's Bear.

"They usually have two goals: get a picture with the Hamm's Bear, and get the Hamm's Bear railed [drunk] to see what else they can milk out of him. It works, for the most part."

Over at the Double Deuce, a Goliath biker clad in a Hell's Angels hat, leather jacket, and T-shirt sits at the end of the bar. But he rises quickly and becomes territorial when his stripper girlfriend shows a bit too much interest in the Hamm's Bear.

"NO CAMERAS OR CELL PHONES," scream the signs, but the Hamm's Bear is no mere regular. Pictures are taken of him with the owner, with the owner's sidekick (who carries out the bartender's suggestion to "grab the bear's crotch"), and with Sherry (no last name, please), one of the dancers who presses her boobs into the Hamm's Bear's face, kisses the Hamm's Bear's nose, and puts her hands all over the Hamm's Bear's fur as the boys on sniffer's row look on and, perhaps, wonder where they can find a bear suit.

"There're only six of these [suits] in existence," says the Hamm's

Bear. "We get offered boatloads of money from collectors for it all the time. The Hamm's collectors come to these conventions, and it's like a *Star Trek* convention. They see it and they want it."

He'd be crazy to give it up, because spend even one night with the Hamm's Bear and the old rock star bromide comes true: women want to be with him and men want to be him. That's certainly the case at the Double Deuce, where the overheating Hamm's Bear quickly straw-shotguns a couple of PBRs and says, "Let's roll."

On the way out, the Hamm's Bear stops for a few last photos with a dancer and a biker.

"See?" says the Hamm's Bear, as if to ask: *Does a bear piss beer in the woods?*

(December 27, 2006, City Pages)

Uptown Bar Blues

SINCE THE NEWS BROKE that the Uptown Bar will cease booking music after Saturday night, the naysayers have come out of the woodwork to explain why it just doesn't matter: the sound system was no good, the area isn't an ideal location for a live music club, and it was hard for bands to get gigs there. Oh yeah—and parking was a drag.

But to me, that is so much nitpicking. Because the Uptown's main attraction, and legacy, can be summed up in two words: no cover.

Ask any club crawler from any other city, and they will tell you that the free-admission policy on most nights made the Uptown an anomaly. A miracle, even. And since the music was that much more accessible, it turned the Uptown into a breeding ground in the truest sense of the word. Not only was it a springboard for local bands to the big leagues (the angle that all the TV stations have taken, as if that is the singular validation of any artistic institution), but more important, it was a place where audiences could amble in and amble out. As such, they were given the opportunity to engage in an experience that has become all too rare in the shoved-down-the-throat musical environment of the '90s: discovery.

People would wander in off the street at midnight after catching a film at the Suburban World or Uptown and stumble upon Nirvana, the Gear Daddies, Babes in Toyland, Soul Asylum, Oasis, the Replacements, Cows, the Jayhawks, or some other future yarn-maker. Among bar-goers, one of the more common refrains was "Meet me at the Uptown at ten, and we'll figure out where to go from there." Some nights, the dates would linger for an hour or so and then head downtown or to the West Bank. Other times, they had no particular place to go, so they closed down the joint.

Of course, the naysayers will dismiss the Uptown's social aspect as a see-and-be-seen scene. But there have been several nights doing this job when I've been on my way back from the intimate confines of the

Target Center or Metrodome, or some other awful "music venue," and I was drawn like a magnet to the Uptown to get my feet back on the ground and my ears back to reality.

It didn't matter who was onstage, it usually sounded pretty good—even if, yes, the sound system didn't. What made the Uptown feel like an oasis was that I would invariably run into someone who would relight my fuse with a conversation about music. And that is a gift not to be sneezed at, because such conversations aren't easy to come by, unless you count industry chitchat, which I don't. For pure intravenous shots of music fandom, there was nothing quite like being blindsided by a barfly, friend, or musician at the Uptown.

I've tried to come up with my all-time favorite musical moment from the little hole on Hennepin. In the end, I couldn't narrow it down. But for some reason, the one that sticks with me most is watching the end of a Vikings–Bears Thursday night game out of the corner of my eye as the Ass Ponys played. Somebody caught a touchdown pass, the Vikings won in overtime, everybody cheered, the TV went off, the band played on, and we still had American Music Club to go.

That was the Uptown's charm. Always cool, but never too cool to be real.

Actually, the Uptown is everything the Vikings—corporate, timid, stunningly predictable—aren't. Outside its doors lurks a world of infomercials: where Fran Tarkenton spews on about finances and fitness, Anthony Robbins makes bettering yourself seem like a haircut, and that lady with the black hair and pink suit tells couples how to fall and stay in love.

Well, nobody at the Uptown ever went for that nonsense. I suppose the common term for the clientele is *slackers*; if that's the case, count me in. But more accurately, they were people who wanted something real out of life. People struggled there. Financially, emotionally. Alcohol was served. Stories were shared. Ideas hatched. There were plenty of real-life soap operas to tune into and great gossip to be had.

I learned about deaths, and births, there. It was a place where people caught up with each other. A place where you learned and came away with a little nugget of barroom philosophy—from the stage or while standing in line for the bathroom—that helped you wake up the next day and face the world again.

Tomorrow night, after the Wonsers and special guests play the last note at the Uptown, all that will end—to a degree. The Uptown isn't closing, so some of the socializing will go on. But without the draw of music, its pull won't be nearly as great. And as all the competing club owners reading this will surely remind me in the coming weeks, the void will be filled.

But as anyone who ever spent a night there hashing out the world's problems or discovering a little-known band knows, the Uptown will not so easily be replaced. For as long as I can remember, I have been going to bars for one thing and one thing only. Music. I've always dismissed the social aspect as frivolous, secondary. But recently, a friend changed my mind. "I like bars because I like being with people," he said. "And even if I'm not there, I just like the idea of bars. The energy."

That was why the Uptown was important. It was a nondenominational church, where life itself was worshiped. And even though I haven't spent much time there in the past year, I liked to think that it was still there, pulsing. That people were there, being forced to deal with one another. Congregating. Jostling. Struggling. Learning. And overcoming, always, the monumental obstacles of bad sound and inconvenient parking.

(April 26, 1996, St. Paul Pioneer Press)

Closing Time

EVERY NIGHT IN OCTOBER, the Uptown Bar is doing its best impression of the Titanic, as patrons bid farewell to the soon-to-be-demolished local legend: at one point or another, the room tilts and all the tables, glasses, silverware, and pub-goers careen down the plank and into the icy waters of the past, as the bands play on.

Okay, that only happens in the mind's eye after a couple of the Uptown's famous Bloody Marys. But come November 2, the lone noise from the Uptown will be that of the wrecking ball (relocation rumors continue to swirl), but for one night anyway—Friday, October 10, 2009—this is the way it was:

10:00 P.M. Asked what they make of the Uptown closing, the six-person crew at Jimmy John's in Calhoun Square offers a collective shrug.

10:05 With the exception of the Uptown Theater's late show of *A Serious Man,* the Uptown is the lone Uptown business hopping tonight. Victoria's Secret is closed. The North Face is closed. Urban Outfitters is closed. Chino Latino's shimmering storefront sums it up nicely: all that glitters isn't soul.

10:10 The Kitchen Window's vast bookshelves reflect in the Uptown's picture window across the street, making the red-spotlighted Mammy Nuns look as if they're playing in a cozy rock 'n' roll library or wing of the Minnesota Historical Society.

10:15 One of the back booths in the front room is commandeered by sisters Samantha Loesch and Molly Barnes, co-owners of Kings, the new wine and beer bar/restaurant that opened two months ago to much acclaim and good tidings in South Minneapolis (and, full disclosure, where I do some work). The irony of the new kids on the block bidding adieu to the old Hennepin haunt isn't lost on many.

10:17 The Mammy Nuns roar on about the medicinal qualities of guitar chords and cords, as local musicians Gini Dodds, Tony Zaccardi, Terry Walsh, Larry Sahagian, Chris Pericelli, and local music fans Tom Hallett, Tom and Fran Willford, Lizzy Leff, Debbie Donovan, Jay McHale, Andy Everett, and dozens more nod and bop along.

10:18 Zaccardi: "I spent my twenty-first birthday here. June 13, 1998. Ian Rans (of *Drinking with Ian* infamy) brought me here for a beer. I was sitting here, having my birthday breakfast beer, and ten feet away Robert Plant from Led Zeppelin stands up and asks the server if there's a record store nearby. [Jimmy] Page and Plant played the Target Center the night before; he was wearing electric-blue clothing. She pointed him up the street, he walked out, and no one said a thing. That was my introduction to the Uptown Bar."

10:20 In a booth near the stage, one guy reports to another that after a couple decades of no communication an old flame has found him on Facebook. Heavy sighs all around.

10:22 Flat-screen TVs on both ends of the bar broadcast endless replays of Alex Rodriguez's game-tying home run off Joe Nathan earlier in the night. Picked scabs all around.

10:23 The single-strip ticker-tape neon sign above the soundboard scrolls along: *Welcome to the Uptown Bar and Café . . . Check out our website www.uptownbarandcafe.com . . . Monday Oct. 5 Western Fifth . . . Tuesday Oct. 6 D-Mine and Lothario and Wise Guyz . . . Wednesday Oct. 7 Grant Hart . . . Thursday Oct. 8 The Idle Hands with The Melismatics and 500 Miles to Memphis and Blue Sky Blackout . . . Welcome to the Uptown Bar . . .*

10:24 Singer Ashleigh Still and a girlfriend walk in but turn on their heels immediately to catch Hookers & Blow at another bar, because the Uptown doorman "was mean to us."

10:25 Joe Henry, from California, via Facebook: "My best night in collaboration with the Jayhawks was a night at the Uptown . . . freezing cold out, fur hats onstage . . . pulled a drunken Dan Murphy onstage to sing happy birthday to him, but we launched into [Soul Asylum's] 'Cartoon' instead."

10:30 Chatter in the back booth turns to bulldozed-but-not-forgotten Twin Cities music landmarks Jay's Longhorn, the Prom Ballroom, Goofy's Upper Deck, Duffy's, etc.

10:31 The Tisdales kick off their set with a blistering kick drum–guitar combo as Hallett tells a friend, "The thing I'll miss most about this place is seeing Tommy Stinson play here every New Year's Eve."

10:32 "When I moved here in 1989, this was *the* place in town," says a sweaty Rob Rule, still amped from his set with the Mammy Nuns. "You could see the Cows and Freedy Johnston and the Gear Daddies and Babes in Toyland. No cover, great food, shitty sound. It was awesome."

10:33 Woman to man in booth: "You like a contrary woman, don't you?"

10:34 "We came here looking for guys with feathers in their caps," says Uptown newbie Margaret Campbell. "We're a little disappointed. There's a distinct lack of hipsters here."

10:35 Mike Wolf, from New York, via Facebook: "I will equally remember: Brick Layer Cake and Today Is the Day in opening slots, each torturing sellout crowds; almost every AmRep band, several times; Scrabble with Franklin Bruno; Mark Eitzel bleeding and in tears; Sun City Girls speaking in tongues; Thinking Fellers Union wearing suitcases on their heads; the 12:45 A.M. call to "HIT THE BRICKS!" and the hash browns with melted hell-I-guess-it-COULD-be-real-cheese on top."

10:40 "It sucks that this will be replaced by another Victoria's Secret or something," deadpans Campbell. "I don't think Victoria's got as many good secrets as the people in this room."

10:45 The server's POS screen flashes the Uptown Bar logo, which reminds a fellow of a time when the Uptown sponsored softball teams—not to mention the sight of Dave Pirner, a ringer for the Twin/Tone–Uptown team, who befuddled a squad of dentists and doctors with his unruly dreadlocks and his unrulier hitting stance.

11:00 Sahagian: "I played on this stage more times than any other band in Minneapolis (with the Urban Guerillas). We were the first band, along with the Wallets, to be booked here as an alternative rock band."

11:30 Onstage, Kruddler singer Shane Gallivan riffs about Molly Ringwald and Robert Plant and concludes with a cry of "F— the Yankees!" to a smattering of cheers.

Midnight Good clothes: bartender in the bright green T-shirt emblazoned with The Clash's first album cover; guy with the Big Money, Inc. jacket; a few straight-outta-Vargas vintage fall female fashions.

12:15 A.M. In the back booth, news about local wiz kids All Mod Cons and their fedoras, parkas, and Felix Unger–like fussiness inspires in at least one bar-goer a bucket-list desire to see *Quadrophenia* on the big screen this fall.

12:30 Paralegal Tammy Belka leans her head through the doorway of the music room and listens to the band. Color her unimpressed: "[The Uptown being demolished] doesn't matter to me at all. I don't have any emotional attachment to this place. I'm just here to see my friend's band. But they serve Wild Turkey, which is nice. There are not a lot of bars that serve Wild Turkey: the Uptown, the Nomad, Stasiu's, the Turf Club, that's it."

1:00 From the suddenly dimly lit stage, Flamin' Oh's singer/guitarist Robert Wilkinson tells the crowd, "This is the only bar I've ever been eighty-sixed from." Then, with a laugh, "You've gotta be pretty f—ed up to get eighty-sixed from the Uptown." Then, with reverence, "We're very happy to be here, and honored and proud to be invited to send this great bar off in magnificent decadent style."

1:10 Sahagian: "Let it die and move on. I'm a dinosaur. I have enough petrol in my body to support a small country. But Angie Dickinson did sit in that booth where your ass is right now. My mom was Angie Dickinson's daughter's psychotherapist, and I showed her around town a bit back then."

1:15 Stickers on the soundboard case: God's Favorite Band, Eclectone Records, Birds of Avalon, Accident Clearinghouse, "Drum Machines Have No Soul."

1:30 The Tisdales' Rich Mattson joins the Flamin' Oh's onstage and instantly ratchets up the ruckus. Wilkinson, wielding the white Gibson he's been playing for almost as many years as the Uptown has been in business, lurches into The Clash's "Brand New Cadillac," pointedly spitting out the lyric, "Balls to you, daddy, I ain't never comin' back."

1:45 As her husband Bob plays keyboards onstage, Beth Burns opines, "Once this goes away, Hennepin and Lake is gonna look like the strip in St. Cloud, which has been the biggest hole in the world forever."

1:55 Mattson: "My first Uptown experience? We left the Alice Cooper concert on Halloween, 1987. Said, 'Let's go check out this Uptown thing.' Run Westy Run was playing. Kirk Johnson was swinging his mic around, and I got smashed in the face by it. I got a black eye from it, but at the end of the song he came over and said, 'You okay, dude?' It was the greatest thing ever. It was heaven."

2:10 Jimmy Johns is closed. Sign on the door reads "Rock Stars Wanted."

(October 12, 2009, Minnpost.com)

Ballad of the Tin Star Sisters

YOU CAN TELL THEY'RE A SISTER ACT because they're wearing matching dresses, pink tulle things that they bought secondhand for forty bucks. It's a Thursday in northeast Minneapolis, she of the boho and working-class bars and century-old churches. And the Tin Star Sisters—also known as two of the three Anderson girls from a small dairy farm outside of Spring Valley, Wisconsin—are setting up on the tiny stage at the 331 Club. It's cubbyholed near the back of the bar, an apparent afterthought to the jukebox.

There are no amps or drums in sight. The dark-haired one, Ivy (Marvel is her married surname), is fiddling with her lone percussion instrument, a hi-hat cymbal. Satisfied, she straps on her accordion, the instrument at the core of so much of this region's most original music, be it the Wallets' art-funk or the myriad polka bands of the Midwest, some of which still take up residence in Nye's Polonaise Room down the road. (Go to the river, take a left.)

The light-brown-haired one, Kim (Anderson—she is not married, and she and her sister wonder why any of that is germane), cradles her xylophone mallets in tattooed arms that testify "2006" as much as the rest of her getup nods "1936." She checks the heel of one of her tap shoes. As they get ready to rock (or not rock, as the case may be) the Sisters exchange the night's first grin, of which there will be many and many variations. This one is the grin of two siblings who have played games and music together all their lives, a grin that says, "Here we go again" and "Can you believe we're getting away with this?"

The accordion wheezes-lilts, the xylophone pretty-plunks. The hi-hat simmers like a caged thing. Tuning up. To the casual chronicler, the Sisters do not look like any classmate in the storied rock 'n' roll high school that is Minneapolis/St. Paul, some of whose iconic photos adorn the walls of the 331. (You can find more of them a few blocks down at the Minnesota Center for Photography's "Musicap-olis" exhibit.)

No. Tonight, as with most nights, the Tin Star Sisters look like a song-and-dance trapeze act.

From the '40s.

In the Catskills.

The Sisters have done the State Fair and burlesque shows, so the prospect of playing to a tough crowd of potential shruggers doesn't phase them. They make their way through their first few numbers, expertly traversing the high wire of their own making. And when Kim hops out from behind the xylophone to do a slip-'n'-slide tap dance near some bemused stool-sitters at the bar, the joint erupts into giddy applause. Ice, broken. Crowd, won.

But how, exactly? Plenty of campy acts have wowed 'em on cutes or charm alone. But the Sisters have songs—both their own and the covers they make their own. A screeching, heartfelt reading of Prince's "The Beautiful Ones." A herky-jerk version of Looking Glass's '60s AM radio hit "Brandy," during which Ivy magically becomes the voice of the forlorn sea wife, waiting for her man as she sings, "My life, my love, and my lady is the sea." A Ramones medley, sung in—*mais, bien sur*—French. A medley that could pander to karaoke culture's cheap seats with its inclusion of Bob Seger's "Night Moves" and Bruce Springsteen's "I'm on Fire" but instead ends up a thing of weird power.

"We're really sincere," says Ivy later. "We only play songs we love. We don't really do things for kitsch."

Over the course of the forty-five-minute set, newbies and vets alike fall under their spell. As the clapping swells at the cusp of the last song, Kim hastily whispers something to Ivy. It's obvious to anyone who's been around the concert biz what she's saying: yank the hook while the suckers have their mouths open; tell the crowd to belly up to the merchandise table. Ivy complies and puts on her best huckster hat. Into the microphone she says, "Oh, yeah. We're the Tin Star Sisters. If you want, we have buttons for sale."

One of the most reliable pop-cult signifiers of the moment is MySpace's "Top Eight Friends" feature. A glance at the Tin Star Sisters' "friends" reveals a few local musicians in the top spots, including wry country medicine showman Mike Gunther & His Restless Souls, and Amy Buchanan, the gregarious grande dame of Cirque de Rouge burlesque. (The Sisters have performed with both of them.) But perhaps the most telling photos are those of Chico and Harpo Marx.

"We don't love the Marx Brothers because they're a family, necessarily," says Kim, nestling close to her sister in one of the 331's back booths before a recent show. "But they do function in a way that's intertwined and supported," says Ivy. "Like, this guy starts it, but this guy finishes it. And I think that's something that's unique to families, the way they can finish each other's sentences or pick up where somebody else left off."

Kim (who is thirty-two years old) and Ivy (twenty-three) are the middle sisters of five siblings born to Barry and Mary Anderson. Their family farm abutted a woods that the kids would escape to at all times of the year, a beach they'd loll on during summers, and a barn where they'd build hay forts.

"It was pretty fun," says Ivy of the Anderson spread. "The one thing I can say about growing up in the country is that there was a lot of free time. Just long afternoons where . . ."

"There weren't a lot of distractions," says Kim. "Except for TV."

"Yeah," laughs Ivy. "After we watched about five hours of movies or watched *Purple Rain* a couple times, we'd go out and embark on a little project for the day."

Both women took piano lessons when they were kids and hated them in turn. But seven years ago, they got serious about their music—or as serious as they get. In an effort to jump-start their career, they went to Mills Fleet Farm and bought some materials for a washtub bass, which their father helped them build.

Kim played the tub, Ivy the kazoo. They recorded a batch of covers (including "Sweet Dreams," by Roy Orbison and "Magnet and Steel" by Walter Eagan) on a Fisher-Price tape recorder they dubbed Mobile Unit One. Then they played it back and analyzed what they liked and didn't like.

"We didn't have the means to play the things that we wanted to play the way we wanted to. [But] it didn't take a lot of training to play the kazoo," says Kim, invoking a creative tenet that guides the Sisters to this day. It's that seat-of-the-pants approach that is the most intoxicating part of the show—along with the charm of hearing harmonies that may have developed in the back seat of the family station wagon, two decades ago.

"That's why people love *The Sound of Music* or *Seven Brides for Seven Brothers*," Ivy says. "We do all get along really well. We always have, although the five of us are all pretty different. We're probably the most different," she says, looking over at Kim. "Or the most alike."

"Which one is it?" says Kim.

Ivy laughs and looks up at the clock. It takes time to put on a pair of fishnets and tune up a ukulele.

Spring Valley is an hour's drive from the Twin Cities, but as has been the case for many others who made their way to the land of a million bands, the Big City may as well have been Oz.

"All our TV stations were from Minnesota," says Ivy. "I remember watching the news, and at one point there was a tornado warning for the metro area. When I looked on the map on the TV, our county was included. And I was like, 'Hey! We're in the metro area! Wow!' I'd never realized I was so metropolitan."

Yet their musical sensibility has less to do with the flannel sensibility of the Uptown Bar and the 7th St. Entry than with a less celebrated side of Minneapolis. It's a history that embraces fan dancers at the old Pantages and accordion waltzes in church parking lots. And it has burbled up in the style of such attic-rockers as Tulip Sweet and Her Trail of Tears, Têtes Noires, Dutch Oven, and ZuZu's Petals.

"We wear these pink sequined tutus," says Ivy, drinking a preshow champagne and warming to the somewhat amorphous topic of vintage fashion as a musical guidepost. "Even though we don't have much consideration for image, getting those pink tutus at a secondhand store was a big catalyst for getting our act together. They had names written in them, and they'd been used by people in the Ice Capades.

"There's this responsibility to do something with this. We've been granted this lucky thing of finding two pink sequined tutus that match us and fit our bodies. It's tied to local history, but in this really vague way, because we don't know anything about them.

"I feel like it's a myth of our making. To get excited about something, you have to feel like there's a story there. So we sort of invent this story behind our own genesis. And we do that about everything. It's like Nye's. It's not just a bar; it's this mythic bar. It's haunted."

So is the 331, which until a year or so ago was a coarse bar with a boardinghouse on the second floor. The pensioners and disability collectors upstairs would take phone calls and pick up their mail at the bar downstairs. The new 331 Club, which is owned by salon entrepreneur Jon Oulman and operated by his son, is becoming the anchor of a new scene. Lining up down the block are the Modern Café, the Ritz Theater (home to Ballet of the Dolls), Rogue Buddha Gallery, and Artrujillo Gallery. Gallery 13 and the Minnesota Center for Photography are within stumbling distance; you could reach Creative Electric in a shopping cart if you could find someone to push you.

And at the center of this scene are the Tin Star Sisters, with their standing Thursday night gig. (Alas, September 21 will be their last show for a while, as Ivy prepares to move to Brooklyn and Kim returns to the University of Minnesota to study landscape architecture. They'll be together again at the end of the year to play a handful of CD-release shows.) It's possible that some folks have made it through the Sisters' six-month residency without ever getting what they're about. Tonight's crowd, though, is in on the joke, or the nonjoke, or whatever it is the Tin Star Sisters do.

After the set, Kim and Ivy retire to the club's backstage area and change out of their tutus into jeans and T-shirts. Ice Capaders into civilians. Wonder Women into drinkers. They sidle up to the bar and order martinis. Boys flutter about. Stevie Wonder is on the jukebox. One of the newbies approaches and buys a button. And in that moment, as they both dig around in a plastic bag looking for the merch, the Tin Star Sisters look as if they have the world by the tail—or at least the sash.

(September 13, 2006, City Pages)

Driftwood Nights

IN HIS BEAUTIFUL 2005 MEMOIR *The Tender Bar,* J. R. Moehringer celebrates the Manhasset, New York, pub he grew up in via the prism of one of its regulars:

> Steve believed the corner bar to be the most egalitarian of all American gathering places, and he knew that Americans have always venerated their bars, saloons, taverns, and "gin mills," one of his favorite expressions. He knew that Americans invest their bars with meaning and turn to them for everything from glamour to succor, and above all for relief from that scourge of modern life—loneliness. He didn't know that the Puritans, upon landing in the New World, built a bar even before they built a church.

Moehringer could have been writing about the Driftwood Char Bar, the warm and trippy South Minneapolis hole-in-the-wall whose many charms and cast of cartoon characters change nightly—hourly, even— and whose flavorful history, roots, vision, and good energy make for a truly original vibe that can drum up echoes of the *Star Wars* cantina, the end of *Casablanca,* Hemingway haunts in Paris or Havana, or any other watering hole of yore you can name.

"Thank you, we loved the music," said one gargantuan Afro-Caribbean gent in a falsetto whisper worthy of Aaron Neville, to bar owner Heidi Fields on his way out the door one night last week, after fast-rising free-funk floaters Pho woke the dead at the Cremation Society down the street. "It's like Chicago or New York."

Better: it's South Minneapolis, situated in the same neighborhood as kindred-spirited homegrown businesses and entities like Curran's Family Restaurant, Anodyne Coffeehouse, Roadrunner Records, and the Kingfield Farmers' Market—not to mention fellow neighborhood pubs Kings Wine Bar, the Lowbrow, and Pat's Tap—and located well within walking or biking distance of hundreds of thousands of city-dwellers who may or may not know that Willie Mays patrolled center field for the 1951 Minneapolis Millers at long-demolished Nicollet Park up the street.

"We're not one of the hip, trendy bars. We're not Northeast," said Larry Sahagian, the former leader of '80s punk-funkers the Urban Guerillas, who spent a decade booking the Cabooze and who, for the past three years, has been seeding the Driftwood with a high-quality mix of local and national singer/songwriters, blues, funk, rock, and punk. "I love music, and Heidi loves music, and the regulars from the neighborhood love music, and that's the bottom line. Music is our life."

Thus far, there are no laminated alt-weekly awards for "Best Neighborhood Bar" hanging behind the bar at the Driftwood (but there are some rad Jimi Hendrix and Pink Floyd posters, and a huge tie-dyed heart on a sheet behind the drum kit), nor have the masses discovered its decidedly not-for-everybody delights. But that doesn't mean something special isn't happening on a nightly basis at the former Westrum's Tavern at 4415 Nicollet Avenue, something you can't get at Applebee's, First Avenue, or Buffalo Wild Wings.

"It's just a nice little juke joint," said Sahagian, of the Driftwood's positively organic nature.

"I always say it's a 'gay-lesbian-interracial-biker-bar-and-hippies, too,'" said Fields, who opened the bar in December 2007 after Westrum's went under earlier that year amid neighborhood complaints about loud noise and drug dealing. What a difference six years makes.

"I love this bar," said Fields, sitting at one of the Driftwood's tables out front, nursing a goblet of red wine and enjoying a cigarette. "I've met so many outstanding people and musicians. This town is full of talent, and I want this place to be a place where they can showcase their talent and hone their craft. A lot of the music we have here is originals. We don't do cover bands. Our main [vision] is you have to do original stuff. I believe in supporting musicians and original music.

"I grew up eight blocks from here. I always knew I wanted to have music here. Through the friendship of musicians, it grew and adapted and changed. I always say that I built the bar, but the musicians and the people who come are the ones who make it. I just provide a space."

She also tends bar, cooks, runs sound, does the books (her background is in accounting), and acts as an open-armed and open-hearted hostess who puts in long hours and face time with her customers. Named for a piece of driftwood that Fields found in Mexico ("something aged, natural, homey, folkic"), the Driftwood at times can approximate a coastal feel, providing a salty landing spot for surfers, sailors, and fishermen of all stripes coming off the lakes for a bump and the sound of music.

"It's safe to say you can travel far and wide all over the Twin Cities and not find a better venue and pure musical talent than you do at the Driftwood," said WCCO-TV news photographer Joe Mears, who hits the Driftwood on his bike after his nightly newscast duties have wound down. "I'm lucky that Nicollet's on my commute, because I get to ride by here and hear the music. I've heard more talented musicians playing here for no cover than what you pay for in some clubs, and I always think the same thing: 'I did not expect to be blown away by a band I'd never heard of before in a little place like this. I did not expect to be here at 1 A.M. when my family's at home and I've got to be up in the morning.' But it's so worth it."

Due in part to America's ever-quickening slouch toward neighborhood gentrification and homogenization, the average life expectancy of a nightclub is two years. Hoboken, New Jersey's storied Maxwell's announced this week that it will shutter its doors July 1 because parking near the bar was prohibitive and live music wasn't nurtured, leading club owner Todd Abramson to comment, "The culture in Hoboken is driven by TV now. A lot of the bars downtown are fighting with each other for who has the most giant TVs. That's what Hoboken nightlife has become."

In music-mad Minneapolis, the Driftwood feels like a secret speakeasy (with plenty of on-street parking) and a one-of-a-kind place you couldn't make up if you tried. Both Fields and Sahagian say they had no template for the club when they started, but it's obvious their experience and hard work have forged that most elusive of endeavors: a true American original.

As such, it takes on a nightly life of its own. Some nights it's dead, with a band or songwriter playing to only a couple of friends and the pool hustlers in back. Other nights it's packed, and, given the minute-by-minute magic it generates, you'd swear you were in the middle of a Hold Steady song, or on Bourbon Street in New Orleans or Sixth Street in Austin, Texas. Either way, the words of the late, great Twin Cities music promoter Sue McLean are always at the forefront of the Driftwood experience: "Live music is good for the soul."

"On any given night, there are eighteen-year-olds to seventy-year-olds here," said Sahagian, who graced a jubilant Driftwood crowd with a cover of Bob Dylan's "Leopard Skin Pillbox Hat" at the club's Dylan birthday lovefest on May 24. "And as long as you go with the flow, anyone will talk to you here. All you have to do is walk up and say 'Hi.' It's a sweet spot."

The sweet spot's foundation is Sunday afternoons/nights with the Shotgun Ragtime Band, who have fired up their marathon Grateful Dead–flavored jams 103 consecutive (and counting) Sundays, a few of which have been frequented by Driftwood alum Nicholas David. Monday night's popular acoustic jam and Willie Murphy's Wednesday night blues jam provide old-school flair, and the rest of the calendar is peppered with up-and-coming local bands—including monster blues-funk band stars-in-waiting Pho, ferocious roots rockers the Lone Crows, and powerful pop punks Space Cats—looking to replicate the success of Malamanya, who took the Driftwood by storm a couple of summers ago.

"Heidi's a real music lover," said singer/songwriter and Driftwood vet James Loney in the bar's basement after a recent set. "She does things on a shoestring, and she still pays you well. That doesn't happen everywhere."

"Bands love playing here," said Fields. "Because of the wood and the vibe, the room itself plays like an instrument. Bands always talk about: 'It sounds so good in here. Natural.'"

After a long day of booking, cooking, ordering food and liquor, and talking to guests, Fields and Sahagian can often be found up in front of the band, dancing, singing, and caught up in the light, heat, and moment. It's *The Tender Bar* at its most tender, and indelible evidence for what makes the Driftwood tick.

"Look at this. There's nothing else around; all the bars are closed now," said Fields late last Sunday as the Driftwood dance floor churned. "A lot of people help me. People pick up the trash outside and clean the sidewalk, because they love it. It sounds crazy, but it's true. Someone brought a bunch of flowers to us and put 'em up outside, because they like this place. It's like a commune here.

"I'd like for this neighborhood to grow. We're on Nicollet Avenue; I'd like to have more and different types of venues so you don't have to go downtown or Uptown. I get a lot of compliments from the neighborhood regulars, like 'Please don't stop.' I have no intention of stopping. I think it's a wonderful concept. Everyone loves music. I'm a Taurus. I'm stubborn. I'm not going anywhere."

(June 7, 2013, Minnpost.com)

FIVE
SHOWMEN'S REST

Are You Lonesome Tonight?

THIS IS A STORY about Elvis Presley. Which, of course, means it is also about O. J. Simpson, picked scabs, Kurt Cobain, repressed memory syndrome, you and me (whether we like it or not), and whatever else, anything else, we want it to be about. But before the story gets started, some real-life Elvis sightings.

At a club show, G. Love (of himself & Special Sauce), the new Philly bluesman with the baby face, stovepipe 'burns, and "sensation" tattooed all over his 6-foot-2-inch frame, evokes a raw sexuality that is just, the tacit barfly logic has it, *like a young Elvis*. In a promo spot for a fall TV special, Jay Leno appears in a King-style gold lamé suit; the next week, Jerry Seinfeld is decked out in what could be the identical outfit on the cover of *Rolling Stone* (head: "The King of Prime-Time Comedy"). At the same time that Patty Loveless is slinging "I Try to Think about Elvis" into the Top 10 of the country music charts, R. Kelly appears in a concert at a basketball arena not far from his hometown of Chicago and teases the screaming teenage crowd with a whole lotta bump 'n' grind. "The police are backstage tonight," claims Kelly, America's newest pop hunk-criminal. "They told us to tone it down a little bit, but let's see what we can get away with."

On the cover of the September 20 issue of the *Globe,* photos of Oprah Winfrey and Elvis as adults and children are offset with the headlines "Top Historian Uncovers Past Even Oprah Didn't Know/ Oprah's Amazing Link to Elvis" (subhead: "Her family slaved for his—they may even be related!"). On the Nashville Network, a distant relative of Elvis's hawks a new book, telling Crook and Chase that he's sure Elvis would have big problems with his new son-in-law, Michael Jackson, because the King "didn't approve of mixed-race marriages."

From a variety of glossies, Lisa Marie and Liz Phair flash separated at birth sneers, while Ween kick off their new album with a dopey rocker called "Take Me Away," in which Gene Ween responds to canned applause with a "Thank you" that stops just short of *Thangew-evehhymusch.* Finally, amid all the chatter about how Cobain's suicide note misinterpreted Neil Young's sentiment about it being better to burn out than to fade away, nobody mentions that the next line of that song is "The King is gone but he's not forgotten."

Forgotten, no: not a chance. Bigger than life, yes. The most prominent of the recent Elvis sightings have emanated from the Rolling Stones' *Voodoo Lounge* tour, now playing at a football stadium near you. Somewhere, barreling down a highway in this great land, is a semitrailer that houses a mammoth inflatable Elvis—dormant, dark, Lilliput's giant tied down, waiting to free itself, poised for its next encore. This past August, at Camp Randall Stadium in Madison, Wisconsin, the strains of the most recent generic Stones single, "Love Is Strong," wafted over the football field while a cornucopia of big balloons came to life. Spilling over the back of the stage were a genie, a cobra, a goat, and, true to the "Budweiser Presents the Rolling Stones" banner, a big white mutt that looked a lot like Spuds MacKenzie.

One of the balloons was Elvis, or was supposed to be: it had the guitar, the sideburns, and the stance, but to me it looked like the Underdog float from the Macy's Thanksgiving Day Parade made up as Eddie Cochran. Or El Vez. Which is to say it was just another giant monster dressed up in anonymous '50s tinsel, like Mothra or Godzilla, so it wasn't even that surprising when the little girl in front of me tugged on her dad's sleeve and pointed: "Who is *that*?" I watched the guy move his gaze from big-screen Jagger to the dirigible. He studied for a moment and finally shrugged his shoulders. He didn't know.

He didn't recognize the iconography. Perhaps not coincidentally, the Stones show, which up to that point had been filled with enough surprises to make it at least amusing, turned sleepy and hollow.

In 1981, Greil Marcus ripped Albert Goldman's lurid bio *Elvis* and the proliferating Elvis disinformation of the day, wishing, simply:

> What we want to know is why a certain person sang in a certain way, and why that touched us, why that simple confluence of circumstances changed the country, and the world—but since those are difficult questions, mysteries that will never be solved but also the only questions worth asking, we can be led to settle for every last quirk, rumor, failing, perversion, and we may be led to believe, finally, perhaps, that the real questions are not so important, or even real at all.

Thirteen years later, produced against a backdrop of a media milieu that more than ever prefers whimsy over accountability, the mere act of asking Marcus's question again ("*Who is that?*") feels not only real and important, but as essential as the answer itself. Which is why Peter Guralnick's extraordinary, just published epic, *Last Train to Memphis: The Rise of Elvis Presley,* is such a revelation. Underdog Elvis serves as a metaphor for how pop culture has twisted the life of Presley—inflate, exaggerate, deflate, pack away for later use—but with *Memphis* (part one of a planned two-volume biography), Guralnick takes us back to a time before Presley was what he has become: a nonperson. Over the course of nearly five hundred pages, Guralnick traces the Presleys' modest beginnings in East Tupelo, Mississippi, and Memphis, from where Elvis shook the world.

With more natural insight and less hyperbole than anything that has come before it, *Memphis* focuses on setting the record straight, be it the exploding of small myths, such as the one about Vernon Presley listening to his son's first public performance at a talent show on a car radio, or larger ones, such as the widely accepted portrait of Sun Records founder Sam Phillips as an opportunistic businessman who co-opted black culture for monetary gain. But more than that, *Memphis* is a loving exploration of not a blimp or a rock star but a fellow human being.

In the author's note, Guralnick—who has written extensively on Presley and is the author of such indispensible pop-music history books as *Lost Highway, Sweet Soul Music,* and *Searching for Robert Johnson*—tells of driving through Memphis one day in 1983 with a Memphis native:

> [She] pointed out a drugstore where Elvis' cousin used to work. Elvis used to hang out there, she said; he would sit at the soda fountain, drumming his fingers on the counter top. "Poor baby," [she said] and something went off in my head. This wasn't "*Elvis Presley*"; this was a kid hanging out at a soda fountain in South Memphis, someone who could be observed, just like you or me, day dreaming, listening to the jukebox, drinking a milk shake, waiting for his cousin to get off work. "Poor baby."

Above all, Guralnick writes, "I wanted to tell a true story. I wanted to rescue Elvis Presley from the dreary bondage of myth, from the oppressive aftershock of cultural significance." Considering the subject, that's no mean feat, and a reminder of a game we used to play as kids—the one where you pick a word and say it over and over until it is reduced to phonics and loses its meaning.

Elvis Presley. Say it fast. Faster. Slur it. Keep doing it until there is no connotation or preconception or residue. What you discover is the essence of *Memphis.* Almost as an afterthought, Guralnick snatches the words *Elvis Presley* from the black hole they've been banished to and catapults them back to the summer of 1954, when a newspaper ad misspelled them *Ellis Presley,* and back to when Presley guitarist Scotty Moore said, of the first time he heard them, that they sounded like "a name out of science fiction."

Guralnick relays such details with an even hand and, refreshingly, makes few attempts at framing them with overimportance. (The book, after all, comes with a built-in foreshadowing device, since the ending is rock history's worst-kept secret.) Likewise, perhaps Guralnick's greatest achievement is his chronicle of the slow—not overnight—development of Presley's talents and the beginnings of rock 'n' roll. There are scenes told with breathtaking clarity, such as the one about an undiscovered teenage Presley skulking around the lobby of the Sun

Records offices, battered guitar in hand, waiting for someone to notice him. Waiting for his chance.

For before he was Elvis the icon, he was Elvis Aron Presley the artist, and in the wake of celebrity, history has all but forgotten that Presley was once a struggling musician, passionate and serious about his art. As Guralnick reports, in Tupelo, Presley studied the career of Mississippi Slim from a distance, and in Memphis, he devoured records until Hollywood distracted him. The long-held notion that the Elvis phenomenon was a force of nature that happened to Elvis Presley is to dismiss the person whose ambition was obvious and intense.

"His energy was fierce; the sense of competitive fire seemed to overwhelm the shy, deferential kid within," writes Guralnick. His first manager, Bob Neal, recalls just how serious Elvis was about his work, immersing himself in stacks of records by Ray Charles, Big Joe Turner, Big Mama Thornton, and Arthur "Big Boy" Crudup. "He had so much drive," said his friend George Klein, "so much determination and energy, he just knew he was going to make it and nothing was going to stop him."

Guralnick thereby shoots down the myth of Elvis as artistic puppet. On the contrary, from the very beginning, the singer was imbued with a stubborn artistic vision: in January 1955, against everyone's advice, he recorded "Heartbreak Hotel," the final version of which flew in the face of the seminal fusion of raw country and R&B that the first Sun session produced, so much so that Sam Phillips deemed it a "morbid mess." And Guralnick expertly conveys a similar picture of Presley cutting "Hound Dog," via the recollections of photographer Alfred Wertheimer, who was in the studio during the first RCA sessions:

"Elvis left his chair and crouched on the floor, as if listening in a different position was like looking at a subject from a different angle. Again he went into deep concentration, absorbed and motionless. At the end of the song he slowly rose from his crouch and turned to us with a wide grin, and said, 'This is the one.'"

From Elvis's very first recording, "That's All Right" in the summer of 1954, it was evident that he had tapped into something extraordinary. When that something was unveiled to the world, the response was instantaneous: pioneering Memphis deejay Dewey Phillips debuted the song on his radio show, and the station was flooded with phone calls and telegrams, so he played it six more times. Clearly, the world was poised to discover—and seize for itself—what Sam Phillips had seen in the kid.

And so the artist formerly know as Elvis Presley became the phenom known as Elvis. Guralnick best illustrates the repercussions of that conversion by chronicling the slow decline of Presley's relationships with his original band, Scotty Moore and Bill Black, as the music becomes secondary to the circus run by promoter and manager Colonel Tom Parker. As Elvis begins to storm America, Moore and Black fade into the background—both in terms of musical significance and within the book's storyline. ("We were just like two mules put out to pasture," recalls Moore.) Similarly, perhaps the book's most revealing subtext is the trajectory of Elvis's career in relation to the stories of the two most important women in his life at the time: his mother, Gladys, and his first serious girlfriend, Dixie Locke.

At the beginning, they are his closest confidantes, his conscience. But as Elvis begins to explode, they also fade away. With a great deal of restraint, Guralnick shows how Gladys metamorphosed from a proud mother into a bitter lover forced to share her baby with the world. (The impression of a hopeless Gladys near the end, health failing and drinking beer in the afternoon at Graceland, is downright chilling.) Dixie is the sweetheart who implicitly understood and loved him, and who, after their inevitable breakup, haunts all his subsequent relationships with women.

Bubbling under the details of Elvis's ascent, then, are unsettling omnipresent memories of the simple life, represented by the presence of—or lack thereof—the mother–adopted daughter relationship that is torpedoed when Elvis finally splits up with Dixie. The two women are reunited, in a sense, at the conclusion of the book, when Dixie, now long married and a mother, visits Graceland, which is teeming with strangers on the night of Gladys's funeral. Elvis, the most famous person on the planet, is newly enlisted in the Army and soon to depart for Germany. It is a pivotal moment in Elvis's life, and the book's most unforgettable snapshot.

"We talked about his mother and rehashed from the time that I'd met her and all the things that we'd done that were funny and silly," Dixie tells Guralnick. She goes on:

And he expressed how special it was just to be with somebody you knew from those many days back that loved you and accepted you for just what you were back then. He said, "I wonder how many of my friends that are here now would be here if it were five years ago." He said, "Not very many, because they are all looking for something from me." And he told me about one of the guys who was singing backup for him at the time who had just given his heart to the Lord. He had been in the world for a long time and was just really messed up, and he told Elvis that he was having to walk away from the life that he was leading, and Elvis said, "I wish I could do that." It was just so sad. I said, "Why don't you? You've already done what you wanted to do. You've been there, so let's just stop at the top and go back." He said, "It's too late for that. There are too many people that depend on me. I'm too obligated. I'm in too far to get out."

I find it impossible to read that, this year, without thinking of Cobain, whose death was likely accelerated because he believed that his own Elvis ending was a done deal. In fact, Cobain is eerily present throughout much of *Last Train to Memphis*, which in truth is the story of the world's first rock star and the prototypical pandemonium that laid the foundation for August 1954 and everything after. Guralnick reports: "'I'll bet I could burp,' said Elvis impishly, 'and make them squeal.' And then he burped and they did."

There is a terrific live recording of Elvis singing "Ready Teddy" that makes it painfully obvious that those squeals and screams came from someplace very private and primal, and Guralnick captures this crucial aspect of that phenomenon with equal precision. Screenwriter and director Hal Kanter tells Guralnick about a flock of fans who mistook his car for Elvis's: "I saw a young girl open her purse and take out a Kleenex, and she wiped her hand on the car, took some dust, put it in the Kleenex, and folded it and put it back in the purse. I thought, 'My God, I've never seen any kind of devotion like this anywhere, about anything.'"

Nothing like what was happening to Elvis had every happened to anyone else, anywhere, about anything. The words *rock and roll*, stitched together, had yet to become obsolete, much less a musical genre, and were still viewed as something dangerous—not Green Day dangerous, but truly dangerous. Elvis had no luxury of a blueprint, unlike Michael Stipe. (In *Newsweek*, on Cobain, the entrapment of fame and the slow-burn climb of R.E.M.: "I don't know if I'd be around today if *Murmur* had gone to number one.") And no one—not Stipe, or Prince, or Madonna, or Michael Jackson—would ever be able to imagine how it felt to be Elvis. How could you?

You might, as Guralnick points out, convince yourself that it is, all of it, an act of God, that your "voice is God's will," not your own. And you might, finally, as the book's most poignant photo captures, bury your head in your daddy's shoulder on the day your mama dies, sob uncontrollably on the steps of your just-purchased mansion as the press corps gawks, and tell this God that you'd give it all up if you could just have her back.

For his book *Hang Time: Days and Dreams with Michael Jordan*, *Chicago Tribune* columnist Bob Greene tailed the NBA superstar over the course of two championship seasons while Jordan was at the peak of his fame. At one point, Greene makes a sweeping attempt at putting his subject into context: "I thought about what it must have been like to spend 1956 with Elvis Presley, both he and you beginning to sense that decades later people would look back and say: 'This was it. This was the seminal time.'"

For a celebrity who has been imprisoned by his fame, Jordan is as good a latter-day parallel to Elvis as there is. But the fact is, there has been no celebrity, artist, or case study quite like Elvis. He was, to drop a cliché, an American original. Today, as his sixtieth birthday approaches, we have become a culture mired in that paradigm, and as a result we demand that all milestones pale in comparison to their predecessors. *Last Train to Memphis* is more, then, than a book about Elvis Presley. It is a book about America, race relations, the music business, the present, the future, and, often, the jealous past. It is the story of a time when the American Dream was something desirable, not detestable; in that sense, it is an important time capsule that reads like a repressed memory syndrome therapy session, and explains why we—you, me, Kurt Cobain—do what we do.

But most of all, it is about magic. Early on, of Elvis's boyhood fascination with the black community in Tupelo, Guralnick writes:

You walked by a bar and barely heard the wailing of the jukebox over the noise of men and women drinking and gambling and signifying the sounds of love. On weekends the churches would be jumping, in a fashion not dissimilar to an Assembly of God congregation when it started speaking in tongues, but with a joyfulness and a sense of celebration, and expelling of emotion that was embarrassing for a closeted young boy to see at close hand—it seemed sometimes as if they were in the throes of a kind of passion that was not to be revealed in public.

Maybe so. Last month, the Stones rolled into Memphis; the day after, in a review of the concert that appeared in the Memphis daily newspaper the *Commercial Appeal* (the paper whose August 17, 1977, headline read, "Death Captures Crown of Rock and Roll—Elvis Dies Apparently after Heart Attack"), there was no mention of Underdog Elvis. And by the time most Memphians were having their morning coffee, the gentle giant, deflated, was back in his cage and rumbling down a highway toward the next football stadium. Nestled in with the goats and the genie and Spuds, Underdog Elvis waited for the next time he would be summoned to perform.

Inside the dark semi, Spuds woke up and nudged his mysterious balloon buddy, who was wide-awake because, as always, he was too jacked to sleep after the show. Spuds rubbed his eyes and looked over at Underdog, who was staring through a cracked panel at the fading Memphis horizon.

"Hey," said Spuds. "Didn't you used to be . . . ?"

(October 21, 1994, LA Weekly)

All Apologies

DEAR FRANCES BEAN,

Just got the news. My sincerest condolences to you and your mother, Courtney, and the rest of the family. I hope you don't find this too presumptuous, but I had to write to you today, even though you can't read yet (while I think of it, have a great second birthday this summer). I wanted to offer my deepest sympathy, but mostly tell you what your old man came to mean to me over the past few years.

And because they found his body and a suicide note in Seattle this morning, I can't write him to tell him. Which is probably a good thing—if I were to say something to him right now, it would probably be something that we'd both regret later. Because I'm so angry I can hardly see.

The truth is, I felt pretty close to your dad. Even though I never met him, I felt like I knew him—just like a couple of million other fans of his band. To me, he didn't seem like a rock star or a genius or a prophet.

He seemed like another fan that you'd hang out with at the bar, a guy you'd talk with about your problems, his problems, about how the band onstage was sounding that night.

That was the thing about your dad's job: when he was at his best, he gave voice to our innermost feelings; sometimes he didn't even articulate them so much as just made us feel them with his raw, pained, angry, sweet, magnificent set of lungs.

The last time I got a chance to hear those lungs in the flesh was last December 10 at Roy Wilkins Auditorium. You would have been so proud, Frances. He was so beautiful. So rageful and passionate. And the band was tremendous.

They were the first punks to wrest the charts from the dinosaurs, and this night they played like it. They proved beyond a shadow of a doubt that they had survived the glare, the guilt, and their own demons.

Flush with the excitement of seeing a group at the peak of their powers, I ran back to the newspaper office and proclaimed Nirvana to be "The Greatest Rock and Roll Band in the World."

Sitting here now, trying to recall that night, only one moment keeps coming back. It is of the encore, in which your dad—wearing a golden mohair sweater and looking very small—sat strumming an acoustic guitar and singing the chorus to an old Vaselines song: "Don't expect me to die for it, Jesus, don't expect me to cry for it."

That memory was interrupted by an MTV interview with your dad they were rerunning Friday. At one point, he said, "The Beatles went from 'I Wanna Hold Your Hand' to 'Sgt. Pepper's Lonely Hearts Club Band.' I'm not comparing us to the Beatles, but . . . I just want to experiment."

That's what I was looking forward to, too, Frances, because the sky was the limit. Just the other day, I was at the record store, and a friend and I were talking about that December Nirvana concert. "Best thing I saw all last year," he said, which I heartily agreed with.

We speculated as to what Nirvana would do next and dissed the holier-than-thou punk purists who labeled them "sellouts" or the old-timers who didn't think they had staying power.

Unbeknown to us, as we dreamed of your dad's future, he was already lying dead next to a suicide note, the bottom of which read, "I love you, I love you, I love you."

He was probably talking to you. And as you grow up, you should remember that. Because in the coming years, your old man will be made into something else. They will make a martyr out of him, and his name will be sandwiched into sentences with names like Jimi Hendrix, John Lennon, and River Phoenix.

They'll say, he even wrote a song called "I Hate Myself and Want to Die." And in the coming weeks, there will undoubtedly be those who will weigh in with the opinion that, as the voice of a generation, your dad had to die for our sins. He had to take one for the team, sacrifice himself for grunge people everywhere, because, like the song says, "every generation has its own disease." And, as it turns out, its own martyr.

But don't you believe them, Frances. Tell 'em the truth. Tell 'em that your old man could have lived if he wanted to—and if he wanted to half as bad as you and I wanted him to.

(April 6, 1994, St. Paul Pioneer Press)

Do You Remember Rock 'n' Roll Radio?

THE RAMONES PLAYED their first Twin Cities concert in 1976 at the old Kelly's Pub in downtown St. Paul. The Suicide Commandos, the local band that formed around the same time as the New York rockers, opened.

The afternoon of the show, a couple of underage kids from Minneapolis, one of whom wore a Ramones T-shirt, drove across the river and parked in front of the bar. The kids had never been to a bar of any kind before, but they were gonna give it a shot. "We love the Ramones," the kid with the T-shirt told the bouncer at the door. "We just want to see the band. We won't drink or anything. Will you let us in? Please?"

It was 5 P.M. The Ramones wouldn't be onstage until almost midnight. The bouncer gave the lads the once-over, propped the door open, and barked, "Get out of here."

Which is what the kids did. But they didn't stop listening to the Ramones. They drank quarts of Mountain Dew and played endless games of foosball while listening to the Ramones' classic self-titled debut album and their follow-up, *Rocket to Russia*. A couple of years later, the kid with the Ramones T-shirt wore it under his gown when he graduated from high school.

A couple of years after that, the kid found himself hauling gear into Sam's (later First Avenue) for one of the many Ramones gigs the kid would see over the years. The kid's big brother's band, the Neglecters, was opening the show along with the Replacements. When the 'Mats finished their set, singer/songwriter Paul Westerberg primed the crowd for the Ramones by saying, "The best band in the world is up next. If you don't think so, fuck ya."

Now the kid is writing a column about the death of Joey Ramone, fifteen minutes after he heard the news, forty-five minutes from deadline. He is thinking about what Paul said. He is thinking about how damn much fun the Ramones were, how insanely fresh they sounded in the mid-'70s.

He is thinking about what it felt like, pogoing to exhaustion, being lifted off his feet at those shows, about the crush of flesh, the shout-along choruses, and the fact that *SPIN* magazine got something right when in its latest punk special edition it named *Ramones* the number-one punk record of all time.

He is hoping that Zippy the Pinhead somehow acknowledges Joey's passing, because the Ramones brought pinhead culture to the masses and humor back to rock 'n' roll. He is thinking about all the people who will be crushed when they hear the news—the musicians, record store clerks, and people like his friend Mary B. Goode, the biggest Ramones fan he knows—who once upon time were all united under a flag that bore the Ramones' unofficial battle cry, "Gabba Gabba Hey!"

He is thinking about the beginning of the Ramones' shoulda-been-classic "Rock 'n' Roll Radio," which crackles with static, and a radio dial searching for something that crackles, something real, and Joey's nasally opening line, "Do you remember rock 'n' roll radio?" The kid is thinking about how much fun it would be to hear that blasting out of the radio today, but he knows that that is not about to happen anytime soon.

More than anything, the kid is thinking about how Joey Ramone always made him feel like a kid, and how he probably always will.

Gabba-gabba-hey.

(April 16, 2001, St. Paul Pioneer Press)

Meeting across the River

THE DISCO BALL SPRAYED dizzy purple flakes on my lap, jeans, and cowboy boots, which were kicked up on a chair of the Clown Lounge in the basement of the Turf Club, the oldest nightclub in St. Paul. It was Saturday night around eleven. Gene Ween was onstage upstairs, preaching the gospel of freaky found family to a packed room of strange but true believers.

A few minutes earlier I had gone out for some fresh air. My friend John Swardson, the night's opening act, was out front on University Avenue having a postgig cigarette. We talked briefly about the latest tragic deaths in the local music family, Buck Hazlett and two of his kids, when our buddy and fellow musician/writer Danny Sigelman gave us the bad word that Clarence Clemons had died after having a stroke.

Too much. It all hit me hard, so much harder than I would've predicted, and I suppose my friends saw it in my face and stammer. "We've got to power through, man!" cheered Danny, flush with the ever-accessible magic in the night that is live music. "We've got to power through!"

Of course. I bummed a cigarette from Swardson and walked down the street to light up in the foyer of Fantasy Gifts, amid the neon lingerie, latex, and lotion in the window. The tattooed love girls were just closing up, and when I wearily asked, as they locked the heavily barred door, if they were off to party the night away, the seen-it-all sex-traders laughed and said, "I'm going to sleep" and "I'm going home to my kid."

Back at the Turf, it was trumpet player and baseball pitcher Paul Odegaard who offered the wisest counsel of the night: "He's gone, but think of how much he gave us."

Leave it to a fellow horn player to put it into perspective—the idea, of course, that the volcanic sounds that erupted from the Big

Man and his instrument are and always have been part of the eternal ether.

But at that moment, I needed to collect myself and get away from the heat and racket, so I descended the stairs into the basement and got a seat in the corner. I was the only one in that iconic man-woman cave, save for the bartender, and, later, a lone couple, so I suppose it was only natural that, as the dizzy purple flakes worked their nostalgic hypnosis that ultimately morphed into a very vivid present, I thought about, well, you.

It's no exaggeration to say that the friendship Springsteen formed with Clemons via rock 'n' roll is part of why I find myself writing these words—first for myself but also very much for any tramps like us who were born to live, in some way, as large as The Boss and The Big Man, whose friendship and bond through music led them from the Jersey Shore to the high seas of life lived at its fullest. They were cowboys, pirates, shamans—and for any kid who ever wanted to experience life beyond the thrill of adventure books, they were a path.

"The night I met Clarence, he got up onstage, and a sound came out of his horn that seemed to rattle the glasses behind the bar and threatened to blow out the back wall," Springsteen said when he was inducted into the Rock & Roll Hall of Fame. "But there was something else, something that happened when we stood side by side. Some energy, some unspoken story. He always lifted me up. Way, way up. Together we told a story of the possibilities of friendship, a story older than the ones I was writing, and a story I could never have told without him at my side. I want to thank you, Big Man, and I love you so much."

Love. That's why my brothers, Jay and Terry, and I found Springsteen together in the mid-'70s. That's why people form bands. That's why people play and immerse themselves in music. That's why Curtiss A told WCCO-TV that he woke up shrieking when he got the news that his old running buddy-turned-super-dad Buck had been killed. That's why it hurt so good the other night when I finally forced myself to snap out of it and join my friend and fellow musician Pete Christensen upstairs at the Church of Ween.

We hadn't planned on attending the show, but Gene Ween needed a keyboard and Pete hauled his down to the club and we ended up staying for the entire set. Geoff Matson, a kid from the audience, joined in on saxophone and ripped it like a hurricane. When he got offstage, I asked him if he knew who Clarence Clemons was. He said no, but when I invited him to join my and Pete's band onstage for our gig at the Stone Arch Festival the next afternoon, he said yes.

After a spirited farewell to Gene in the basement dressing room, Pete and I split for Whiskey Junction to catch up with my brother Terry, who had just finished his set with the Belfast Cowboys. The three of us had been tooling around the lakes the night before when the iPod shuffle landed on "Spirits in the Night," the song Clemons sat in on with Springsteen that fateful night they met in the early '70s. When my brother saw me, his epic horn section still ringing in his ears, he buried his head in my shirt and sobbed.

The next day Pete and I played our gig, Matson the sax kid showed up and howled like the second coming, and as we sat on a sandbar on the river after the gig, I thought about the day Clemons called me.

It was a Saturday afternoon, a couple of years ago. I was puttering around the house when the phone rang. On the other end was my friend Jackie Heintz, a St. Paul girl and super Springsteen fan who, along with her mother Jeannie, had formed a friendship with Clemons over the years that found them visiting him at his Florida home. My first CD had just come out, and I loaded up the Heintz gals with some swag to give to the E Street family.

"Hey, Jim," said the Big Man. "I wanted to call and thank you for your music and the T-shirts. What a nice gift. Blessings to you, my friend."

Back atcha, Big Man. See ya in the stars.

(June 12, 2011, Minnpost.com)

SIX

MIX #2
TEENAGE KICKS

One Love

THIS IS A GHOST STORY. On Tuesday, June 26, at exactly 1:30 P.M., my wife and I were driving in our station wagon north on 35W when the alternator snapped. The engine seized up and coughed and finally quit, and I coasted off the exit to a dead stop in the middle of South Thirty-fifth Street in Minneapolis, between Stephens and First Avenue.

That area of the Twin Cities usually gets mentioned in newspapers only when bad stuff happens, but I want everyone to know what went down that afternoon, the hottest of 2001 so far: Bob Marley showed up.

That's right—Bob Marley, the reggae mystic who rose from unspeakable strife in his homeland of Jamaica, was moved to sing about joy in the face of the sort of human catastrophe unique to Third World countries, and became a voice of oppressed people everywhere. He died in 1981 at the age of thirty-six, but I swear, he was there. Granted, I may have been suffering from sunstroke, and I may have been the only one who heard him, but you're going to have to trust me on this because my wife can't back me up. She didn't hear what I heard.

She'd hiked off to fetch us a tow truck while I stayed with the wagon, which was immovable because the battery was fried. I was stuck. Right in the middle of the street. The emergency flashers didn't work, so I stood behind the car and waved the other drivers around me, and that's when I heard Marley the first time.

"Hey, bro, you need a push?" asked a death-skinny punk-rock guy who walked by me with a pronounced limp and a purple cane and his punk-rock girlfriend.

"No thanks, bro. It's locked up. Stuck in Park. Thank you, though. Thanks a lot." That's what I said. That's what I said as I stood out there in the ninety-five-degree heat, sweat pouring from my head like a spent lawn sprinkler, for twenty-five minutes. And do you know how many times I said that?

Twenty-five. I counted. Twenty-five people in twenty-five minutes. Twenty-five people slowed down in that heat and traffic and took the time to talk to me. Twenty-five times I said, "I'm cool," or "I appreciate it," or "Muchas gracias," to the point where, after a while, I started grinning stupidly because I felt like an urban parrot.

Or a guy who'd just seen Marley's ghost.

He was black, white, brown, yellow, young, old, male, female. Guys with tattoos who looked like they'd had a few. Guys who looked at me like they wanted to kill me. Guys who looked like they wanted to get to know me (a lot) better. A guy who came out of his house to ask me if I needed help and who, a few minutes later, came back out and put his family of four and two overflowing laundry baskets into a cab.

A muscular guy in a 2Pac T-shirt who wanted to chat as much as help. A woman who looked like she put on her clothes to come out of her apartment just to see if I was okay. A wiry old Rastaman who walked by, offered to push, and despite the haze in his eyes looked like he could push a tank uphill.

A couple of teenage girls who offered me their water bottle, a soccer mom who offered her cell phone. A Hispanic family in a pickup and a businessman in an SUV, both of whom asked if I needed a lift.

A beautiful goldilocked woman around my age who, when she smiled her sunshine smile at me after I told her my wife had gone for the tow truck, made me think that there might not be a better place to be in the whole wide world at the moment than standing out there on that hot tar.

That's where I heard it. On the hot tar. On a Minnesota afternoon that felt like a Jamaica afternoon. It was Marley's "One Love," written in 1962 for his then-girlfriend Rita, not long after Jamaica won its independence from Britain. The song that the BBC named, in 1999, "the anthem of the millennium." The song penned by the songwriter who, in Africa, China, Latin America, and many parts of the United States, is bigger than the Beatles.

It was the damnedest thing. I'm telling you, it came not from a few cars, but from every single car. They pulled up beside me, and "One Love" sprayed out of their speakers in the form of torso-rattling hip-hop, genteel classical, militant metal, earthy R&B, peaches-and-cream country-western, sweet salsa, urbane jazz, buttery folk.

Twenty-five different car stereos. Twenty-five different versions of "One Love." Twenty-five different people who took a second on the hottest day of the year to ask a stranger if he needed help.

Which he did. And he is here today to thank them all again, even the ones who just waved or thumbsed-up, even the two who said, "Get the (bleep) out of the way!"

Marley once said, "Reggae music is music of the people." At the moment, there is a creeping sense that there is no music, or government, of the people, and the despair about that is palpable. Beyond that, personal isolation and headlines attached to horrific news stories make people fear that there is no goodness in the world, no common bonds, no future.

But last Tuesday, twenty-five people rolled down their windows and reached out to touch someone they'd never seen before and would probably never see again. Why? Maybe because they wanted to do a good deed, or because they wanted to revel in the fact that the sun was finally out, or because somebody did a good deed for them once, or because that's how they were raised, or because that's Just. What. You. Do.

All I know is that when that tow truck showed up, I was sorta disappointed, because it felt like we were all just getting to know each other.

A couple of hours later, my wife and I borrowed our neighbor's car and took the kids to the pool. On the way, we came upon a woman whose car had broken down. My wife rolled down the window and asked her if she needed help. She said she didn't, and my wife told her the same thing had happened to us earlier in the day.

That was little consolation to the woman, whose three kids were crawling all over her. But as we pulled away, the whole thing prompted me to tell the kids the story of the Good Samaritan, which I botched horribly because it's been so long since I've heard it and because the sound of "One Love" was still mixing me up.

The one part I got right, though, is that the Good Samaritan comes in the form of ordinary people, strung-out people, sexy people, rich people, poor people, tired people, lonely people, sinners, saints. And if you listen, sometimes you can hear them all singing the same song, like the one Bob Marley sang at Madison Square Garden twenty-one years ago.

That was the last time he sang "One Love," but I was wrong about this being a ghost story. Ghost stories are about dead people.

(July 6, 2001, St. Paul Pioneer Press)

Ooh La La

I'M NOT SURE WHEN I first suspected that the Faces' "Ooh La La" is the perfect song, but I felt the same way at the 400 Bar the other night, when John Munson and his cover boys in Meltaway did it. The set was a vocal-rich showcase of pretty covers of songs by the likes of Elvis Costello, Trip Shakespeare, Ron Sexsmith, and Brian Wilson, but when they broke into "Ooh La La," the room lifted.

Seriously. Everyone stopped what they were doing, even in the back, just as I've seen it happen before: at the Faces' farewell concert at the Minneapolis Auditorium in 1975, and at several Soul Asylum shows in the early '90s, when those guys would do "Ooh La La" as an encore and send everyone home with, well, souls asylumed.

The Front Porch Swingin' Liquor Pigs do it regularly at their Friday night gig at the Viking Bar, and when they played it on New Year's Eve, a couple of barflies close to this column report that, with 2001 lurking just around the corner, goose bumps broke out as the entire joint sang the chorus of, "I wish that I knew what I know now, when I was younger, I wish that I knew what I know now, when I was stronger."

If you don't know the song, you should, because it's as good as it gets. It succinctly sums up life and how to live, but it also grasps the mystery of same. Despite originally disowning the song, Rod Stewart recorded a surprisingly cool version of it a couple of years ago (the original is sung wizenedly by bassist Ronnie Lane), and it perfectly concludes the finest ode-to-outsiderdom-disguised-as-a-teen-movie, *Rushmore*.

But why, exactly, is "Ooh La La" so indestructible, after almost thirty years? Musically, it's because the melody rises, then rises some more, like an especially loud flock of geese heading south. Also, its melody is irresistible, the way all great pub sing-alongs are irresistible.

Mostly, I'd say the song survives so vividly because of the sentiment in the title, which manages to bring together the three amigos of "C'est La Vie," "Que Sera, Sera," and "You Can't Always Get What You Want." It's a fascinating thing to ruminate on, because the singer's wish for wisdom is entirely unfeasible, since ultimately everyone has to glean such knowledge, get to where they're going, alone.

So the question is posed, even as we sing along: what, exactly, do we know now that we would have wanted to know when we were younger?

Not a thing, if you ask me, because no one could have told me anything when I was younger—not only because I wouldn't have listened: I already knew everything.

"Ooh La La" is sung from the perspective of a grandfather telling his grandson about what he's learned, but he ultimately throws his hands up in the air, concluding, "Poor young grandson, there's nothing I can say. You'll have to learn, just like me, and that's the hardest way."

Be that as it may, elders will always attempt to impart knowledge to youngsters, whether the youngsters want to hear it or not.

Here's my shot, to the teen wizards of tomorrow. This is what I've learned. This is the advice I would have given to the younger, stronger me, had I asked. Or, at least, this is what I came up with when I dusted off my (vinyl) copy of "Ooh La La" the other night:

Try to find yourself, but don't worry if you get lost along the way, because that's what's supposed to happen. Make mistakes. Experiment. If you find something you like, share it with the class. Cherish it. All of it. You never know when someone you love isn't going to be around anymore. Embrace it. All of it. Even the emptiness.

Sleep in, then seize the day. Get a job, any job. Work hard. Quit a job, any job, spontaneously, dramatically, at least once in your life, because it is exhilarating.

Live it up. Cry at the credits. Slide your feet on defense.

When adults ask you how school's going, give the poor suckers a break. Let them in.

Don't be so hard on yourself. Don't be mad at the world, because it's bigger than you and it will hurt you, which is not the worst thing that can happen to you. Don't get mad at the old people running this country; get even. Don't let anyone dismiss your music, and don't believe anyone's story of golden youth other than your own.

Go to school dances and games, even if you think they're mindless. But unless the spirit moves you, don't ever cheer, "We've got spirit. Yes we do! We've got spirit. How 'bout you?" because teen spirit smells.

Get some spirit anyway.

Pray. Party. Try harder. Slack off. Be sarcastic six days a week, but on the seventh day, rest. Contradict yourself, early and often. Search and coast. Be cautious and fearless.

No pressure, but change the world. By always saying what you feel and think, even if it's hard, even though they'll laugh at you and call you names, because the alternative will slowly, surely kill you. That's how.

Play the field, but keep your eye on the ball, because you never know if the girl or boy you just met is going to be your wife or lover or best pal or inspiration.

Make as many platonic friendships with members of the opposite sex as possible, because they're like good snow tires: they respond well to slippage, and they last.

Listen, really listen, to as much music as you can possibly get your ears around. There are secret treasures to be had, ways of living to be ingested, like Tsar's "Teen Wizards," my favorite song the radio won't play. And, while you're at it, download John Prine's "Hello in There," which will make you feel bad about how you treat, or don't treat, old folks.

If it doesn't, see a doctor.

Turn off the TV; it's crap. Never give up on the radio, but don't be a lemming. Read. Write. Rage. Against the machine and the dying light. Closely study the work of Ferris Bueller (*Ferris Bueller's Day Off*), Tammy Metzler (*Election*), and Harold Chasen (*Harold and Maude*).

Question authority, but make sure they're good questions. Make your mark. Do something that's never been done before. Live for the moment, but make plans for more moments you can live for.

Talk to somebody, anybody, about your dreams. And your problems. Especially your problems.

Don't do anything stupid—or too stupid, anyway. Life is a cabaret, my friend, and remember: both the good times and bad times give you soul, so let the bad times roll.

Talk to your parents, or guardians, or aunts, uncles, or grandparents. They're old, not dead, and most of us remember what grade school, high school, and college were like. Vividly. Painfully. Happily.

Hold your parents' hands once in a while as you walk through this life, even if you haven't in years, even if it makes you feel a little silly. Pretend you still need them. Do something with them on a Friday night, like charades or Scrabble or the St. Clair Broiler, even if it makes you feel uncool.

Because the fact is, you are uncool, and no matter what you think, you never will be cool, because feeling awkward is part of the trip. Nobody ever really gets over it: they just cover it up. Your uncoolness is just especially exposed now, but I promise, it won't always feel like your whole body is on fire.

Which is both good and bad, so burn while you can.

Stick to your guns. Mind your manners. Talk to strangers. Don't be chicken. Lighten up. Love thy neighbor. Look out for the other guy. Memorize this, or not, then eat it, pass it on, or fill in what's missing for you.

And when all else fails, ooh la la.

(January 28, 2001, St. Paul Pioneer Press)

This Is the Sea

CALLING SOMETHING A "MIRACLE" these days can get you laughed right out of the cynics' club, but there's no other word for what happened at First Avenue around 10:15 Saturday night.

The Waterboys were onstage, having returned to the scene of their most recent inspirational service of March 28. Among other things that night, the Irish-British band's singer/songwriter, Mike Scott, memorably sang, "That was the river, this is the sea," giving voice to anyone who may have been going through a profound winter funk and/or midlife crisis, as the dicey past (the river) slipped into the looming future (the sea).

Six short months later, the funk and crisis and future and sea belonged to everyone. Before the show, a fan told Scott that the Waterboys' performance of "This Is the Sea" had helped him grow up, to which the singer responded, "Glad to be of service."

Now the fan found himself near the front of the stage, listening intently again as Scott sang, over an electric guitar that sounded like banging shutters in a storm, "I'm not through with my changes / I've got a long way still to run / I'm gonna play this show even if nobody comes."

The main-room floor was packed but neighborly. Up front, two neighbors/best friends from St. Paul danced together. Jen was driving, a mom; a woman I will call Sue was drunk, an attorney; and early in the set, Sue told an acquaintance that she has been going through some personal problems. The acquaintance told Sue to join the club, because that pretty much describes the universe, 2001.

Sitting in his wheelchair behind Jen and Sue was a guy named Chris. Introductions were made over the decibels and drinks, and Chris, a paraplegic whose main expression of gratitude for the music was the occasional snap of his fingers, told everyone when they asked that he could see just fine. The feeling was that Chris wanted to be part of the crowd, maybe blend in, and most of all, hear what the great Scott had to say.

"Since September 11, a lot of things that used to seem important don't seem so important anymore," Scott said. The people at the lip of the stage stood with their arms folded, drinking up the words and songs as if Scott were an adoptive mother ladling out homemade stew. The love crackled from the stage, unregulated and unmistakable, and infected every body—able and otherwise—that put a finger in its socket.

The songs held huge meaning and healing. "Bring 'Em All In" was an incantation to fill the heart with as many lovers or soul mates as one can hold. "Dumbing Down the World" cut like an ax, a cheerleader for philosophy and spirituality. At the end of a typically extraordinary "Whole of the Moon," Scott sang, impishly, purposefully, repeatedly, "I picture a rainbow."

The band lurched into the lusty "I Know She's in the Building," but Scott, who had given a kindred poet's shout-out to Prince earlier in the show, stopped and restarted it, because it wasn't "sexy" enough. Then it was: caring but rough, too. "Maybe tonight!" he teased. "Maybe tonight!" He was playing both matchmaker and warlock; the miracle was looking for a couple of willing souls to inhabit.

Scott played guitar solos that bled and sang songs such as "The Pan Within" as if he knew it might be the last time he'd sing anything to anybody, or anything that would ever mean as much to anybody. "Fisherman's Blues" packed its usual dreamy-pub wallop, and then, just like that, they were gone. End of show. A few minutes later, after the crowd had whooped and clapped itself into vermicelli, they were back. Encore. "This Is the Sea."

As the guitars and drums bubbled and boiled, Sue, in that full-on-drunk-but-fully-in-the-moment mode, took off her shirt. Now wearing a white tank top T-shirt, she raised her arms above her head freely, blissfully. Scott snarled above her, a blue light bathing him as he screamed the lyrics this time, "You're trying to remember how fine your life used to be / That was the river, this is the sea."

Sue closed her eyes and writhed the writhe of a soul unleashed. She was dancing with Jen, but mostly with herself, letting the current move through her. Finally, Jen let go. She took a few incredulous steps backward, in order to watch her friend transform into a beautiful creature she had never seen before.

As the band unfurled its song of courage, Sue sidled up next to Chris's wheelchair. The two neo-strangers exchanged a glance in the semidark, then Sue closed her eyes and let the music guide her. She put her hands on Chris's shoulders, then grabbed the handles of the back of the wheelchair, and sat in his lap.

The drums and bass were tribal now, and Sue was arching her back, her shiny brown hair swinging wildly to the beat and nearly touching the dance floor. "She has a brother who is paraplegic," Jen shouted to me over the building roar, as Sue's arms rested on Chris's shoulders, as Chris's head banged on the wheelchair headrest, his small body jostling puppet-like, in great ecstasy. He was in danger of falling out, but he didn't because Sue knew what she was doing.

They danced like that for three minutes or so. When the song ended, the band stood at center stage bowing. Sue and Chris had their arms around each other as Scott told everybody to take care of themselves and each other and promised to return next year.

On the floor, superlatives and good-byes were exchanged. Outside the club on the sidewalk, people were sobbing and hugging. "Did you see that?" they said. "Did you see that last song?" Maybe they saw their own miracle. Maybe they saw the same one.

Because that's what it was, a miracle. What else do you call the sexiest, most loving dance you've ever witnessed? What else do you call a sweet-smelling rose that sprouts so effortlessly, with such timeliness, out of this stench of broken bricks and mortar?

No, there is no other word for it, and there is no reason not to believe that many more like it aren't on the horizon, because everything that came before it was the river and that was the sea.

(October 18, 2001, St. Paul Pioneer Press)

All My Life

SHE HAS A PENCHANT for drama queenery, but this time the shrieks were legit: the eraser was stuck up her nose. That's what happens when a girl three days away from her fifth birthday pretends an eraser is a nose ring and inhales. Now her brother was screaming, her mother was freaking, and she—she was doing both, because I'd bloodied her nostril trying to get the thing out with a tweezers and a flashlight. It was bright blue. I could see it.

I packed her up and drove to the emergency room. The admitting nurse said kids stick peas and beads up their noses all the time, which made me feel better. Part of me figured we'd be in and out of there in a couple of hours, but another part, the ER vet part, knew better. After signing her in and getting her fitted with a hospital ID bracelet, I found two chairs by the aquarium. She ogled the fish and, with giddy escape-from-bedtime mania, talked about *Finding Nemo*. I settled in for the long haul.

Make that "girded myself": the emergency room is anything but settling. It is a holding tank of ambiguity, a purgatory between death and life, and, like airports or bus terminals or Laundromats or the sidelines of kids' soccer games or any other place where you find yourself trapped with yourself, and in its dull captivity, you take stock of all the things you've done and haven't done, the perfect father or husband or person you haven't been, and you start living Evan Dando lyrics like "I'm so impatient for a new sensation, God knows what I thought I'd do. I bit my own sweet heart in two."

Talking about restlessness here. Talking about the feeling that happens when the universe forces you to put the brakes on and you realize yet again that you're a greedy bastard, that love and family and music and friends should be enough, but at the moment they're not, because at the moment you aren't feeding that voracious harpy that taps you on the shoulder at the oddest hours to remind you that there are people better than you who are creating art and scoring touchdowns and having passionate love affairs and helping the poor and then there's you. A distracted fuckup who apparently can't keep his daughter safe from herself, much less the world, stuck in a waiting room with a bunch of sick and tired zombies watching reality television and reading months-old magazines and half-listening to your daughter talk about fish and books and cartoons and school and Grandma and why this and why that and why this again and why that again and will it hurt and you feel bad for not being all there but you listen to it all the time so there are times when it Just. Becomes. White. Noise.

Then there are other times when absolutely the only thing you want out of life is to see a blue eraser come popping out of her right nostril.

We killed the first three hours by going to the bathroom seven hundred times and drinking at the fountain six hundred times. We read books and blabbed and hurry-upped and waited. Then the nurse showed us to our curtained-off cubicle, which housed a bed and a TV that had four channels, all of which carried news of teenage shootings, so we left it off. For the next hour, I told her stories of the other times I'd been in the hospital with her, about the time her uncle ran around the block wearing only his saddle shoes, about the time her grandpa, etc. She wanted more. Her eyes were wide and fixed on mine and happy to have me all to herself. Captive.

I helped her off with her clothes and put her in a tiny hospital gown. She sang songs and poked her head out the curtain at the other patients, most of whom were seniors who lay unconscious on gurneys. She crawled on the floor and asked what everything in the room was for. We were both calm and terror-free. I told her that if she jerked her head around when the doctor tried to get the eraser out, the doctor might need to give her a shot that would put her to sleep so she wouldn't jerk. She didn't complain, but her eyes welled up with tears and trailed up to the bunny on the ceiling, which she decided at that moment she hated.

The doctor came in. He didn't introduce himself, but his name tag said Brian Jones. I resisted the urge to make any cracks about Rolling Stones and swimming pools, so as not to interrupt the reassuring monologue he was giving. He told me about the CPR move we'd try first and told her, "Daddy's going to give you a kiss and blow into your mouth." Which is what I did, but it produced no eraser—just snot, blood, tears, and the sourest there's-therapy-in-my-future look I've ever seen on her face.

She bolted upright. I hugged her to my chest and wiped her tears with my T-shirt. Brian Jones took another look up her nose and reached for the first of the four pairs of tweezers he'd try for the excavation. He made an exploratory dab. She jerked her head away. He did it again. She did it again. He left the room for a few minutes and came back with a nurse and a Q-tip swabbed with numbing gel. The nurse put her in a gentle headlock, I pinned her legs down, and she started screaming for her mom.

Brian Jones put the swab up her nose and she bucked like he'd just put electroshock pads on her chest and yelled, "Clear!" I could only see her eyes, which howled with daddy-betrayal, but now the entire hospital could hear how much sh-sh-she w-w-w-anted to go home. Brian Jones put down the swab and gently inserted tweezers #2 in her nostril. With artful expertise, he calmly navigated the flesh around the opening and peered in. No luck. He backed away and left the room. She sprang up, got on her knees, and affixed herself to me like a koala bear to a tree, which was good, because in that position she couldn't see what Brian Jones was holding when he came back in the room: a tray of utensils like the ones Jeremy Irons used in *Dead Ringers*.

He unwrapped the sanitary paper from the tray and sat on the edge of the bed. Another, male, nurse joined the female nurse, and they both took hold of her head. She went wild. The female nurse called her sweetie, the male nurse told her about his dog Hershey, but she wasn't buying any of it. Her screaming hit first-Wednesday-of-the-month levels as Brian Jones dug in with tweezers #3. Her eyes bore into mine with rage and blame. I pressed down on her legs, kept talking to her, and told her everything was going to be okay, even though I was starting to realize she'd have to go under the knife. After a few minutes of gentle burrowing, Brian Jones backed away and sprinted out of the room. The nurses unclenched her head. She got on her knees and tried to make a break for it.

I picked her up, held her on my lap, and wiped the sweat and tears off her face. Brian Jones came back into the room with tweezers #4—a small scissors, actually, with a tiny fishhook meant for those hard-to-reach-spots. As we pinned her down, she started writhing and weakly screaming, "No, no, no! Daddeeeee!" All the adults said the same thing, which at this point—twenty minutes after our first kiss— sounded like bald-faced lies: "It won't take much longer, honey." Brian Jones adjusted his glasses with a newfound purpose and dove in. C'mon, baby.

She arched her back as the nurses held her head in a nurse vise grip, and I held her ankles and listened to high-pitched tales of Hershey the dog, and people all around us murmuring about that poor little screaming kid in there, and just as I started to think it was going to be the knife at worst and the shot at best, Brian Jones uncoiled from her face, like a gardener pulling a weed. "There it is!" we all told her in unison. Brian Jones held it up. It was huge and blue and by far the most beautiful thing I've ever seen come out of a nose. She crumpled into my arms and whimpered.

They gave her a Popsicle. We signed out and thanked the nurses and anyone else we could thank, but we couldn't find Brian Jones, who was off putting out another fire. It was almost midnight.

We drove home along the perfectly quiet city streets and didn't play the radio. I held her hand and told her how good she'd done. She sucked on her Popsicle and made me promise to tell everybody "every detail" of our adventure. And every time I have, somewhere in the background Evan Dando's been singing, "All my life I thought I needed all the things I didn't need at all / All my life I thought I wanted all the things I didn't want at all."

(October 8, 2003, City Pages)

Beautiful Day

WE HAD THE RADIO UP LOUD a couple of Fridays ago on the way out to the Onan Observatory in Norwood–Young America, easily the best stargazing date of the spring and summer. It was all-request day on the Current (89.3 FM), so I asked the fourth grade BFFs in the back seat what they wanted to hear.

After a short conference, they decided on their song. I got on the cell as the sun was going down over the prairie and much of the traffic on East Hwy. 212 was streaming against us into town. I couldn't get through to the studio line, so I called a friend and asked her to make the request via email. She called back, double-checked the names of the BFFs, and said she'd do her best.

In a "Science of Facebook" chart in *Time* magazine last year, happiness was deconstructed like this: an ideal happy individual has ties to: a next-door neighbor (happiness quotient: +34 percent); a friend living within a mile (+25 percent); a sibling living within a mile (+14 percent); a friend of a friend (+10 percent); a coresident spouse (+8 percent); a friend of a friend of a friend (+5.6 percent). The data, of course, do not account for your various sundry happy misanthropes and lovable loners, but you get the idea.

The chart ran through my head as the deejays—two old friends whose unbridled passion for sharing music has led them to doing it, and therefore bringing people together, for a living—played "Monster Mash," a tune from my youth that recalled a time before iPods and personal playlists, when hearing your song on KDWB or WDGY was the most instantaneous and thrilling way to connect with the universe.

We pulled into the parking lot of Baylor National Park and the girls ran off to the playground. I sat in the car, drinking in the impossibly green and already dazzling pastoral scene, scribbling in a notebook, and making notes on my tape recorder. The sun was going down, the moon was coming up, and the girls were on the swings, kicking their legs in the air to take them higher, higher, higher, when the first few notes padded out of the car door speakers.

I couldn't believe it. I jumped out and yelled across the field. They waved and took off like a shot, two athletic girls with smiles the size of the horizon, running at me and filling the windshield with all their unbridled vibrancy and U2's "Beautiful Day" blasting out across the universe.

They got to the car before the first chorus kicked in. They didn't say much. They listened closely. Their eyes crawled around the scene. They wanted to know if the deejay had said anything yet, which he hadn't. They climbed on the roof of the car and watched some boys play catch with a football as Bono instructed them to acknowledge the moment, to not let the beautiful day get away.

I told them that because of them, "you two girls, right here, right now," all over the world—Minnesota, New York, China, Seattle— people were listening to this redemption song of freedom. Together. More crawling eyes.

As the tune faded out, deejay Mark chimed in, "It's a beautiful day for stargazing. That's what Helen and Julianne are doing with Papa Jim, on their way to check out the stars."

That's an exact quote. I know, because I left the tape recorder running. I won't bore you with every daddy detail, or how many times I've played it since, but let's put it this way: "Beautiful Day" has never sounded more beautiful, mixed as it was with those preteen giggles and all that pervasive joy, hope, grace, and a scream-along to "what you don't have you don't need it now, don't need it now, don't need it now."

(May 14, 2008, Southwest Journal)

Dear Sam,

Someone passed onto me your prose on our show. They don't write em like that anymore. Every night we step on stage we aspire to tear — lose those feelings of strength of connection w/ our hope to leave our audience a little stronger, happier and wised-up. Besides untold riches and glory it's the only REAl reason for carrying on giving a show. But it's a good one.

[signature]

SEVEN
THE BEAUTI-
FUL ONES

The Gold Experience

EARLY ONE MORNING in February 1993, I walked out of Minneapolis Glam Slam, where Prince, as he was then known, and the New Power Generation had performed an impromptu concert. It was a three-set marathon, a greatest hits revue that included a version of "Purple Rain" that had the patrons on the floor waving their arms back and forth religiously. Just like in the movie. Just like in the past.

When it was over, I made my way across Fifth Street, and as the Minnesota air freeze-dried the dance sweat on my face, I turned up my collar to an entirely different kind of coldness: after establishing himself as one of the most fiercely innovative musical forces in American culture over the past decade, Prince, it seemed, had little left to offer but star power, showmanship, and fuzzy nostalgia.

And the truth is, since I'd seen it happen before, I can't say I was all that disappointed. Instead, I took comfort in the fact that I'd borne witness to the little rocket's ascent more than a dozen times in clubs: at First Avenue (then Sam's) in 1980 the night before he and the *Dirty Mind* band went to Los Angeles to open for the Rolling Stones; in 1981 at an amazing free-form jam the night after the *Controversy* tour stopped at Met Center; in 1983 at the Minnesota Dance

Theater performance at First Avenue where much of *Purple Rain* was recorded; in 1984 the week *Purple Rain* was released; in 1987 at a warm-up for the *Sign o' the Times* tour; at Glam Slam in 1990 working out material for *Graffiti Bridge,*; and on and on and on.

But as I walked from the club to the parking ramp that night, I admit to feeling a certain smug sympathy for the nouveau Prince fans who'd just got done paying their respects in the court of His Royal Badness. Because more than anything, the Glam Slam gig reminded me of the times I'd seen Ray Charles and James Brown—in dinner theaters. Entertaining shows, to be sure, but like all such experiences, the music was framed by the specter of pale imitation and a little voice that nagged, "You should've been there when . . ."

Overnight, then, it seemed as if Prince had prematurely signed on with this relic club, trading spontaneity for choreography, risks for hits, genius for just good enough—all of which is and always has been anathema to his legendary appetite for self-experimentation. At the time, the word on the street was that Prince was old news, that he'd been displaced by an army of new jacks who couldn't run with him on a real instrument if their entire collection of vinyl samples depended on it.

Which is why, when the strains of "Purple Rain" finally faded that night and I watched Prince take his bows, I wondered if he suspected what I did. I wondered if he realized that the stuff was just this side of stale, and if he had it in him to challenge himself again. Nobody could blame him if he wanted to coast after all these years, but as I watched him run through an admittedly mind-blowing array of old hits, another, very distinct, impression took hold: that he was bored out of his skull, and he was purging himself of his past.

Fast-forward exactly one year later. Prince is no longer Prince but a symbol/glyph, and everyone, including me, thinks he's gone off the deep end. Later, he'll tell Alan Light from *Vibe* magazine that he knows people will make jokes about it—he even accepts that aspect of it—but that the name change is a way to draw a very clear line between him and the comfort of his past laurels. Weirdly, I get it. On a gut level, I understand his desire for his music to grow, his need to move on, and his thirst for personal growth. Maybe it's because he and I are the same age and grew up in virtually the same neighborhood, but in my thirty-sixth year I likewise discovered that true knowledge doesn't come easy; it requires a process that the psychotherapist calls "hard work" and that Prince calls panning for "gold."

Which is to say that Prince doesn't represent the past but possibility. In February 1994, he emerged from an intense writing and recording seclusion and threw a party ("The Beautiful Experience") at Paisley Park to commemorate the release of "The Most Beautiful Girl in the World" single. That's when I first heard much of the material you now hold in your hands—including the marvelous cartoon dance workout "Now" and the Al Green–kissed "Most Beautiful Girl." The ninety-minute performance was a gritty, lean, and supremely nasty coming-out baptism that, unlike the Glam Slam gig a mere twelve months prior, revealed Prince to be a past-jettisoning, forward-thinking world citizen capable of howling lines like "Hooker, bitch, 'ho / I don't think so," and then, with genuine badass squirreliness, "Light us up and take a hit."

Which, as a matter of fact, is exactly what I did. As often as possible. Last summer, Prince and the NPG set up shop for a week in Erotic City, the small annex in Minneapolis Glam Slam's upper deck. Typically, they'd start at about 2:00 A.M. and play until 3:00. All my cronies from the old days had long since given in to their skepticism and bailed from the purple magic bus, so my friend Theresa was the only one I could ever talk into going. One night we were joined by 150 people. The next, four hundred. One night, he lay on his back and played feathery blues guitar for twenty minutes; the next, he bounced off the NPG horns like a tireless, tenacious Muscle Shoals band leader; the next, he led three hundred people on a scavenger hunt out to Chanhassen for a full-fledged concert at Paisley Park.

It was exhilarating, and exhausting. Theresa and I would drive home from those gigs dazed and bemused and go to sleep with the birds chirping and the sun coming up. The next day, we'd call each other up. Did you hear this? What was that lyric? What's up with the spiritual vibe? I was floored by the band—bassist Sonny T., drummer Michael Bland, keyboardists Tommy Barbarella and Mr. Hayes—and the balance they struck between well-drilled professionalism and off-the-cuff jam-ability. After a July Glam Slam gig, Theresa said she thought "Pussy Control" was just another one of Prince's sexist throwaways; I thought that was too easy. I defended it as a light-hearted and raunchy take on the power of womanhood.

We bitched, wondered, and danced. Yeah, we were hooked, I suppose in the same way that any Prince fan gets hooked, but because it was all new material and we were hearing it as works in progress unfettered by the usual cheese, it was more exciting than just superstargazing in a small club. It was, as we often said those nights in June and July, like discovering an underground band that nobody had ever heard of before.

In retrospect, it was exactly what I needed. I'd spent much of the past year of my job at the St. Paul *Pioneer Press* covering the music of despair, and I was sick of everybody being so damned serious. I wanted to have some fun. Prince and the NPG did it; they made me laugh and think and twitch. And there was something else.

After spending the past few years cultivating personas of soft-rock balladeer, electrifying dancer, and public relations goofball, Prince returned to doing what he does better than almost anyone else on the planet: playing *guitar*. Upon first hearing Jimi Hendrix's "Purple Haze," Bruce Gary wrote that "it was as if all the soul music and rock 'n' roll I'd ever heard had become this raging flood." That quote stuck in my head night after night as Prince consistently nailed my jaw to the floor and swept us all up in his own raging, gushing, flash flood.

As the summer wore on, Prince started showing up for more impromptu gigs at Glam Slams in Miami and Los Angeles, and the grapevine reported that he was performing this brilliant new material side by side with covers by Stevie Wonder, Sly Stone, and Salt-N-Pepa. He's never made a secret of his passion for musical history, and you can clearly hear the bridging of those three generations folded into these grooves. It's there in the anthemic utopian vision-meets-celebrity vulnerability of "Gold," in the hard-won socially conscious confidence of "We March," and in the jubilant noise that is "Now." Pissed off and playful all at once, it also contains a genuine bitterness and anger at the media that cuts through on "Billy Jack Bitch."

As that track illustrates, *The Gold Experience* is, if nothing else, raw and real. And in case you haven't been paying attention, that's big news. One of my main complaints about so much modern R&B is that everything sounds so unremittingly chipper; even supposedly sad torch songs are rendered with a glossy detachment, an antifeeling. No such problem here: "Shhh" is a melancholy blues-gospel jam built on a tangible bed of longing, while "I Hate U" is a messy, anguish filled kiss-off that stems from a paradox (desire versus spite) that more polite art usually avoids.

Above all, Prince wants it known that this is a record about the fight for freedom—personal, artistic, political—but anyone with half an ear can suss that much out. During the making of it, he was enamored with Betty Eadie's book *Embraced by the Light*, a first-person narrative on near-death experience, and that theme also peppers the record, most explicitly on the reincarnation dream "Dolphin." It is also implicit on several other tracks that ponder birth, death, life, and rebirth, and one man's own expectations and perceptions of himself.

To me, the most fascinating aspect about these twelve songs is that they come from a human being who, like you and me, struggles day in and day out, but unlike you and me, does so in a very public forum. And that public flailing makes the music somehow resonate even deeper and transcend the confines of good beats and hitmaking. It is the sound of an artist at odds with himself, his world, his past, present, and future. Who would've guessed that such a sound could be this big, bad, and joyful?

More than anything, throughout my own *Gold* experience I heard a unique, and uniquely potent, mix of purpose, celebration, and fear. There is a palpable sense of urgency here, as if Prince knows that time is running out for all of us to make connections with ourselves and the outside world. Don't believe me? Listen to the scream in the middle of "Endorphinmachine" or the guitar solo on "Gold" that concludes the album. The two things they share are desperation and liberation. Listen. Cue 'em up, back to back. Hear it? He isn't showing off; he's searching. Again. And like never before.

(July 1995, liner notes to Prince's record The Gold Experience)

Salesmen and Racists

I CAN'T REMEMBER financial advice, recipes, entertainment news, computer stuff, statistics, trivia, names, dates, brands, or my own family's history past a certain point.

But I can tell you exactly where I was when I read the review of the first Clash record that made me want to write what you're about to read. It was in *Rolling Stone*. It felt important, like the simple act of one person writing his truth about music could change the world.

It came out at a musically bland time much like this musically bland time, but after I read it, I was convinced that nothing was ever going to be the same. For a while, it wasn't. And now here we are. Post-rock. Mope-rock. Dip-hop. Poop-pop. Take Belle and Sebastian. And Dave Matthews. Please.

Well, I believe it is time for a change. As I said last month, I believe in rock 'n' roll—again, not as a genre of music, or as a relic, but as a living, breathing organism that simultaneously nurtures/soothes the savage beast and rejects/embraces everything that has come before it. Furthermore, I believe that the best rock 'n' roll unites not divides us, and in this time of widespread distrust about how music reaches our ears I want to say something I've been wanting to say ever since I plopped down in that green corduroy couch in my father's den to read *Rolling Stone* that hot summer night twenty-three years ago.

I have seen the past, present, and future of rock 'n' roll, and his name is Ike Reilly.

Whose friend and confidant I have been over the past twelve years, a fact that only killjoys and corpses will have a problem with. The hope here is that the rest of us, those with blood still running through our veins, will get over such conflicts of interest and be inspired by Reilly's major-label debut when it is released in five short weeks, and hear what I hear: a meteoric batch of songs that says something fresh about who we are, who we were, and who we wish we were. And by *we*, I mean Americans.

That's what Reilly's record could be called, because it is about all of us—old, young, white, black, purple, rich, poor, in debt, in doubt. But it's not called *Americans,* or even *Ex-Americans,* the name of one of Reilly's greatest as-yet-unrecorded songs. It's called *Salesmen and Racists,* because in the end that is what all Americans are, every last one of us, since making a buck and stirring the melting pot are the two things that have kept this train a-rolling all these years.

Let me tell you what I know about Reilly. He drives a Crown Victoria police cruiser, which makes various cameo appearances in his songs. He's had his nose broken a bunch of times, once in Paris. He's got a crooked smile and hot blue eyes that, in the right light, make him look a little deranged. He's big-hearted, loyal, and genuinely street smart, and he writes songs the way he talks—with Technicolor language that has been known to offend the easily offended.

He's got a great memory and a million true stories, like the one about his buddy the priest's first gig, his Irish drinking pals, a wheelchair, and a fleet of cop cars.

Then there's the one about him mixing *Salesmen and Racists* in a Los Angeles studio next to Britney Spears and *NSYNC, whom he said were "really nice." Spend five minutes with him, and you'll realize that something of everyone he has ever met—every fat cat and homeless person he held the door for while working as a hotel doorman in downtown Chicago for twelve years—has rubbed off on him and stuck.

He has lived his entire life in Libertyville, Illinois, whose most famous son is Marlon Brando. Reilly can tell you all the local Brando lore, like when the Wild One drove his motorcycle through the high school. But while Brando went to Hollywood, got fat, and made awful movies, Reilly stayed in Libertyville, raised a family, ran marathons, drank, smoked dope, made music, got sick of it, and built a studio and a business from the ground up.

Then he got sick of that, and he and his guitarist/keyboardist/coproducer Ed Tinley holed up in that studio and made what I like to call the next—and maybe last—great American rock 'n' roll record.

The songs on the album, when cranked in the car or headphones, tend to explode in the imagination. This is what I imagine: Reilly standing on the scrap heap of phony youth culture and the too-cool-to-feel indie-rock scene, screaming, "Children, I belong to you." Patriots and expatriates in airports, singing, "Do you need anything from duty free? I gotta get out of the USA." The Man in Black and an all-star chorus of rappers singing, "Hip-hop has blown my mind, John Cash has done his time."

The whole wide world making home videos of their families and friends singing along to the one that goes, "Put a little love in it, before it brings you down." Pubs everywhere swaying to the one that goes, "Drinks all around, for my wasted friends." Ersatz lovers singing to each other through the ether, "I don't want to be alone with you, but I don't want to be alone."

Sensational St. Paul boxer Matt "The Predator" Vanda, with whom Reilly shares a certain fighter's spirit, training to the one that goes, "He went from featherweight to flyweight to phantomweight to welterweight to helter-skelter middleweight." Secret Service agents cracking up at the one that goes, "They voted you in as the talk of the nation, now we're drinking to your assassination."

I also imagine what it will be like this week at the Turf Club, where Reilly will perform an unprecedented four-night stand starting Wednesday, and where he and his band (Tinley, drummer Dave Cottini, bassist Tommy O'Donnell, and guitarist Phil Karnats, who together look like—what else?—a cabal of tough, cocky, gregarious, and slightly unhinged Chicago guys) played its debut show May 12.

It was terrific, and historic, but if their sixth show together (June 9 at the 7th St. Entry) is any indication, this is the week that people will one day brag to their club-crawling grandchildren about: the four nights we watched a great new band blossom before our eyes and before the world got to them.

The Turf is also where Reilly and I met up with my brothers Jay and Bird and my friend Craig on the night of March 11. Reilly had sent me the finished record two days earlier, and we wanted to celebrate. So the five of us sat at a nearly empty Turf over a pitcher of Guinness, talking about the record, our health, our work.

Finally, 'round midnight, I suggested we listen to the thing. Reilly was reluctant, but we made him do it. Bird drove. Jay rode shotgun. Craig, Ike, and I were in the back seat, in that order. We pulled out of the Turf parking lot, picked up our buddy Tony, and cruised the side streets and parkways as big, bushy snowflakes kissed the cities. Six guys. Married, divorced, fathers, nonfathers, working stiffs, and one next big thing. To us, anyway.

The third time we listened to the record, Craig, drunk, leaned over Reilly and talked to me as if Reilly weren't there and proclaimed the record to be "an epic." Someone said, "This is gonna kick Springsteen's ass back into the studio." Someone else said, "[Screw] Springsteen."

We drove for almost three hours. We gazed out the windows at the cities we'd grown up in, at their landmarks and neighborhoods, as visions of the Summer of Ike danced in our hearts. We sang, lustily, "Let's take a drink, let's take a ride." We sang, quietly, "I wanna be the one that you crave, and then I want to chase you away."

Mostly, though, we listened. To all those scruff-of-the-neck-grabbing guitars, tricks, drums, tangents, raps, horns, strings, and joy-making melodies. To "Commie Drives a Nova," "Angels and Whores," "New Year's Eve," and all those other raunchy, romantic tunes about lust, love, and life, and the one that ends with Reilly singing about "salesmen and racists and football stars, all hanging out at the hotel bar," over an organ grinder tinkle.

Earlier that night, I had picked up Reilly at the hotel bar. We sat there for an hour and talked about the record, a record we'd been talking about for four years, ever since he sent me the first of many demos he and Tinley recorded. We talked about our dreams for it. I told him, "There will be some day down the road when we'll go, 'It happened. Here we are. It actually happened.'"

Neither one of us could articulate what that meant exactly or what specific brass ring we imagined that day would bring, but I can now. If you've read this far, if you're plopped down on something like a green couch in your father's den, and you believe a single word you've just read, that day is today. Children, I belong to you.

(June 24, 2001, St. Paul Pioneer Press)

Put a Little Love in It

LAST WEEK I WROTE, "I have seen the past, present, and future of rock 'n' roll, and his name is Ike Reilly."

Turns out I may have undersold him.

How good were these shows? If you were there, and you didn't quite get it, which is sort of hard to imagine, let me put it this way: these shows were so good that everyone who was there and paying attention will never forget them. So good that a year from now, people who weren't there are going to be lying about having been there, or lying about having not cared about being there.

But I wish everyone could have been there, because there is nothing more important than an out-of-nowhere burst of feeling good about yourself and your fellow man and the future.

Most everyone who was at the Turf last weekend will know what I mean by that, because everyone I know is still grasping for words to describe what happened.

Check out a few of these e-mails:

"I remembered the phrase *burning joy* used by the priest last week during his homily about John the Baptist. I understood what the priest meant on Sunday, and last night, this morning, I experienced it." (Carol)

"'Duty Free' is my favorite sing-along song of the past ten years—I literally screamed myself hoarse." (Brad)

"Best band on the planet? They might be in the midst of a four-night stand at the Turf." (Patrick)

"Magical." (Brianna)

"I'm trying to remember the last time I felt this way about someone, and I finally came up with the first time my buddy Rudy turned me on to Elvis Costello's *My Aim Is True*." (Dan)

"It was f—ing amazing." (A guy from a local record shop)

Like that guy, others were doing what rock fans do in the face of the lack of sufficient adjectives: dusting off musical references and milestones that haven't been dusted off in quite some time. Springsteen at the Stone Pony. Replacements at Duffy's. Dylan at Newport. Nirvana at the Uptown. Yikes.

For me, the whole four-night stand was, no exaggeration, the most extraordinary club residency by a band I've seen since Prince's Erotic City shows in '94 and the Replacements' five-night stand at the 7th St. Entry in 1986.

You know Andy Uzendoski and Andrea Swensson? The prom couple who appeared in this column a few weeks ago? They were there, flipping out. *Pulse* writer Tom Hallett brought his eleven-year-old son, and playwright Craig Wright brought his twelve-year-old son, Louis. Their fathers wanted them to see history, and that is exactly what they saw. And I hate to be the one to tell them, but these youngsters might spend their entire lives haunting clubs, trying to duplicate the blue moons they ran into last weekend.

Let me try to explain. Each night's set was different from the night before. In terms of spontaneous combustion, Thursday was the most magical, because the band was much tighter and much more confident than Wednesday, which served up a pretty ordinary set that was fine but earthbound and, frankly, had me a little down afterward.

Thursday was another story altogether: the room felt different from the outset. By 11 P.M., there was a tangible current of electricity in the air, and the band fed off that energy and found its groove right out of the gate, and near the end, Reilly's giddy, triumphant face had me choked up during "Whatever Happened to the Girl in Me?" At the end of the night, he played five songs in the basement on his acoustic guitar for three *Minnesota Daily* arts writers who, one can only hope, kept good notes.

Friday night was equally ridiculous, with Reilly setting up on the floor and starting with acoustic versions of "Hail! Hail!" and "Put a Little Love in It (According to John)," and finishing with a guttural full-band version of "Put a Little Love in It" that had me and Tea and Sympathy singer/songwriter Alicia Corbett looking at each other across the bar and clutching our hearts, as we watched Louis absolutely possessed by this song of hope and elevation.

By then, the band had evolved, in short order, into a dangerous, sexy force of nature unto itself. Coupled with Reilly's clarion voice, timeless and timely songs (including a devastating new one called "Get a Gun") and the crowd's creeping realization that these guys want to sell records and be part of the system so that maybe they can beat the system, they took off like a shot.

I need to tell you something here: in the mid-'90s, I put together a benefit for an AIDS hospice at First Avenue. Reilly and his band drove up from Chicago and played a terrific set on a terrific bill that included Pleasure, Joe Henry, Slim Dunlap, the Tropicals, and the Gear Daddies.

At the end of the night, when Reilly and his mates were piling into their van to drive back to Chicago, he wouldn't even let me give him gas money. That's the kind of guy he is. Which is only one reason why I'd take a bullet for him. Drive the Bronco for him.

But I wouldn't lie for him, because that would insult both of us and, most important, you. But I'm not lying: this is it. Rock 'n' roll. As good as it gets. He's singing about us. He's singing about the culture and the future of America.

The politicians and CEOs may have given up, or lulled us to sleep, but this tough-as-nails little songwriter from Libertyville, Illinois, hasn't. Wednesday is the Fourth of July, and he is one of the biggest patriots I know. He is not giving up. He signed twelve-year-old Louis's drumstick like this: "Keep Going." He signed my six-year-old son's drumstick like this: "I love you, Henry."

I don't even know if any of this makes sense anymore, so let's go to the highlights: the crowd (hipsters, hippies, moms, dads, punks, kids, students, poets, playwrights, musicians, lawyers, ink-stained wretches) screaming, singing, crying, "Put a little love in it, before it brings you down."

Bassist Tommy O'Donnell and guitarist Phil Karnats playing each other's axes at the end of the euphoric "White Man's Blues (Boat Song)." Drummer Dave Cottini almost eating his cymbals during "Hip Hop Thighs #17," and guitarist/keyboardist Ed Tinley taking on the stage persona of, as one observer put it, "Bob Stinson with an M.A."

The entire floor pogoing wildly to "Last Time," and then swaying, Irish pub–style, to "My Wasted Friends." Then, on the final night, as the mini–mosh pit swelled around Reilly, who had jumped offstage to sing the encore of "Commie Drives a Nova," a professional rock critic drunk on tequila and love and a dream weekend come true, pouring a beer over Reilly's head.

Photographer Jay Smiley was there, shooting the whole thing, and I think he got a picture of that moment, and I usually don't care about stuff like this, but I want a copy of that picture.

I might frame it, because what I was doing was baptizing him. Thanking him. Saying good-bye. Because it is never going to be like that again. Reilly's major-label debut *Salesmen and Racists* hits stores July 31, and after that, it is going to be a hell of a ride. And to all 1,400 people who were at the Turf last weekend, you have earned some serious bragging rights.

Good for you. Good for all of us.

(July 1, 2001, St. Paul Pioneer Press)

Magic

I DIDN'T HAVE A TICKET to the Springsteen show as of 3 P.M. last Friday, and show time was 8 P.M., and, well, I was starting to come to grips with the notion that I'd blown it, and that staying home with the family and dog and watching the Wolves–Nuggets and *Criss Angel— Mindfreak* was all in all a pretty good second option. I started talking myself into agreeing with the ticketless pals who'd justified their loss over the past few weeks, saying that they weren't going because of the ticket price ($95), the venue, the been-there-done-that do-re-mi. Still, it was Friday night . . .

A friend suggested I look on www.backstreets.com, the Springsteen fan site. Within five minutes I was talking with a woman named Kim from the western suburbs who said she had an extra general admission ducat and that she'd meet me at Xcel Center, door #1, in an hour. I dumped the kids on my neighbor and called my wife at her new job and asked if she minded if I spent the anniversary of our first date with nineteen thousand other hotties, and she admitted that she was bummed because she wanted to go to the show but gave me the go ahead, and as soon as I hung up I had a skip in my step and the money moment of *Badlands*—"I wanna go out tonight and find out what I got"—ratcheting up from my solar plexus.

I hit the cash machine and the highway and got to the X and did the deal with Kim, who showed me what line to get into for the neomythical wristband lottery that determines which lucky 470 people get to be in the front section of the arena floor. At that point, I would have done anything Kim said: I was in. I was flying, on my own, unencumbered by anyone else's needs or any semblance of a schedule. Some friends were meeting for a preshow beer at Patrick McGovern's Pub on West Seventh Street, but I ran into some of my hardcore Bruce fan friends who were getting in line, so that's what I did—with about four thousand other people hoping to get closer to the stage, the altar, the party.

I won the lottery.

So did some guys whom I'd just met, just like back in the day when we'd all spend the night together waiting in line for Springsteen tickets and then reconvene months later at the show. So did a bunch of new comrades—musicians, writers, photographers—whom I met through hootenannies and live music this year, and so did several old friends. There was Jackie and Jeannie Heintz, the St. Paul mother-daughter team of Bruce fanatics. There was James and Brianna and Brianna's dad, Brad, who wondered aloud if this might be the last time we see Clarence Clemons, who, after two hip replacement surgeries, was looking typically badass but frail. There was Alexa Jones and her mother, Vicki, both of whom I met this year.

Last week Alexa wrote a beautiful piece about life and death that gets at what it felt like to stand around with all these people, waiting for the E Street Band to hit the stage. Her thesis graph: "Maybe I don't go to church or have a religion in the traditional sense, but I believe in the spirit of life. That energy that pulsates through your guts and mind and out into the world, into another person, can't disappear when the body is gone. It's electricity that's released into the air, maybe the heavens."

Heaven this night was a hockey arena, where our group was joined by Paula, a Brooklyn-born mother of three, including an autistic child and a U.S. Marine serving in Iraq. Tough girl. St. Paul girl. Republican, I'm pretty sure. Had nothing but good to say about Norm Coleman, who got the arena built where her beloved Wild play.

In short order, I learned that Paula's mother died when she was nineteen, and that she adopted and raised her five siblings. She's from a family of cops and firefighters, a number of whom walked away from the twin towers on 9/11. This night she was on her own, too: her husband had told her to go have fun, and so she was. She had that *Lords of Flatbush* thing going on in her voice and said, "Get a couple more beers in me, and I'll be talking like Rosie Perez."

I sprinted up the arena steps to take a preshow piss and get a beer and ran into one of my oldest Springsteen running partners, Rita, and her sisters, and moments later found myself standing in the beer line with Paul Molitor and his sister, and moments after that ran into Dan Wilson, whose soul-igniting existential anthem "Free Life" was heard a few days earlier by the ten million viewers of *Dirty Sexy Money*.

It was around this time, with the flickering arena lights signaling the start of the concert, and all this oneness shuddering through the place, and all these people I love inside and outside that pit pulsing through me, that I had the very real sense that everyone you meet prepares you for the next person you meet, and that all we're ever doing in this life is meeting and remeeting ourselves—not a stranger or an acquaintance or old friend or new lover, but the latest version of the new or long-lost you.

The old dogs hit the stage with "Radio Nowhere," with Springsteen growling, "Is there anybody alive out there?" to a Greek choir, and then, less quotable but perhaps more salient in the media miasma of know-it-all pundits and opinions we find ourselves in, "I just wanna hear some rhythm."

When they lurched into "No Surrender," I wedged myself behind Alexa and Vicki and steadied myself. Martin, Jason, Jen, and Kyle had my back. I raised my beer and prayed along, "We made a promise, we swore we'd always remember, no retreat, baby, no surrender." Springsteen looked right at me, the guy with the chalice held aloft, and grinned and nodded.

When it was done I touched my face, and hell if it wasn't wet with tears. I can name the last time I cried, and trust me it was a long time ago, but the pushing-sixty little garage rocker with the Telecaster-on-fire who described his job on *60 Minutes* as, "I make grown men cry and women dance" got me. Again.

I am not making this up. I am not exaggerating, and you can yawn or make fun of me or Springsteen, but the shit really, truly, was flowing from him into me, and I know I wasn't alone. I was flat-out lifted. It was intense, as life-changing as it had been when I saw him the first time at Met Center in 1978 when I was nineteen. It felt more important this time, because I have kids, the world is in the shitter, and the voice in my head that says I'm not always on my game, not always inspired, not always doing the best I can, was quelled by an echo of my best self, and the music allowed me to forgive myself and showed me yet again how to be tougher than the rest of my former selves and keep going.

That is why I write. That is why I write this today: to let anyone who happens to read this message in a cyberbottle know that Bruce Springsteen is barnstorming North America, changing the world, ripping open the wounds of America, making it better, and when he's gone, when he leaves the arena or the world, that feeling lives on, just like Alexa said, and I'm glad she did, because I was starting to think it was just me.

I spent the last part of the show walking around and listening from different spots and checking out other raptured faces, which were especially so during "Living in the Future," the chorus to which ("None of this has happened yet") dances with the message of the new Joe Strummer film, *The Future Is Unwritten*.

Around the end, I returned to the military mom, did the bump with her, and put an ice cube down her back. Then I did an Irish jig to "American Land," said my good-byes, and went over to McGovern's, where I walked through the place several times in my "South Minneapolis" T-shirt, which prompted huge St. Paul guys to bang shoulders with mine. I kept going, daring anyone to pick a fight, break my spirit, break the spell.

It hasn't happened yet. Maybe it never will.

(November 5, 2007, Reveille magazine)

A couple of weeks before Christmas that year, I received a handwritten card from Springsteen. One of the highlights of my writing life, and I quote: "Dear Jim, Someone passed on to me your piece on our show. They don't write 'em like that anymore! Every night we step onstage we aspire to tear loose those feelings of strength and connection and joy. We hope to leave our audience a little stronger, happier, and wised-up. Besides untold riches and glory, it's the only real reason for continuing on. But it's a good one. Best, Bruce Springsteen."

EIGHT
MIX #3
HEART AND SOUL

I Still Haven't Found What I'm Looking For

I BELIEVE IN BELIEVING in something, so what I have come to believe in most after all these years is rock 'n' roll.

I believe there are those who will believe me to be ancient and almost medieval for making such a statement, but I believe rock 'n' roll to be not a genre of music but an all encompassing force that simultaneously forsakes and embraces all that came before it and all that has come since.

I believe it to be the sound of freedom, liberation, the human spirit unshackled. I believe in the Kingdom Come and then all the colors will bleed into one.

I believe in electric guitars ringing, chiming, screaming. I believe in last call, drinks all around, and the first cup of coffee in the morning after a hard day's night. I believe in torn jeans, T-shirts, leather, tattoos, punk-rock girls, trouble boys, drummers who look like cats clawing out of a corner, and lighted cigarettes propped up on the end of guitar necks like incense sticks.

I believe U2's Bono when he sings, "I believe in you."

I believe in sock hops and raves. I believe in lyrics that don't make sense, songs that get better after ten plays in a row, hip-hop beats that curl toes and tongues. I believe in suburban teens finding homilies in Napster, suburban parents finding miracles in home stereos, city slickers finding gold in headphones, and all of them connecting to the same giant antenna in the heavens.

I believe rock 'n' roll saves lives.

I believe in fire in the belly, passion in the back seat, snare drums that sound like cannon shots coming over a ship's bow, and singers, writers, and poets who spill their guts, open their veins, make us laugh, show us the way. I do not believe in "post-rock" or music that makes me feel numb or dumb.

I believe I am starving for a rock band to blow the roof off an arena, the way I believe U2 will blow the roof off the Target Center on Tuesday night.

I believe I am not alone. I believe we the people have had it with Fake. I believe that more and more of us are rising up and saying what John Lennon sang many years ago: "Gimme some truth."

I believe U2's Bono to be one of the fed-up folks. I believe he is on the great explore, and that he will be until the day he dies. I believe his is one of those lives that was saved by rock 'n' roll and that he believes he has a debt to repay. Which I believe he has done already, if only with "I Still Haven't Found What I'm Looking For." Which I believe people, including its makers, will sing, listen to, and glean guidance and comfort from many years after all of us have shaken, rattled, and hummed off our mortal coils.

I believe U2 believes in roots, the kind that on Tuesday will invisibly extend from the Target Center stage across the street to First Avenue, where U2 played its first Twin Cities concert in 1981. I believe Bono has a good memory. I believe that is why he called Joey Ramone on Good Friday, and why two nights later, a few hours after Joey died, U2 encored in Portland with the Ramones' "I Remember You."

I believe bands like U2 inspire faith. I believe it is no coincidence that Joey Ramone passed into the great beyond while U2's "In a Little While" played in his hospital room. I believe that many people who believe in U2 are of many faiths—some devout, some fallen away, some returning to the scenes of their crimes.

I believe "Stuck in a Moment You Can't Get Out Of," which was inspired by the suicide of INXS singer Michael Hutchence, helps the forlorn to remember that This Too Shall Pass.

I believe the most enlightening lyric I heard on the radio this winter also came from U2, one I would wish upon anyone who periodically wrestles with various funks, depressions, and blues-to-be: "It's a beautiful day, don't let it get away, it's a beautiful day, don't let it get away."

I do not believe in nitpicking when it comes to matters of the heart, which is what the U2 stage is shaped like for this tour. I believe people who pay almost $100 to stand in a basketball arena with twenty thousand other ordinary/flawed/uninspired souls who have been yearning to sing along to a verse such as, "What you don't have you don't need it now, what you don't know you can feel it somehow," are getting a bargain.

I believe that Tuesday night, Bono will be proved correct in his assertion in *SPIN* magazine that the reason many of the Elevation 2001 Tour tickets are general admission is that "in the U.S., the experience of seeing U2 was never a physical one the way it was in Europe. There, the whole floor would lift up. It was intoxicating."

I believe in being lifted up. I believe U2 embodies what Thomas Jefferson said in 1816, which still haunts true today: "I hope we shall crush in its birth the aristocracy of our monied corporations which dare already to challenge our government to a trial of strength, and bid defiance to the laws of our country."

I believe our corporate government is not acting in our best interest, and that all the hollow entertainment it sponsors is no mistake. I believe the powers that be want us driven to distraction, to quarrel among ourselves, so they can do their bidding in peace and under the cloak of darkness. I believe that U2 is not about to let them get away with it.

I believe that the Irish musicians could help save us from ourselves, if we just listen to their dreams of a better world, born as they are of their homeland's eternal strife: Sinead O'Connor, Van Morrison, Mary Coughlan, Mike Scott, and all the others who have firsthand experience in overcoming a culture of bureaucratic repression through magic.

I believe America has a hole in its soul. I believe U2, the fighting Irish, can help fill it. I believe them to be a bunch of tough bastards. I do not believe in false idols, like the Smashing Pumpkins' Billy Corgan, who upon the breakup of his band said, "Fighting the Britneys of the world just got too hard," or some nonsense.

I do not believe in giving up. I believe in fighting for what's right, and good, and dangerous, and dirty, and true. I do not believe that U2 believes that rock 'n' roll is dead, or that it is a genre, or nostalgia. I believe that if rock 'n' roll will one day join the dinosaurs as a cultural signpost and as a viable spiritual path, then U2 is not going down without a fight.

I believe it to be less lofty than all that. I believe Bono when he sings, "I'm just trying to find a decent melody, a song that I can sing in my own company."

I believe that something like the Holy Spirit flows through people like Bono, who I believe believes he has a job to do, which he has exhibited countless times through his music, his good nature, his trips to Bosnia and beyond, his induction speech for Bruce Springsteen into the Rock & Roll Hall of Fame, and through what he wrote in Q magazine last year:

> I was thinking about Bob Dylan the other day, trying to define what it was about him that I respect so much, and what came to me was a line by the poet Brendan Keneally from the "Book of Judas," a line which I used for guidance on the Zoo TV tour but which I realized applies to Bob Dylan throughout his whole career. The line is: The best way to serve the age is to betray it.
>
> That is the essence of Bob Dylan: not just as simple as being on whatever the other side is, because that's just being a crank, and cranks at the end of the day aren't very interesting, because you always know their position. Dylan was at one point in time the very epitome of what was modern, and yet was always a unique critique of modernity. Because in fact Dylan comes from an ancient place, almost medieval.

I believe U2 to be cut from the same cloth. I do not believe their bigness gets in the way of their realness. I do not believe that rebellion or shocking the next generation is the sole function of rock 'n' roll, and I believe that those who seek to do so through obvious means have missed the point entirely and are trying too hard. I believe in melody and mini-anthems and maxi-anthems and goosebumps and confusion and rage and rapture and ballads and bashers and buzzing amps and bum notes.

I believe in zoot suits and Beatle boots and Louis Armstrong and the Stones' tongue and *London Calling* and Chuck Berry and neighborhood record stores and all-ages nightclubs and no cover and that new Fatboy Slim video with Christopher Walken dancing on the ceiling.

I believe in the Dairy Queen worker who told me he always gave free ice cream to anyone wearing a Rev 105 T-shirt. I believe in looking out for the other guy. I believe everyone should stop saying "That rocks" about things that absolutely do not rock.

I believe if you care, you rock. I believe if you care about where this world is going, where all of us are going, not just you, then you rock.

Which is to say that I believe in rock 'n' roll. Which is to say that I believe in you, and vice versa.

(April 29, 2001, St. Paul Pioneer Press)

Peace on Earth

SHORTLY AFTER ELEVEN A.M. this morning, I stood outside a classroom at my daughter's preschool, talking to a mom who had come to school early to pick up her daughter. "I just want to touch my girl," she said.

Another was crying. The red in her eyes matched the red in her "I Voted" sticker she wore over her heart. She was worried about her husband, who was in transit from his job. Others talked about Pearl Harbor, revenge, racism, and what to tell their kids.

I put on some music. Specifically, I put on U2's *All That You Can't Leave Behind,* the record that has offered me more guidance in the past year than anything else I've heard or read. I went straight to track eight, "Peace on Earth," and started driving.

"Heaven on earth, we need it now," sang Bono. "Sick of hearing, again and again, that there's gonna be peace on Earth."

As the acoustic guitars padded away and the organs chimed, a surreal sight flooded my windshield on this, the morning of International Peace Day: an electronic marquee on a freeway overpass screaming, "Mall of America Closed." The faces of the few other drivers around me looked waxen. For miles I looked for smiles, a sign of one soul who had not been ruined by the morning's events.

I got off the freeway and parked by the side of the road to listen and watch. A woman worked on her garden. A man delivered flowers to a house. A jogger dodged a FedEx truck, a woman strolled her baby, a couple of punk rockers sat outside a coffee shop, the sun was out. Business as unusual. "No one cries like a mother cries for peace on Earth," sang Bono as a bright yellow school bus tooled by.

I started driving again and found myself heading toward the church I grew up in, the one I spent so many years half-praying in, the one I hadn't been to in years. When I got there, it was as quiet as the city streets were eerie. I sat down in a pew near the back and then did what an older woman, the only other person there, was doing: got on my knees.

When I got home, I turned on CNN, turned down the sound, and turned up the music. The TV screen was crippled with chaos, and Bono, whom some of my friends hate because they think he's an egomaniacal do-gooder, was singing about it. I was glad to have him.

Great song. Again, it's called "Peace on Earth." I played it at least thirty times today, and it wasn't nearly enough, because to my way of thinking, it should be coming out on every radio station in every corner of the globe, twenty-four hours a day for the rest of whatever we call our lives.

(September 11, 2001, St. Paul Pioneer Press)

The Ballad of Paul and Sheila

I AM STANDING in the northwest corner of Lakewood Cemetery in Minneapolis, in front of a silver monument that looks like a heart, a broken heart really, and I am thinking about how wrong the world has gone, how Minnesota Mean it all feels. I'm thinking about how much everyone I know misses the man I've come to visit, how sick I am of sitting around waiting for change, and about what might happen if I ask you to do something, which is what I'll do in a minute.

Like most Minnesotans, I met Paul Wellstone once. It was at the Loring Playhouse after the opening night of a friend's play. He and Sheila were there, offering encouragement to the show's director, Casey Stangl, and quietly validating the postproduction festivities with his presence: the Junior Senator from Minnesota and his wife are here, we must be doing something right.

The year before (1990), I'd written a column for *City Pages* encouraging all local musicians and local music fans to go vote for this mad professor the following Tuesday. He won, and, as many have said since, for the first time in my life I felt like we were part of something that had roots in Stuff the Suits Don't Give a Shit About. That is, we felt like we had a voice, like were getting somewhere, or like Janeane Garofalo's villain-whupping character in *Mystery Men,* who memorably proclaimed, "I would like to dedicate my victory to the supporters of local music and those who seek out independent films."

After the election, Wellstone's aide Bill Hillsman told me he believed my column had reached a segment of the voting populace that they were having trouble reaching, and that it may have helped put him over the top. I put aside my bullshit detector for the moment and chose to believe him, just as I choose at this moment to believe that music and the written word can still help change the world.

When I introduced myself to Wellstone that night as "Jim Walsh from *City Pages*," he broke into that sexy gap-toothed grin, clasped my hand and forearm, and said, with a warm laugh, "Jiiiiim," like we were a couple of thieves getting together for the first time since the big haul. I can still feel his hand squeezing my forearm. I can still feel his fighter's strength.

For those of you who never had the pleasure, that is what Paul Wellstone was—a fighter—despite the fact that the first President Bush said upon their first encounter, "Who is this chickenshit?" He fought corporate America, the FCC, injustice, his own government. He fought for the voiceless, the homeless, the poor, the little guy—in this country and beyond. He was a politician but not a robot, an idealist but not a sap, and if his legacy has already morphed into myth, it's because there were/are so few like him. He was passionate and compassionate. He had a huge heart, a rigorous mind, a steely soul and conscience, and now he is dead and buried in a plot that looks out over the joggers, bikers, rollerbladers, and motorists who parade around Lake Calhoun daily.

Paul and Sheila Wellstone and six others, including their daughter Marcia, were killed in a plane crash on October 25, 2002. I remember where I was that day, just as you do, and I don't want to forget it, but what I want to remember even more is October 25, 2003. So here's what we're going to do.

We're going to start something right here, right now, and we're going to call it Paul and Sheila Wellstone World Music Day. It will happen on Saturday, October 25. On that day, every piece of music, from orchestras to shower singers, superstars to buskers, will be an expression of that loss and a celebration of that life. It will be one day where music—which to my way of thinking is still the best way to fill in the gray areas that the blacks and whites of everyday life leave us with—rises up in all sorts of clubs, cars, concerts, and living rooms, all in the name of peace and love and joy and all that good stuff that gets snickered at by Them.

Now. This is no corporate flimflam or media boondoggle. This is me talking to you, and you and I deciding to do something about the place we live in when it feels like all the exits are blocked. So, first of all, clip or forward this to anyone you know who still cares about grass roots, community, music, reading, writing, love, the world, and how the world sees America. If you've got a blog or Website, post it.

If you're a musician, book a gig now for October 25. Tell them you want it to be advertised as part of Paul and Sheila Wellstone World Music Day. If you're a shower singer, lift your voice that day and tell yourself the same thing. If you're a club owner, promoter, or scene fiend, put together a multiact benefit for Wellstone Action (www.wellstone.org). If you're a newspaper person, tell your readers. If you're a radio person, tell your listeners. Everybody talk about what you remember about Wellstone, what he tried to do, what you plan to do for Wellstone World Music Day. Then tell me at the e-mail address below, and I'll write another column like this the week of October 25, with your and others' comments and plans.

This isn't exactly an original idea. Earlier this year, I sat in a room at Stanford University with Judea and Michelle Pearl, the father and sister of *Wall Street Journal* reporter Daniel Pearl, who was kidnapped and murdered by members of a radical Islamic group in Pakistan in February of last year. After much talk about their son and brother's life and murder, I asked them about Danny's love of music. He was a big music fan, and an accomplished violinist who played with all sorts of bands all over the world. Unbeknownst to me at the time, Pearl was also a member of the Atlanta band the Ottoman Empire, and his fiddle levitates one of my all-time favorite Irish jigs, "This Is It," which I found myself singing one night last fall in a Sonoma Valley bar with a bunch of journalists from Paraguay, Texas, Mexico, Jerusalem, Italy, and Korea.

The Pearls talked with amazement about the first Daniel Pearl World Music Day (www.danielpearl.org), the second of which happens this October 10, which would have been Pearl's fortieth birthday. I told them about attending one of the first Daniel Pearl World Music Day activities at Stanford Memorial Church, where a lone violinist silently strolled away from her chamber group at the end, signaling to me and my gathered colleagues that we were to remember that moment and continue to ask questions, continue to push for the dialogue that their son and brother lived for. I vowed that day to tell anybody within earshot about Daniel Pearl World Music Day and later figured he wouldn't mind a similar elegy for Wellstone, who shared Pearl's battle against hate and cynicism.

Wellstone didn't lead any bands, but he led as musical a life as they come. He lived to bring people together, to mend fences—which is what music does so effortlessly. When he died, musicians and artists were some of the most devastated, as Leslie Ball's crestfallen-but-somehow-still-beaming face on C-SPAN from Williams Arena illustrated. Everyone from Mason Jennings to Larry Long wrote Wellstone tribute songs in the aftermath, and everyone had a story, including the one Wendy Lewis told me about the genuine exuberance with which Wellstone once introduced her band, Rhea Valentine, to a crowd at the Lyn-Lake Festival. Imagine that, today.

So ignore this or do whatever you do when your "We Are the World" hackles go up. I'd be disappointed, and I suppose I wouldn't blame you; in these times of terror alerts and media celebrity, I'm suspicious of everything, too. But I freely admit that the idea of a Wellstone World Music Day is selfish. That day was beyond dark, and to have another like it, a litany of hang-dog tributes and rehashes of The Partisan Speech and How It All Went Wrong, would be painful, not to mention disrespectful to everything those lives stood for and against.

No, I don't want anyone telling me what to think or feel that day, or any day, anymore. I want music that day. I want to wake up hearing it, go to bed singing it. I want banners, church choirs, live feeds, hip-hop, headlines, punk rock, field reports, arias, laughter. I want to remember October 25, 2002, as the day the music died, and October 25, 2003, as the day when people who've spent their lives attending antiwar rallies and teaching kids and championing local music and independent films got together via the great big antennae of music and took another shot.

I am standing in the northwest corner of Lakewood Cemetery in Minneapolis. In front of the silver broken heart, three workers stab the fresh sod with shovels and fumble with a tape measure. Flowers dot the dirt surrounding the statue base. I pick up a rock and put it in my pocket.

The sprinklers are on, hissing impatiently at the still-stunned-by-last-autumn citizens who work and hope and wait and watch beyond the cemetery gates. The sprinklers shoot horizontal water geysers this way and that. They are replenishing patches of grass that have been browned by the sun. They are telling every burned-out blade to keep growing, and trying to coax life out of death.

(August 6, 2003)

This e-mail blast flew around the state and beyond and resulted in Wellstone World Music Day tributes in seventy-five cities across the globe, and a second WWMD the following year. In grand fashion, both shined a light on the Wellstones' memory via every stripe and strain of music. Unforgettable.

Signed, Sealed, Delivered

AS PRESIDENT-ELECT BARACK OBAMA gave his victory speech on the big screen at Arnellia's, the bar's owner and namesake, Arnellia Allen, sat at her favorite perch—on a stool near the cash register. Flanked by a few friends and family, the normally reserved Allen wore a wide grin and took up the packed bar's chant of "Obama" as the television beamed images of America's new First Family to the world.

"I'm in shock," said the sixtysomething Allen. "I'm very excited, but it's a little hard to believe. I felt like this day would come one day, but I never thought I'd live to see it."

Arnellia's is St. Paul's oldest African American–owned business, and its clientele is largely black. Tuesday, a crowd of twentysomething hip-hop fans gathered at the club to hear live crews throw down as older Arnellia's regulars celebrated the historic election near the flatscreen in the corner with drinks, catfish, and chicken wings.

"I totally did not believe that I would see a black man as President of the United States," said St. Paul resident Michelle Bowie. "It's a miracle, almost. It feels like a miracle. I'm very proud of the whole Democratic Party. It feels like everybody is coming together, and that makes me very happy."

Across the bar, music promoters Ronald and Joyce Ligon of Minneapolis wore matching Obama T-shirts and danced jubilantly to the pummeling beats.

"It feels like a new beginning for everybody," said Ronald. "It's not just for one race. Let me put it this way: I believe this is an opening to heaven."

"I'm forty-two years old, this is my first time voting, and this is just a historic moment for me," said Joyce.

In many ways, it was just another night at Arnellia's. People drank and danced and played it cool, but underneath the business-as-usual clubbing vibe simmered the knowledge that America had elected its first African American president.

"There's no other night like this night. Tonight is history night," said Bowie.

"It feels like the first time I had sex, that's how excited I am," said Shawn Suggs, twenty-four. "I feel like I can do anything."

"It's what's up, you know what I'm saying? It's about time, it's overdue," said a huge twenty-two-year-old man who was bellied up to the bar and, inspired by Joe the Plumber, wanted only to be identified as Joe the Hustler. He sat next to Kimberly Johnson, a St. Paul child care worker. The two wore matching black T-shirts emblazoned with photos of Obama, the Reverend Martin Luther King Jr., and the word *Legacy*.

"This man right here was killed," said Johnson, pointing to the picture of King. "I was born in 1968, the year he was assassinated. We were just being able to use white public restrooms around then. We've come a long way. A long way."

That sentiment wasn't lost on thirty-nine-year-old forklift operator David Hall, who sported a beatific expression on his face and an "I Voted" sticker on his chest.

"I didn't vote for [Obama] because he was black. I voted for him because he would be the best president," said Hall. "I served in the military. I was in the Army. I'm the quartermaster over at the local VFW. I've got a beautiful family, my wife's wonderful, and this means something to my kids. It's about our future . . . .

"Our community, we're used to the legal system letting us down," he said. "I'm used to [things] going wrong. I distrust the system so much, but this is the first time I've seen the system work in my life, and I'm forty years old. That's harsh, but it's true. It's a relief. It's a relief to say, 'Finally. Something right happened.' But not right just for me, for everybody."

As the night wore on and the club filled with more revelers, music promoter Joyce Ligon collared a reporter and wanted to relay some more information:

"We're bringing a tribute to Stevie Wonder here, February 28, right here at Arnellia's."

On cue, from the big screen televising the festivities from Grant Park in Chicago, came the unmistakable strains of Obama's campaign song: Wonder's "Signed, Sealed, Delivered."

(November 5, 2008, Minnpost.com)

Love Is the Law

MY BUDDY JOE AND I are fathers and husbands and freaks, so when we heard our mate Rick was playing in the Four Pints Shy house band at the Renaissance Festival, we knew we had to carve out a Sunday to gather the tribe, smoke cigars, drink beer, and return to a simpler time, when the only concerns of the day involved jousting, slaying dragons, and worshipping fair maidens.

In short order, after confronting Death in the street and drinking with Sneaky Pete the Pirate in the pub, we ended up at the King's court, surrounded by the king and queen, their loyal subjects, and about a hundred other punters. Emboldened by the smoke and drink, I rose to my feet.

"Sire, I am but a lowly worm, indeed a knave, but I have a pressing issue that requires the court's wisdom," sayeth I, in my worst medieval Irish.

The king looked at me like I was an unplanned pregnancy. Swords clattered. Heads turned. Silence fell. Apparently improv is not part of the gala's routine; I would be lying if I said I did not fear for my life.

"Permission to speak, Sire?"

"Permission granted."

"Sire, my friend Joe and I here love each other deeply, and we come to you today for one thing."

"If he is your lover, then kiss him for all to see," said the king.

I pecked Joe on the cheek. Lo, the crowd did want more, so I planted a soft one on Joe's bemused cigar-chomping lips. This seemed to satisfy the king's prurience.

"Sire, may I continue?"

"Proceed."

"Sire, if it pleases the court, Joe and I come to you today hoping for your blessing. There is nothing wrong or evil about our love. We want to be married but will only do so upon your command."

The king looked a wee bit nervous. Ye Olde Hot Button.

"My Lord, if it pleases thee, does the court accept—nay, embrace—our love?"

The king looked at his subjects. The subjects looked at the king. Somewhere a few miles away, the Archdiocese of Minneapolis and St. Paul was preparing to unleash a mailing of four hundred thousand antigay marriage DVDs to Minnesota Catholic homes as a way of "stopping gay marriage in its tracks" before the November elections. Talk about evil. Talk about medieval.

"Kiss him!" the king repeated, pandering and buying time. I girded my loins, puffed on my cigar, quaffed my ale, and felt the memory-sting of incense in my nose from my days as a funeral-serving altar boy in the Catholic Church.

"We are not trained monkeys, Sire, with all due respect. No. We will not kiss upon anyone's command but our own. If I am being impudent, send me to the guillotine now. But before you do, we await your ruling. Does the king, in his infinite wisdom, sanction our love? Does this court acknowledge a legal union between two men or two women?"

The queen looked to her king.

"Forgive me, m'lady," I said, bowing. "I know you want to get on with the festivities." The queen bowed back. After a moment of silence, the king made his decision.

"This court sanctions and welcomes all love!" said the king, his words wafting out over the western Minneapolis suburbs.

"The court welcomes all love!" I repeated and raised my chalice. The crowd responded with raised chalices and hefted a hearty three-round cheer of "Huzzah!" into the warm autumn air.

The next night, still feeling my ancient roots, I dialed up Hollywood's latest version of Robin Hood. Most memorable line, from Lady Marion: "Father, I prefer my prayer to be in churches when they are emptied of people."

(October 2, 2011, Southwest Journal)

Toxic

WHAT'S THAT YOU'RE WRITING? You're a what? A critic? You're gonna write about what you think about Britney Spears's concert in the newspaper? Is that a fun job?

Did you like the concert? You did? Me, too! That's weird, because lots of old people hate Britney. It's like they're jealous and they forget what it's like to be a kid, so they do what it's been doing on Holidazzle: rain on our parade.

Wanna know what I think? I'm like every other ten-year-old girl. I love Britney. Some people say she's a prostitute or a product, whatever, but I say she's THE BEST, better than Marilyn Manson Monroe, or whoever you really like, and I can prove it.

Tonight's concert at the Target Center, which was soooo tight, was almost SOLD OUT. There were sixteen thousand people here, which is A LOT of people. I told you she's THE BEST.

Half the fun was looking at all the people. They gave us little American flags when we came in. One really cute high school guy wore an "I [heart] Britney" shirt and a Hill-Murray hat. A mom and her two daughters wore matching Catholic-girl skirts, just like in the ". . . Baby One More Time" video, which sorta creeped me out. A boy my age was dressed like Elvis. Lots of girls my age wore "Rock Star" T-shirts.

When she came onstage, it sort of hurt to actually see her, you know? She looked so hot. Her hair was really big. She wore lots of costumes. My favorite was a gray leather spacesuit that looked like it was part of her skin. There were lots of dancers who looked like fairies and cats and devils. There were bubbles and fire and confetti and sparklers and bungee cords.

I think she was lip-syncing. My favorite songs were "I'm a Slave 4 U" and ". . . Baby One More Time" and "Oops I Did It Again" and "A Girl Not Yet a Woman" and "I Love Rock 'n' Roll," which she copied from Joan Jett, whoever she is. The weirdest part of the whole night was how she went "Whooo!" after almost every song.

She didn't slap hands with any of us. It was sort of like we weren't there. Or like she was making a video she had already made. I didn't like it when she came out dressed like a ballerina and sang, "I was born to make you happy," like girls are supposed to be weaker than boys. I think she looked at me when she said she was proud of our nation's heroes.

She has really pretty eyes. I waved my glow stick at her the whole time, even when she was offstage, changing her costumes, which took almost as long as when she was onstage. My head and throat hurt from screaming so much, which is what everybody was doing, which made it really LOUD. Lots of parents wore earplugs.

The concert started with a big ol' Pepsi commercial and ended with a big ol' Pepsi commercial, which bores me because I HATE Pepsi and LOVE Coke. You know what she said at the end? "You're THE BEST." I know she probably says that to all her audiences, but I think she really meant it. I wonder if she ever gets sick of being so popular.

Oh, this is my dad. He hates Britney—excuse me, "Barbie," as he calls her. He thinks he's really funny. But he DID take me to the concert. What a grouch. He wouldn't let me use his binoculars all night. It was like they were glued to his eye sockets or something.

Now he says we have to hurry home to see Mom. I have a feeling she'll have THAT LOOK in her eyes when we get there. She'll say, "Hey, cowboy, how was Britney?" and make me go to bed right away. I think they still make out. Ewww!

Well, I should go. It's past my bedtime. Unless you can get me backstage, that is! Okay, well, it was worth a shot. Maybe someday I'll be famous and you can write a story about ME.

It was very nice meeting you. Hey! I'll read your report—oops, I mean "review"—in the paper tomorrow! Say nice things about Britney, okay? That must be a fun job. Is that a fun job?

THE BEST? I bet. Tight.

(November 30, 2001, St. Paul Pioneer Press)

I Am the Cosmos

AT THE CONCLUSION of an opening set that included music-fan odes "Big Star Big" and "Let's Give Tennessee Credit for Music," Slim Dunlap asked the crowd of a thousand at First Avenue Thursday night, "Are you psyched for Big Star? Yeah, you better be; we have to treasure this evening."

That we did. Countless geezer acts may be making the rounds these days, but absolutely none inspires the sort of passion, or reverence, that Big Star does. The Alex Chilton–led Memphis band made three records in the late '70s and promptly split up, re-forming in 1993 with Posies singer/bassist Ken Stringfellow and singer/guitarist Jon Auer, who replaced original members Chris Bell (who died in 1979) and Andy Hummel. Their First Avenue performance was the foursome's first in two and a half years, and the first of a three-stop tour that travels to Chicago and Memphis this weekend.

First Avenue's big screen rose to the sound of who-woulda-thunk-we'd-ever-see-this? squeals, revealing the front line of Chilton, Stringfellow, and Auer, and drummer Jody Stephens, who launched into a sizzling guitar-baked version of "In the Street" (now known as the theme from Fox's *That '70s Show*). Chilton looked great—close-cropped hair framing a bald spot, lean, mean, and keen—and spent the evening jousting with the front rows and inhaling secondhand smoke ("I just quit smoking, so I gotta get my fix").

No rock icon he, just an animated waifish figure in jeans and a T-shirt, playing noisy, sinewy guitar and some of the greatest songs ever committed to vinyl. Before a lovely reading of "When My Baby's beside Me," Chilton said, "Have we ever played here in Minneapolis? I can't remember."

The fact is no. Which, in part, is why Thursday's show was so special. Over the past two decades, Chilton has performed several times in the Twin Cities—some memorable, many not. He has even come through town with his re-formed '60s group the Box Tops (whose biggest hits were "The Letter" and "Cry Like a Baby"), but this was a chance to hear all those great songs in one big, hour-plus blast.

The only question was, how would they sound? Could they live up to the records, which have been burned into their listeners' subconscious for twenty years? Yes, they could. One after another they came—"The Ballad of El Goodo," "Back of a Car," "Daisy Glaze," "Baby Strange," "Don't Lie to Me," "Feel," "Thank You Friends." Auer delivered a stunning version of Bell's signature teen-dream piece "I Am the Cosmos," with the chorus's "Yeah, yeah, yeah" harmonies soaring up to the mossy First Avenue ceiling and falling back to earth like angel-kissed moon dust.

One of the night's highlights was the transcendent "Jesus Christ," which Chilton snottily dismissed. "We wanted to write a Christmas song, and this is the best we could come up with—but don't be fooled. We don't believe any of this [stuff]." He semi-smirked his way through it, but not even Chilton's pessimism could ruin a song that has made it onto every Christmas mixtape worth its salt. The set included buoyant takes on the Kinks' "'Til the End of the Day" and Todd Rundgren's "Slut," and when the descending guitar riff to the Big Star classic "September Gurls" crackled through Chilton's amp, it was as magical a moment as any that has occurred in that storied room over the past thirty years.

Just ask anyone who was there. Diligent pop historians and famous Minnesota musicians shared floor space with newbies who discovered Big Star's Memphis soul-by-way-of-Abbey-Road pop through tapes made by older and cooler friends. They hung on every note and sang along to lyrics they've only heard alone in their bedrooms, cars, or living rooms. Big Star never made it on the radio, so there has never been a chance to partake in the mass shared communion that is so central to the rock experience.

Until Thursday night.

After "Hot Thing," an intentionally cheesy new song that could be the centerpiece to a teen-lust movie sound track, and the final blues-rock encore of "Don't Stay Out All Night," it was over.

As the clock neared 1 A.M., and a few stragglers danced around a pile of garbage being swept up by the First Avenue grounds crew, Chris Dorn of the late, great local pop-rockers the Beatifics lingered at the bar, savoring the moment, and summed up how many felt: "I can die happy now."

(May 7, 1999, St. Paul Pioneer Press)

Georgia on My Mind

I LOVE GOING TO HEAR MY BROTHER sing and play music with his band, St. Dominic's Trio, Tuesday nights at Nye's Polonaise Room, which a few years back was named "BEST.BAR.EVER" by *Esquire* magazine.

Every week, those guys fill the room with love and entertain the troops with a sweet strain of soul music that makes a body never want to leave. They're so good at it. I often sit back in a booth or on a stool these nights, counting blessings, listening to the music, watching people, eavesdropping, and staring into the crystal balls of neon, mirrors, and liquor bottles.

The truth of the matter is that live music and a couple of beers calm my scattered nerves as nothing else does, much in the same way that R.E.M.'s "Everybody Hurts" never has failed to. Last night at Nye's, I watched a middle-aged couple from Houston make out like teenage banshees in the front booth as St. Dom's made Siamese twins out of The Who's "Substitute" and the Flaming Lips' "Do You Realize?"

After I expressed my great admiration for their public display of affection, the kind that Minnesotans too rarely engage in, my friend Debbie and I ended up dancing to the double-dip depression blues with the Texans, who presented us with their cowboy/girl hats at the end of the night.

It was a night like that a couple of months ago when I found myself sitting alone at the Nye's piano bar with Mike Mills, bassist for R.E.M., who was in town for a show at the Varsity Theater with the Baseball Project the next night. Hovering around the piano were Mills's bandmates Scott McCaughy, Linda Pitmon, and Steve Wynn. They were the only people in the bar, save for Corky tending the front bar, and Mike, Nye's omnipresent and ornery piano player and sing-along host.

I said hello to the group and sat down next to Mills. He and McCaughy sang a spirited "Mac the Knife." After which I suggested to Mills, who was nursing a gin and tonic and looking as forlorn and far away from home as any traveling salesman ever has, that he sing "Georgia on My Mind."

"That's a good idea," he drawled. We thumbed through the laminated pages of the songbook together and found it right there on page 71, the Hoagy Carmichael–penned heartbreaker that was written in 1930 and has been the official state song of Georgia since 1979. Mills's friends were meandering around the otherwise empty room, so it was left to the two of us to carry the tune out wistfully into the muggy Midwestern night.

When it was done, Mills turned to me and, feeling an uncommon connection, said, "Do I know you?"

Not really, I said, even though I did—through his music, etc. What I know for certain, however, is that, as I write this, the late, great Vic Chesnutt is singing in my headphones his balls-tripping version of "It's the End of the World As We Know It (and I Feel Fine)" from *Surprise Your Pig: A Tribute to R.E.M.*, and I'm remembering how R.E.M. was a beacon for independent music and art at a time when trailblazers were needed, and how they helped introduce me to so much good music, including Chesnutt, Hetch-Hetchy, Jack Logan, the Chickasaw Mudd Puppies, the Dashboard Saviors, Beggar Weeds, and more.

It crawled from the south, to be sure, Flannery O'Connor's South, perhaps, under the direction of the college rock town of Athens, Georgia, and bellied all the way up to the Twin Cities, where R.E.M. became adopted sons, touring nonstop and playing at Sam's, First Avenue, Harriet Island, the State Theater, Met Center, the Xcel Center, and one memorable night at Midway Stadium—which I'm remembering fondly now that R.E.M. has announced that they're calling it quits as of today.

(September 22, 2011, Minnpost.com)

It's the End of the World As We Know It (and I Feel Fine)

THERE ARE TIMES when nature and art intersect at such a ridiculously perfect moment it verges on the surreal. One of those times came Saturday night at Midway Stadium in St. Paul. But it didn't happen when the first lightning bolt lit up the sky, as Michael Stipe was in the middle of a spontaneous, good-humored tirade against corporations.

"I fucking hate Nike," the R.E.M. lead singer said. "We could talk about Target. My friend Heather lives here, and she says Target was one of the first companies to embrace equal rights for same-sex partners. I never go to Wal-Mart. I always go to Target."

BOOM!

Nope, it wasn't at that point, when thunder and strobe-lightning hit simultaneously, prompting Stipe to apologize to all the corporations-with-friends-in-high-places he may have offended. Nor was it when he warned the crowd that "there's a lightning storm coming this way, so we have to cut things short because we don't want anything bad to happen. Take off your shirts and enjoy the rain."

Which is what he, the rest of R.E.M., and their fifteen thousand fans did. But that wasn't the moment, either. Nor was it during the main set, when R.E.M. played like a band reborn. They wove through a crisp, tasteful two-hour set that drew heavily from their new album, *Up,* and most of their back catalog. Moody old chestnuts like "Fall on Me" and "The One I Love" were played with the same verve as the wistful "Daysleeper," a terrific new song called "The Great Beyond" (written for the forthcoming Andy Kaufman biopic, *Man on the Moon*), the forbidding "The Apologist," the demure "Sweetness Follows," rockers "Star 69," "Crush with Eyeliner," and "Gardening at Night," and their classic anthem to possibility, "Man on the Moon."

Nor was it when the pool ball–headed Stipe proved that he has become one of rock's most engaging frontmen. Part ballerina, part Sinatra mime, he squeezed meaning from every possible syllable and cut the figure of raging young bull that would do any hardcore punk band proud.

And it wasn't when a train choo-chooed behind the stage, and Stipe ad-libbed the "train conductor" chorus to "Driver 8," or when he chatted about mosquitoes, or when he went into a short but lovely cloudburst-inspired version of Creedence Clearwater Revival's "Have You Ever Seen the Rain?" which burst into "Losing My Religion."

It was when the skies opened up in earnest during the last song—you can't make this stuff up—"It's the End of the World As We Know It (and I Feel Fine)." With lightning crackling every few seconds, and sheets of rain pouring down, Stipe asked the crowd, "How do you feel?"

To which the drenched faithful roared, "Fine, fine, fine." They thrust their hands in the air and danced, reveling in the baptism of wonderful coincidence, and in the knowledge that R.E.M. was alive and kicking and more precious than ever.

(August 22, 1999, St. Paul Pioneer Press)

NINE

MINNEAPOLIS CONFIDEN- TIAL

Geese of Beverly Road

HANG AROUND WITH MY BUDDY Pete Christensen long enough, and he's liable to play you one of his favorite songs, "Geese of Beverly Road," by the National. It's a classic light-from darkness tune whose chorus dreams, "Hey love, we'll get away with it. We'll run like we're awesome, totally genius."

That childlike spirit of escape and adventure has been at the heart of the forty-six-year-old welder, artist, musician, husband, and father of three for as long as we've been friends and neighbors. He's fond of referring to human beings as "creation machines" who make their own reality through intention, self-awareness, and the power of positive thinking, and damned if it doesn't work. To wit:

Last year when he needed a truck to haul some of his welding and music gear, Pete put out the word to the universe in the form of the thought balloon, "Create Truck." He's always had a penchant for finding value in the abandoned and underused, and reimagining what could be. Lo and behold, in a matter of days and after a minimal amount of networking, he secured an old Ford F-150 pickup, given to him by friend via the forces of serendipity.

This spring, as the snow melted and the soil burst with new life, he cast out the same incantation for a tractor. For the past few years, his inner urban farmer had been yelping to get out, and now he wanted to appease it with a tangible piece of country living in the city.

"From my age on—I was born in 1966—I got to see the family farm get squeezed out of existence," said Pete, who grew up in St. Paul and spent summers on his grandfather's farm in Oklahoma. Like many city kids, he admits to being haunted by the romance of farm life, and a work ethic beholden to Mother Earth and the change of seasons. "There's a thirty-year lapse in farm kids growing up, knowing how to fix stuff, knowing how to ride animals and take care of husbandry and crops. It's down to a handful now. But Minnesota right now is an island of fertile crop growth, while the rest of the country is in a drought. And for me, this tractor represents Minnesota and its fertility—in work, science, art, and agriculture."

It's all about roots, in other words, so it's no surprise that Pete—an accomplished keyboardist—finds himself part of a resurgent insurgent country music movement currently sprouting new crops in the Twin Cities and beyond. Last month, he was in Northfield recording with his friends Matt Arthur & the Bratlanders when he mentioned his tractor dream to guitarist and graphic artist Doug Bratland, who had a 1957 Minneapolis Moline 335 Utility tractor in his garage just taking up space. The two worked out a deal—Pete bartered some welding work in exchange for the tractor—and the bright yellow chariot with the cherry red rims was his:

> It's like a small thirty-to-fifty-acre tractor. But it was a workhorse, built right here in Hopkins and in Minneapolis on Lake Street, and when I found that out, that kicked my butt, man. I've spent the past month learning about the Minneapolis Moline, and I'm so stoked it was built here, because in the past few years I've fallen in love with Minneapolis and everything it offers, all the creativity and artistry.
>
> I've spent forty-plus years looking for passion in something, and to all of a sudden have it stumble out of a barn in Northfield . . . .

Now all I want to do is drive it around town, even though I'll probably get in trouble for it.

For a time the main rival of tractor behemoth John Deere, Minneapolis Moline was a tractor and farm machinery equipment company headquartered in Hopkins, with production plants on Lake Street (off Hiawatha Avenue) and in Hopkins and Moline, Illinois. Its heyday was the 1930s, and production ceased in 1970.

Pete's tractor hadn't seen any action for decades, so he towed it to a mechanic pal's shop in Hopkins. Over a couple of beers, the two men tuned it up, "gave it some TLC," and got it up and running. He pulled up in front of my house a couple of Thursdays ago, to double-takes from the neighbors and the 4B bus driver, and, with a grin the size of a freshly swathed cornfield, proclaimed, "I'm probably the first person to drive a tractor from Hopkins to Minneapolis in fifty years."

Thus began a series of what he calls "joy rides" around town. If you've seen him, as so many have in the past few weeks, you know it's no exaggeration when he says it's changed his life.

It's like a joy machine. People wave and give the thumbs-up, and they know you're [messing] with the system. But it's more "Yee-haw!" than "Breaking the law!" People get out of your way, stop what they're doing and smile, and jump up and down, and take pictures, and ask questions.

It's universal, and it's cross-cultural. Kids go crazy. Old-timers come up to you, almost with a tear in their eye. You just kind of shock their world, you just upset the program.

You don't want to be a nuisance, but you want people to see this Minneapolis history. It kind of trumps this Mitt Romney circus-fest and this Barack Obama circusfest. I've tuned that out. People have yelled at me for doing it, and I don't care, because my life is trumping that, and I say, if you don't like what's going on, create your world.

I mean, you can spend billions and billions on a war machine that creates total destruction, and be part of that, or you can drive a tractor through a town and create joy, instantly. What do you choose? It's a no-brainer.

Last Saturday, Pete's tractor was the hit of his Forty-seventh and Aldrich neighborhood block party. He rented a wagon, bought some hay bales, and toted families down the street, to the Rose Garden and around Lake Harriet. It was the tractor's first public appearance, upstaging even the visiting fire truck, whose captain wanted to trade rigs with Pete on the spot. That's when he realized the nerve he'd struck in himself wasn't his alone.

"At the very least, if I pull that tractor out even one day a year, I know that that thing leaves people better off. Minneapolis is better off for it being here. If I drive around the lake, I guarantee a hundred people will smile, or laugh, or jump up and down, or talk, when they normally wouldn't have done that. I know from experience that this thing has the power to do that," he said. "I keep saying, 'Someone's gotta do it. It might as well be me.' I'd love to just drive it across the state. I love being on it. I've found it to be nirvana for me."

(October 15, 2012, Southwest Journal)

Greetings from Lake We Be Gone

IT'S THE FIRST SUNNY FRIDAY afternoon of spring, just hours after school has been let out, and on Burnout Hill overlooking Lake Nokomis's north beach, twenty-year-old Keith is practicing his own version of predicate logic: "There's some pretty hot babes at some of the other lakes, but this one—Nokomis—is the best. Know why? Because there's too many fags at the other lakes."

"But the way I look at it is like this," he says, switching philosophical gears. "For every two fags in the world, that means there's two more babes for me. Know what I mean?"

Welcome to Lake We Be Gone—where the men are men and the women are rated.

Located a Frisbee's throw away from the Hiawatha Golf Course and tucked behind East Minnehaha Parkway between Forty-seventh and Fifty-first Streets in South Minneapolis, the Lake Nokomis Parkway every summer transforms into one huge spring-break bash—an Aquatennial parade of hormones and heavy metal. Over the years, Nokomis has made a steady separation from the trendier, more urban, yuppie-infested south lakes Harriet/Calhoun/Isles, and taken on a distinct decidedly blue-collar image.

The Nokomis crowd consists of fourteen-to-thirty-five-year-old kids—metal heads, nymphs, frat boys, sorority girls, local metal musicians, models, and morons. The core is made up of South and Roosevelt High kids, but they come from everywhere—Blaine, Richfield, Chanhassen, Bloomington, Edina, Coon Rapids, Minneapolis, St. Paul. And they come with one purpose: to cruise.

As the only area lake with a two-way parkway, Nokomis is the most conducive for, as Agent P. C. Gillies of the Park Police says, "All the kids driving around in their cars and staring at each other." Imagine *American Graffiti* meets *This Is Spinal Tap* meets *I Like to Watch,* and you're in there.

Some, like Duane, a young Jon Bon Jovi look-alike, claim they do more scoring than staring. "You know what I like best?" he asks, of no one in particular, as he struts down the walking path with his pals, the so-called Nokomis Rockers. "I like it when a girl drives by with a guy at the wheel and she's checking me out. That's the best. The *best*."

Down the road apiece, past Burnout Hill and the parking lot full of vans, is a second hill, the focal point of the Nokomis experience. On a day like this, with the sun slowly sinking, the hill is covered with tanning bodies, many of which sit upright, scoping out the action on the strip below. Trucks roll by deliberately. Suburban starlets in convertibles make quick, cool eye contact with urban bikers. Somewhere, from the parking lot maybe, Tone-Loc sings about doing the wild thing and Alice Cooper roars through a stop sign, howling about being eighteen, a boy, a man, and liking it.

So what does it all mean? A poet might be moved to call Nokomis's second hill "an amphitheater of the flesh." If pressed, a sociologist might explain the players' "You watch me, I'll watch you" behavior as the learned mating ritual of the MTV generation. But to Brenna, a young girl with a perfect tan and worldly gaze, the baby oil and pot-scented knoll is one thing and one thing only: "It's a meat market," she says with a slight giggle. "We come here to meet guys. Guys with long hair. The longer the better."

"Sundays are the best," says Brenna's partner, Carrie, she of the perfect big hair and skeptical smile. Brenna and Carrie sport identical white bikinis and identical gold necklaces. They've been friends for three or four years, best friends since they both went through treatment two years ago. Both are fourteen years old.

"Sundays are good because everyone's hung over from Friday and Saturday nights, and all anybody wants to do is kick back and watch," explains Carrie. "Everybody comes on Sundays."

If the Nokomis Rockers are party animals, the Park Police are their chaperones. The relationship is a classic rebel–authority clash that adds tension to the hanging-out game. Because the cops haven't achieved official officer status with the Minneapolis Police force, the kids call the Park Police "Rent-a-Cops," and the cops issue tickets to the kids for everything from standing in the street to putting speakers on top of cars.

"The kids kind of take the lake over in the summer, and it's really hard," says Gillies. "We have to try and take it back from them so they don't abuse the area. The citizens complain a lot about the traffic and the stereos playing loud and stuff like that, and we've got to enforce everything we can down here. There's a lot of drugs and alcohol that goes on, stuff you don't really see. So we've got to keep everyone under control."

Compared to the nights, Lake We Be Gone days are tame. When the sun goes down, the flirting turns seedier and more desperate, as the cops strictly enforce the lake's ten o'clock No Parking ban. The curfew's effect is not unlike lighting a short fuse on the mob's collective libido. Take, for example, a group of ten or fifteen frat boys we'll call The Brothers Johnson who spend their weekend nights on the parkway curb, grabbing their crotches ("Johnsons," as they say) in salute to passing carloads of females. "We gotta get some signs with numbers," one frustrated Johnson brother complains. "We definitely need a better [rating] system."

The urge to merge may be Nokomis's main attraction, but the thing that sets it apart from other area lakes is the sound track that accompanies the action. The poet might say that if Nokomis was a rock band, it would be Iron Maiden to Harriet/Calhoun/Isles's Fine Young Cannibals. The sociologist might make a case for rock being the single most defining aspect of adolescence, concluding that the Nokomis Rockers' practice of playing their boxes at full volume is an integral part of courtship.

Then again, it could simply be a matter of, as one seventeen-year-old glamorite says, "liking loud music played fast."

From every nook of the parkway comes the sound of metal. Queensryche versus Def Leppard. Anthrax versus Poison. Vixen versus Hanoi Rocks, and most of the time, KJJO and ZROCK drown out KQ92. The occasional Top 40 hit wafts its way over the lake ("We don't do Madonna here," says one Coon Rapids rocker), but metal is clearly king of Burnout Hill. And on top of the hill sits one band.

Metallica.

"They're the best, they just are," says Chad, seventeen, with a laugh, astounded at the very nature of the "Who's your favorite band?" question. He peers out from under a shock of brown bangs, looks at his friends, and rolls his eyes. "They play fast and good. And they ain't posers."

By unanimous vote, Metallica is the drug of choice at Nokomis. It seems as if every third T-shirt sports the. . . *And Justice for All* tour itinerary, and from every other car blares "Blackened" or "To Live Is to Die."

"They pretty much started heavy metal," Kris, eighteen, says. "I saw them, and it was the best concert I've ever gone to see. A lot of people get down on them because they sing about suicide and death and stuff, but it's a fact of life, and there's no way anyone can get around it. They express things that none of the other metal bands express. Guns N' Roses are close—but that's different. Metallica sings about depressing times. And these are depressing times."

Maybe so, but you'd never know it by visiting Lake We Be Gone. From now until late September, the Nokomis Rockers will enjoy a carefree summer of music, tanning, cruising, and running from the Park Police.

Back on Burnout Hill, Keith is finishing his conversation with a reporter. "What paper is this story going to be in?" he asks. "The *Minnesota Daily*? Really? I went to school over there for a year. I got three credits the whole year. Three credits."

He laughs, burps, and checks his tan. "Yeah, the U. Now there's a place with some hot babes. Yessir, some very hot babes over there at the U, 'specially this time of year. Not too many fags, either. Know what I mean?"

(May 19, 1989, Minnesota Daily)

Phantom of First Avenue

AS HAS BECOME THE CUSTOM at First Avenue's annual Halloween party, they'll be handing out prizes for best costume tonight. Some of the partygoers will come as ghosts, but at least one regular of the downtown Minneapolis nightclub won't need a costume.

It was 1991 when Molly McManus first laid eyes on the ghost of First Avenue. It was approaching 2 A.M. after an ordinary Tuesday night edition of Club 241, and McManus, the club's bar manager at the time, was closing up. After making sure the doors were locked, she climbed the stairwell to the upstairs bar to check the bathrooms. She went into the men's bathroom and turned off the urinals. Then she went into the women's bathroom.

"That is definitely a hot spot," said Valerie Cenedella, whom McManus succeeded as bar manager. "Every night, the women's bathroom was just this huge challenge for me. You would walk through there, and with all the mirrors you'd see things. Things would catch your eye, and if you ever were brave enough to stop and look, there would be nothing there.

"I'm not always susceptible to that kind of stuff, but there was something definitely there. It was physically tangible; you could just feel it. It was like, 'Okay, I'll be gone soon. Just don't hurt me.'"

McManus surveyed the women's room, as she had hundreds of times before. Bathroom check was the least enjoyable part of her job, because she never knew what passed-out drunk or other character she might stumble upon. She poked her head into the first stall. Nothing. The second. Fine. The third, and the fourth. So far, so good.

Until she opened the door to the fifth stall.

Before it was a nightclub, First Avenue was the site of the old Greyhound bus depot, where vagrants would spend many a night sleeping on the wooden benches, a few of which are still used in the bar. Before that, it was a livestock stable where sheep and cattle were slaughtered. Before that, a school playground.

Some say it is built on holy land, and most anyone who has ever worked there will tell you that it is haunted. Legend has it that a young woman either committed suicide or died from a drug overdose in the bus station. On a bench.

"There are millions of stories," said longtime First Avenue employee Matt Gerhard. Among the tales is of the time in 1983, when Gerhard and another employee were guarding the film equipment overnight for the production of *Purple Rain,* and all the lights in the place went berserk for thirty minutes.

Former employee Oscar Arredondo recalls the night a solitary balloon made its way around the vacant club, up from the dance floor and past the women's bathroom, and settled at his table with a circular gust of icy air. "It was like someone was leading it by a string," said Arredondo. "Normally, I was skeptical about most of the stories that other employees told me. But the weird thing about this was the cold air, because it was a warm summer night."

Others report flying ashtrays, bottles, and boom boxes, drastic changes in temperature and depth perception, a laughing gangster emerging from the wall, unearthly sounds in deejays' headphones, ghostly manifestations, the sound of braying sheep in the basement, legless dancers rising from the dance floor to shake their torsos with club patrons, and an after-hours seance during which 257 channeled dead children claimed that "there is a bad thing in the club."

Of course, this could all be the product of a bunch of overactive imaginations who've had one too many late nights or . . . spirits.

"I've been there some pretty odd hours, and I've never seen anything," said stage manager Conrad Sverkerson. "But that doesn't mean anything. There have been some pretty credible people who have worked here over the years who have seen some pretty strange things. You wonder what's going on."

"I've seen a couple of the manifestation things, and I've never seen it manifest as anything other than a woman," said club deejay Rod Smith. It is an assertion that lends credence to one of the most oft-repeated ghost tales, of the night two employees were minding the box office at the 7th St. Entry, First Avenue's smaller sister club.

As club lore has it, a woman in a green army jacket, long blonde hair, bell-bottom jeans, and bare feet walked out of the Entry, smiled at the two employees, strolled into the main room, then vanished before their eyes. It is a familiar figure to Molly McManus, who, four years after it happened, still vividly remembers the night of her brush with the ghost of First Avenue.

"I opened the door to that stall and saw a woman hanging up there," said McManus, who now lives in Phoenix. "She was wearing a green army jacket and had long hair. It wasn't anything gory or anything: she was just hanging there with her neck to one side.

"What I thought was that it was a real tragic incident. I thought someone had hung themself. I thought, 'Oh, God, what am I gonna do here?' It was more that than anything. I was just freaking out. And then I looked back, and there was nothing there.

"I didn't run, but I was really shaking. I finished up as soon as I could and got out. I didn't tell a lot of people about it right away, because it was so weird. But after that, I would never, ever be in the building alone. Daytime, nighttime, never."

Doors open at 8 P.M. tonight. First-place prize for best costume is $241. Good luck, but if the visitor in the fifth stall decides to make an appearance, you haven't got a prayer.

(October 31, 1995, St. Paul Pioneer Press)

Winter of Our Swedish Fiddler

EVERYONE SHOULD LIVE THE DREAM Joel Bremer lived over the past three months. Everyone should pick a spot on the map, fall in love with its music and people, soak up every last bit of it until bursting and exhausted, and then spend the rest of your life dream-bragging about it to anyone who'll listen, and forever wanting to do it again.

As you read this, Bremer is winging his way back to his hometown of Vasteras, Sweden. He landed in South Minneapolis a few weeks before his thirty-first birthday on December 13, and it's no exaggeration to say that his time here made for as magical a mutual admiration society as I've been witness to, one that undoubtedly inspired my friend Melissa Stordahl to post as her Facebook status update the other morning, "'I feel that there is nothing more truly artistic than to love people.' —Vincent Van Gogh."

To that end, Mr. Sweden has been a gift to many of us who suspect that we live in a rare city and rare time but who also sometimes take it for granted. Which is to say he inspired a lot of us; so much so that his loving Swede-Gone-Wild spirit is already the stuff of legend, song, and Facebook fan page (Joel Bremer Is My Shaman, thirty-one fans and counting).

"He took this town by storm, and he stole our hearts with his sweet nature, upbeat attitude, superb musical talent, and genuine smile," wrote songwriter Jennifer Markey in a post–Bremer Valentine's Day gig note. "He also gives great hugs, and he'll tell you if your instrument is out of tune. Joel and friends gave me my Kick in the Pants, and it won't be soon that their footprints wear off my ass, too."

The Minneapolis–Bremer lovefest started in February 2007, when Bremer came to America for the first time. He played a Swedish folk fest in Sonoma, California, and the festival's organizer suggested he travel to Minneapolis to play the Midwinter Folk Fest at the American Swedish Institute in Minneapolis. There, Bremer became fast friends of Paul Dahlin, a Kingfield musician, husband, and father who in 1985 founded the American Swedish Institute Spelmanslag.

Bremer knew little about Minneapolis before visiting. He loved the Replacements, Prince, the Jayhawks, and the touring Swedish fiddlers from Minnesota he'd met at gigs in Sweden. He knew the town had a reputation for "good alternative culture," and he'd seen *Fargo*. But it was his meeting with local fiddle fairy Eliza Blue in 2007 that ignited Bremer's love affair with the Minneapolis music scene.

"I was thinking about my own playing when I played with Eliza at Palmer's two weeks ago: 'Wow, this is some beautiful stuff I'm playing, and it's all because I met Eliza and started to play with her. It would've never had happened otherwise,'" said Bremer the morning before his flight out Wednesday. "Musically, I have discovered, for me, a new way of playing music. I had never played with any singer/songwriters or any bands before I met Eliza. I mostly just played traditional Swedish music before that. To just stumble into a new way of playing after many years as a musician and to feel that you're good at it has been very exciting. It's been liberating and exhilarating. I've taken big chances, it has paid off, and I've learned so much from it."

Bremer was inspired to play violin when he was six years old, after his parents took him to see the local classical symphony, though he hasn't played much classical music. During his visit to Minneapolis this time, he performed and/or recorded with Eliza Blue, Brianna Lane, Romantica, the Bitter Spills, St. Dominic's Trio, Charlie Parr, Teague Alexy, Slim Dunlap, and David De Young. He frequented the Electric Fetus, Treehouse Records, Cheapo's, and Roadrunner for "fifty or seventy" CDs by local artists.

How do you say *carpe diem* in Swedish?

"I've seen more incredible music in three months . . . . I've never gone out to see this many shows, ever," he stammered. "And it's been local stuff all the time. The musicianship and quality are higher, and you can see it in small bands that put out records by themselves, and in my mind there are so many bands like that that are among the best things I've heard and should be well-known internationally.

"That is one part, and the other is the amazing community. It seems to be a big enough place to have this big variety and lots of different stuff going on, and it's small enough so it's real easy to connect. Everyone knows each other in a real good way, and it's big enough so you don't have to be in each other's faces all the time. It's just this fantastic community feeling and this amazing thing going on here, and everybody should know about it."

(February 18, 2010, Southwest Journal)

All These Weeks

THE SUN WAS BLAZING and going down slow over Lake Harriet one day last week, and I was worshiping at my favorite place of meditation and music making, the Lake Harriet Rose Garden.

I was making like the singer/songwriter hero of my youth, John Denver, quietly playing my guitar and softly singing my favorite new song to the birds, trees, rabbits, and squirrels, perfectly lost in the tune, nature, sunset, and moment, when three silhouettes—a young couple and a dude with a pro camera—came out of the sun and approached me.

I nodded in their direction, staying focused on the song. Tall boy silhouette took petite girl silhouette's hands, they started dancing, and I made the song swing a little more. "Mind if I take some photos of you with them?" asked the guy with the big lens. I shook my head "No," told him to go ahead, and upped the volume a little.

Summer in Minneapolis, just the four of us. Sunset, exploding. Babbling sparkling fountain waters, harmonizing with the heartfelt music, sweet breeze, and lilting songbirds. Airplane, roaring two thousand feet above us. Her, gazing up at his square strong jaw and into his eyes. Him, cradling her. Them, whipped. Them, looking like they want to devour each other right there on the lush lawn. Me, lucky little songsmith.

Off in the distance, a wedding party in formal suits and dresses traipsed through the green, green grass of our hometown and the psychedelic flora of the natural world. On the Facebook party on my computer back home, photos of giddy newlywed friends morphed with the trending news of the day: the upcoming sixtieth wedding anniversary of my mom and dad, Ann and Jerry Walsh, and the engagement of my niece, Sara Marie Brown, to the love of her life, Joseph Ciesla, a handsome young musichead and Harvard man whom all the ladies in the family have determined to be a catch of the highest order. In front of the fountain, on the bench whose plaque commemorates the memory of my late friend and neighbor, Karl Mueller, a couple of twenty-something women talked animatedly, their legs and arms and futures entwined right here in gay marriage–friendly Minnesota.

Yep. True story. Love was and is in the air, young love in particular, and as I sang I could feel the young lovers' palpable chemistry and desire, and I thought about the words of my therapist friends who preach to their experience- and communication-starved clients that sexual intimacy is the single most important ingredient of true love, and of something I read recently, in a piece by psychologist and blogger Mei Mei Fox and her husband.

"It's a romance, not a 'relationship,'" the couple wrote in their breezy but valuable *Huffington Post* piece "Ten Signs You've Found 'The One.'" "You should feel swept away by your relationship. You ought to want to scream about your partner's awesomeness to the world . . . . Some people say you don't need an initial spark of sexual attraction to form a satisfying and enduring romantic relationship. We disagree. When you first meet your person, there ought to be Fourth of July–worthy fireworks."

No argument here. I ended my song, a new one that attempts to express the loneliness of our techno-connected world, and as the music faded the threesome shyly thanked me and started to go politely on their photo-shooting way. I stopped them and, after sussing out that they were making engagement photos, I told them I had another song for them, a love song I'd written, and they settled back into each other's arms.

I played "All These Weeks," a romantic diddy I wrote about falling in love and getting to know someone, and sang it with all my heart, because this was my wedding gift to them, and the best gig of my life. In the olden days the job of the town songwriter and singer was a sacred one, well respected and revered for its role at celebrations, weddings, funerals, and other rites of passage, and rarely have I felt so minstrel-worthy than when these two kids slow-danced and looked lovingly into one another's souls.

Then the silhouettes moved on, and I kept playing. I was happy for the moment to have simply happened, and for their names to remain a mystery to me forever. Just as I was getting comfortable with the idea of letting it all be, the trio returned to the scene of our make-out session for some more photos by the flowers. I got the photographer's information and asked him to send me some shots, which he did.

Their names were Nate and Katie, but for all their erotic romantic energy and fast-spreading good vibes they could've been Huck and Becky, Orpheus and Eurydice, Johnny and June, Romeo and Juliet, or Lancelot and Guinevere, and no matter what version of love you subscribe to, no matter how many times your heart has been lifted or broken, their hopeful love sprang eternal and gushed forth like fountain waters on a perfect summer day.

(August 14, 2013, Southwest Journal)

TEN
MIX #4
FUNKY CEILI

Free Your Mind . . .

THE FIRST TIME HE SAID IT, George Clinton didn't even remember what he said. It was 1967, and his band, the Parliaments, was performing at a club in Boston called the Sugar Shack. The Parliaments came well before Clinton's trailblazing Parliament–Funkadelic collectives of the '70s, a doo-wop outfit that eschewed the genre's matching sweaters and three-piece suits of the day and opted instead for helmets, fencing masks, and robes that were more in line with the era's burgeoning psychedelic movement.

The first time he said it, George Clinton was tripping on acid. The Parliaments were experimenting with a raw melange of slow, dirty blues and embryonic funk. That night at the Sugar Shack, the band was laying down an especially nasty groove that was bathed in moody minor chords and bumped along by their leader's cosmic comic-book ad-libbing and hallucinogenic-inspired Beat poetry.

The first time he said it, George Clinton might well have lost it forever to the moment, were it not for an artsy-fartsy college friend "who talked to me about Nietzsche and Ayn Rand and all that stuff." The kid had made a habit of sitting in the audience at Parliaments' gigs and meticulously scribbling down verbatim passages from Clinton's improvs. After the Parliaments ended their set at the Sugar Shack, he presented Clinton with a scrap of paper. It read:

"Free your mind and your ass will follow."

"To me, it was nonsensical and pseudo-philosophical, and I cracked up every time I heard myself say something like that," Clinton says by phone from his 178-acre Michigan homestead, where he lives with his wife of three years and two of his grandchildren. He went on:

> Years later, I realized things flow through you that you don't even have to know what you're talking about. But I was like everybody else: I learned later that it does mean something. I mean, I write lyrics all the time, and I knew it had a flow to it, but it's deeper than I even thought it was. Because now, everybody thinks that was genius to be able to do a record like that. When he came up to me and said, "This is what you said," I believed him, because he was knowledgeable. So whatever, if he said it meant something, I thought, "I'm gonna keep it."

Good thing he did. Since that fateful night, "Free Your Mind and Your Ass Will Follow" (which turned up on the seminal 1970 Funkadelic album of the same name) has become a cry of liberation in the '80s and '90s: En Vogue's cleaned-up (antiseptic?) reprise of it was a chart-topping smash last year, the Clinton–Red Hot Chili Peppers performance of it was a highlight of last year's Grammy Awards show, and it is currently invoked by rock critics and headline writers all over the world, at the clip of (and this is a modest estimate) twenty times per week.

To be sure, Clinton hasn't lost a single shred of relevancy in the '90s. And the same fire that informed the funky politics of the early Parliament–Funkadelic records burns brightly in *Hey Man . . . Smell My Finger,* Clinton's second album for Paisley Park/Warner Bros.

"The whole album is about the media—who chooses the news and how it gets filtered," he explains. "News shapes our perspective and points of views and designs our reality. It tells you what you believe and what you think. The media have that kind of power, and it starts to look like martial law is inevitable."

The civil rights erosions that are tackled on "Martial Law," as a matter of fact, are the first thing heard on *Finger*, followed by the slyly pointed "Paint the White House Black," in which guest stars like Yo Yo, Humpty Hump, and Dr. Dre lobby for Clinton (Dr. Funkenstein and the Supreme Overlord of the Downstroke, by any other name) to bring the funk platform to Washington.

But "White House" is no mere pop-politico fantasy, since the funk candidate can deliver the goods. My half-hour chat with Clinton last week touched on: the lottery, the Rodney King verdict and the L.A. riots, the drug war, gangsta rap, feminism, *Jurassic Park* and DNA cloning, Sly Stone, conspiracy theories, David Koresh, abortion, the bias wars (gay versus straights, blacks versus whites, males versus females), education, the Beatles, the space program, UFOs, the Kennedy assassination, America's police force versus its citizenry, the job draught, youth, and last but not least, teachers—whom Clinton believes "should be the highest paid people in the world."

And it's not just interviews. *Finger* touches on at least as many topics, with Clinton's main agenda being the combating of the "over-mediafication" of America: "We just want to disprove all of the myths, first of all, about planned obsolescence; that it's got to be over because you're over thirty or thirty-five. Everybody believes that—the radio stations literally say that you're not of our demographics unless you're of a certain age. If you're not young, you're outta there. And we're saying, 'You don't determine that.'"

At fifty-two, George Clinton could be the poster child for youth as a state of mind. Countless hip-hoppers have sampled Parliament–Funkadelic records, and Clinton's popularity rating has never been higher, not to mention his energy level: he recently completed work on a four-CD live album that chronicles Parliament–Funkadelic in all its incarnations from 1972 to 1993, and he's currently in the studio working on a new album from the Parliaments. Then there's the legendary four-hour show he and the P-Funk All-Stars bring to the Cabooze tonight and Wednesday. The secret to his stamina?

I only sleep four hours a night. If I sleep five, then I have to sleep eight. I always have been like that, but I'm glad, because I see everybody else have to do the whole eight hours, and I'm groggy as hell when I sleep that long. That's leisure-to-death when you sleep that long. The longer I sleep, the more tired I get.

So I've saved my energy up for real, just to be here for when the nostalgia part kicked in, and hip-hop made our job real easy. We were just waiting for it to happen; I knew it would. Like, as a band, we've been out the last three years kicking up a storm and working harder than we've ever worked, because we knew that it was gonna happen. And we're ready to bang it for another twenty years if we have to.

(December 14, 1993, St. Paul Pioneer Press)

Grindstone

> *I am out to sing songs that will prove to you that this is your world and that if it has hit you pretty hard and knocked you for a dozen loops, no matter how hard it's run you down or rolled on you, no matter what color, what size you are, or how you are built, I am out to sing the songs that make you take pride in yourself and your work.*
>
> **—Woody Guthrie, WNEW radio broadcast, December 3, 1944**

WHEN WOODY GUTHRIE WROTE this passage, Franklin Delano Roosevelt was staking his claim to fame as the most popular president in the nation's history. On December 3, 1944, the Great Depression was but a bad memory, and World War II was just months away from grinding to its atomic-powered conclusion.

When Uncle Tupelo recorded their kindred-spirited *March 16–20, 1992,* it had been a year to the day since George H. W. Bush's approval rating reached its all-time high. On March 16, 1992, pundits were haggling over what to call the country's economic slump—a recession or a depression—and the initial popularity of Operation Desert Storm was fading fast.

These days, more than any other days, there's a greater number of people homeless, out of work, or working at jobs they're either drastically overqualified for or categorically uninspired by. And once upon a time, troubadours like Guthrie roamed this land, passing down solace and songs from one working generation to another in the classic folk tradition. Though its pulse may be weak these days, that tradition is still alive, surviving only in spite of itself, having recently been reanimated (antifolk), co-opted (*MTV Unplugged*), and mocked (*Bob Roberts*).

Which, given the context, is why Uncle Tupelo's exquisite *March 16–20, 1992* (Rockville) sounds like a miracle to me. Unlike the band's first two albums, *No Depression* and *Still Feel Gone,* the Peter Buck–produced *March 16–20, 1992* is an all-acoustic songbook that combines Farrar/Tweedy originals with interpretations of folk and gospel standards—not exactly a savvy career move for a college rock band on the buzz bin cusp. Highly unfathomable though it may be, it is also one of the best—and most important—records of 1992.

And the same thing could have been said about it in 1932. In other words, *March 16–20, 1992* is as timeless as it is timely. Where Guthrie cut his teeth on the Depression and Oklahoma, Jay Farrar and Jeff Tweedy learned their lessons in working-class St. Louis, and their tales of how disenfranchised Americans play out their pain are just as authentic/applicable in the '90s as Woody's were in the '30s.

From the time clock–watchers who live a "slow-walkin' death" in "Grindstone" to the third-generation miner in "Shaky Ground," Farrar/Tweedy's world is populated by worthless, hopeless lives. They're all here: the autoworkers in Flint, the meat packers in Austin, the stockbrokers on Wall Street, the miners on the Iron Range. Never named, but never very far away. And while *March 16–20, 1992* breathes hardest through its characters, it isn't above explicit political commentary: there's the traditional union call to arms "Coal Miner," the evergreen "Satan, Your Kingdom Must Come Down," and Farrar/Tweedy's own "Criminals," a positively crippling piece about the ability of powers-that-be to manufacture class warfare.

But the album's most chilling moments explore the aftershocks of despair and how they creep into workers' playtime. In "Wait Up," a spent factory worker calls home from the night shift to his lone strength-giver, his drowsy wife. "Honey, please wait up for me," he pleads. "I need you more than I need sleep." And in the breathtaking "Black Eye," a nobody makes himself feel like a somebody by getting shiner after shiner: badges of honor to prove to him and his brothers that his dull self is anything but.

Finally, the album's centerpiece is a classic reading of the traditional "Moonshiner," in which the singer's still life is reduced to living day to day, drink to drink: "The whole world is a bottle, and life is but a dram. When the bottle gets empty, Lord it sure ain't worth a damn." In other words, when promise promises you nothing, there's a certain nobility to giving up. It's a song about slow death, and *March 16–20, 1992* is a record that comes along once in a lifetime. Listen. Woody Guthrie's ashes are all over it.

(November 4, 1992, City Pages)

Windfall

PACHYDERM STUDIO IN CANNON FALLS, Minnesota, is a thirty-five-minute drive from the Twin Cities. Barns, cornfields, and silos rise up from the prairie flatland. The studio is tucked away off a two-lane county road that leads to few, if any, of the modern-day amenities (i.e., bars and restaurants) usually required of the long-term recording experience. Inside, the sound room is flanked by enormous floor-to-ceiling windows that look out onto a hill of pine trees, their branches weighed down by freshly fallen snow. It is a fairy-tale cottage, an amphitheater of wilderness, the ideal record-making retreat.

The studio's small foyer holds the building's lone concession to music-biz glitz. Hanging on the wall above a coffee table and across from a modest kitchenette are gold and platinum records of projects hatched at Pachyderm—Nirvana's *In Utero,* Live's *Throwing Copper,* Soul Asylum's *Grave Dancer's Union, The Beavis and Butt-head Experience*—an alternative rock hall of fame. But poetically, on this frigid January night there rests on the coffee table a copy of the *Country Music Encyclopedia,* stolen from the East Lake branch of the Minneapolis Public Library.

The thieves are the members of Son Volt, who are holed up at Pachyderm for a few days with country singer Kelly Willis. As producer Brian Paulson sits in the control room mixing Willis's "Fading Fast," a song slated to appear on the sound track to Winona Ryder's new film, *She's Not There,* a pin-drop of a jam session has broken out in the recording room. Singer-guitarist Jay Farrar sits on a piano bench with his acoustic guitar, bookended by Willis and bassist Jim Boquist. They slide into songs effortlessly, no particular place to go, no threat of one-upmanship. Willis's and Farrar's voices melt into each other like butter and brown sugar on oatmeal, the same way they did on Townes Van Zandt's "Rex's Blues," their duet from last year's *Red, Hot, and Bothered* compilation.

At first, it's just the three of them, playing evergreens by Loretta Lynn, Tammy Wynette, Gram Parsons, Kitty Wells. Drummer Mike Heidorn ambles in, leans on the piano, and absent-mindedly taps a tambourine before grabbing a banjo. Multi-instrumentalist Dave Boquist arrives after putting his toddler son Shane down for a nap in the adjoining house and picks up a mandolin. Lyrics and guitar parts are guessed at. A language is formed. A spell is cast. When Farrar begins the chorus to an old Merle Haggard song, the verse gets mumbled, but everyone knows the chorus, or enough to belt it out: "I'm proud to be an Okie from Muskogee, a place where even squares can have a ball."

Times being what they are, Son Volt are squares. Their debut album, *Trace,* is a throwback to squares-in-their-own-time the Byrds, the Louvin Brothers, and Creedence Clearwater Revival. In a musical milieu starved for authenticity, Farrar and Son Volt are the real deal, and at the forefront of a small but growing army of country screwups such as Blue Mountain, the Bottle Rockets, Tarnation, the Geraldine Fibbers, and the now-defunct Jayhawks. That *Trace,* a dense, damaged soundscape of lost-highway imagery and emotional breadcrumbs, has sold a relatively paltry fifty thousand copies doesn't bother its makers, who measure success not by modern-rock airplay or *120 Minutes* appearances but by how effectively they contribute to an ongoing tradition.

The center square, Farrar, grew up in tiny Millstadt, Illinois, and attended high school in the nearby East St. Louis suburb of Belleville, an industrial town whose most famous exports are Stag beer, Jimmy Connors, and Buddy Ebsen, a.k.a. Jed Clampett on *The Beverly Hillbillies.* For Farrar, who worked on a farm and in his mother's used-paperback store, small-town life proved both suffocating and inspiring. "A place like Belleville can definitely make you feel isolated," he says the morning after the Willis session, poking at a breakfast of scrambled eggs, toast, and coffee at Rick's Ol' Time Café in Minneapolis. "There was a sort of ever-present drive to just get out. And being in a band provided the means to do that."

Farrar's father, who worked for the Army Corps of Engineers, collected old cars and musical instruments, and a bounty of mandolins, banjos, guitars, and accordions jammed their household. The youngest of four boys, Jay picked up the guitar at age eleven, and his parents and his brothers—John, Wade, and Dade—have all played or still do play. "His whole family can be quite a good band," confirms Heidorn, whose older sister Kelly married Dade (they've since divorced). "It's very musical when you go over there. You always pick up the guitar or piano, and Pop always has an accordion or harmonica. It's quite fun."

Fun, yes, but the twenty-nine-year-old Farrar admits it might also have been something of a crutch. "There was quite a bit of noncommunication involved, growing up," says Farrar. "Except on a musical level. But it's better now. We communicate a lot easier than we did."

Farrar's noncommunication partially contributed to the 1994 demise of Uncle Tupelo, the seminal country-rock band Heidorn and Farrar cofounded with Jeff Tweedy, who has gone on to form Wilco and release his own album, *A.M.* Farrar says he sent Tweedy a note to express his admiration for the Wilco record, but the high school buddies haven't talked, as Tweedy puts it, since "the last note Uncle Tupelo played."

"It's kind of strange, but we went through a lot of mercurial times together," says Farrar. "So I'm sure at some point we'll probably see eye to eye again and do something together . . ." That sentence, like most of Farrar's sentences, trails off. In both conversation and concert, his eyelashes flutter like a fighter's hands fending off jabs to the face. He seems much more comfortable asking questions—trying to turn an artificial situation like an interview into something real, like a conversation—than answering them.

Farrar has been described as painfully shy ("I'm not a joke teller," he understates at one point; "I guess I don't exude a whole lot of personality"), and in public, such reticence has been construed as stage fright. "Yeah," he says. "Not necessarily, though, because—I don't know. I have the same sort of trouble expressing myself one on one, so it's only partial stage fright." Still, playing music is his preferred mode of communication. "It can be a cathartic thing to do," he says. "There are a lot of things you can say with music that are harder to say verbally."

Which is largely the appeal of *Trace*, a picture book of road images and sepia-tone snapshots that starts off with "Windfall," a timeless song built around the timeless chorus, "May the wind take your troubles away." "That was written after I had come off the road with Uncle Tupelo," Farrar explains. "At that time, the idea of getting in a car and driving alone appealed to me."

After Uncle Tupelo broke up, Farrar moved to New Orleans with his high school-sweetheart-turned-fiancée, but returned to St. Louis because he missed his family and the change of seasons. Before recording *Trace*, he spent time driving from New Orleans to St. Louis, where Heidorn lived, and Minneapolis, where the Boquists reside. Along the way, Farrar forged a strong alliance with the Mississippi River, a bond that is positively mud-baked into all eleven tracks on *Trace*.

"It just allowed for a lot of time to reflect," he says of his journey. "There weren't a lot of distractions, so it was good in that sense. Just to have time alone." As breakfast winds down, Farrar smokes cigarettes and puts his gum, which he had stuck to the side of the ashtray, back in his mouth. When he says good-bye, that voice, so richly confident on the Uncle Tupelo and Son Volt records, is almost a whisper. It's the whisper of a man out of his element, a paradox that perhaps only musicians can appreciate.

"If you've played music for a long time," says Dave Boquist, sitting at a Mexican restaurant that night in Minneapolis, "the songs, the music, the instruments all become part of your family. Your confidants. Sometimes I think that it's possible if you're outside of that environment, it's sort of like being without something you're close to. I know I go nuts if I'm away from my music, or my instruments, for a long period of time. I'm somewhat miserable."

Maybe people who play music are drawn to it out of a very basic need. Maybe they just need something to do with their hands.

"Some people don't, but a lot of people do," he says. "Some people are very cerebral and can dream a little. We do manual labor."

(April 1996, SPIN magazine)

Ballad of El Goodo

SITTING IN THE MSP AIRPORT terminal this time last year, I spotted a slight, solitary figure carrying a cheap Hefty bag of a guitar case. As the figure made its way toward me and the gate, where his outgoing flight to Chicago waited, the shuffling gait and pock-marked face came into unmistakable focus—this was Alex Chilton, pop's patron saint of the '80s.

Pop's patron saint sat down next to me, laid the guitar at his feet, and opened a book, though I can't for the life of me remember what it was. I'd met him twice before, once when he and Paul Westerberg were working on the Replacements' "Nowhere Is My Home" at Nicollet Studio, so when I tapped him on the thigh and reintroduced myself, the conversation was easy. We talked about mutual friends, books, and guitars; he said he was on his way back from Minot, North Dakota, where he'd been performing at an oldies show that featured an ad hoc version of the Box Tops, Chilton's first band.

"Jim, do you have any pot?" he asked, in that sweet Memphis drawl, and after we went to the phone booth and contacted a mutual pal, I told him that I once sang for a band that had covered "The Letter," which had been a number-one hit in 1967 for the Box Tops, and "Bangcock," a 1978 solo Chilton tune. Checking the *Cash Box* charts, pop's patron saint's eyes lit up. "Did you ever put 'em on a record?" visions of royalty checks dancing in his head. I told him no, we hadn't, but that I thought I had them on tape somewhere. He wasn't interested.

The survival instinct exhibited in the exchange is the nervous tic of a man who has had to make a living while enduring lives as teen idol, cult hero, living legend, and yes, patron saint. The three records Chilton's early-'70s group Big Star recorded were disproportionately extensive in their influence. Everyone from the Soft Boys to Trip Shakespeare has cited them as influences; the Bangles, dB's, R.E.M., the Dream Syndicate, Dumptruck, and the Replacements have all performed or recorded Big Star songs, and the 'Mats' ode to Chilton was the high point of their 1987 *Pleased to Meet Me* LP.

One morning last week, I woke up pop's patron saint at his Memphis home with a phone call. After he got situated, we talked about his upcoming visit to Minneapolis (backed by a three-piece band tomorrow, Uptown Bar; Friday, 7th St. Entry) and the Alex Chilton legend—a mantle with which he doesn't seem to be even the slightest bit uncomfortable. Still, one gets the feeling that Chilton (whom one acquaintance describes "as full of himself as anyone I've ever met") would rather be a musician than an enigma.

"Hype has a lot to do with it, I think," he observes, of his pervasive influence on the '80s pop generation. "You know, I think there's a certain mentality that young guitar players [have]; that when they hear those [Big Star] records, they think the sound of the guitars is . . . neat. And I can understand that, I guess."

Starting at age sixteen, Chilton scored seven Top 40 hits with the Box Tops, from 1967 to 1969. But his memories of those days are far from fond:

> I've never really felt attached to the Box Tops material—I always felt *detached,* because the people in the band were basically puppets for producers. And the only reason that I did it was so that my parents wouldn't send me back to school. And the money was good.
>
> I mean, it could have been fun, but the whole scene that I was involved in kind of made it not too comfortable. Because I didn't enjoy what I was doing, you know? I didn't agree with [the direction of] the band; I didn't care for where these people's heads were at all. It was the late '60s and '70s, and we were doing these kind of strange, bizarre combinations of country and the blues. And I liked the '60s British bands, and I liked a lot of the California late-'60s bands, that sort of stuff.

Chilton's disinterest eventually led to the Box Tops breakup in 1970, and to the formation of Big Star, which he says was infinitely more fulfilling. After recording several solo LPs in the late '70s he retired, and pop's patron saint spent much of the first part of the past decade working odd jobs as a janitor, dishwasher, and a self-professed "tree guy" (gardener/tree trimmer). He kept busy by producing and playing guitar with Memphis mainstays Panther Burns, and, in 1985, Chilton returned with the EP *Feudalist Tarts* and began touring.

He's since released another EP (*No Sex*) and LP (*High Priest*); he has plans to record again in the fall, and nowadays he spends most of his musical hours producing and shuttling between Box Tops and Alex Chilton gigs. But truth be told, his recent recorded legacy hasn't come close to approaching the Eucharist that was Big Star. Still, the man has traveled through more valleys in his forty years than, say, Michael Jackson, the most obvious analogy to Chilton's child-star-turned-adult-spaceman case. And if anything, pop's patron saint has become secure with his resultant eccentricity.

"I don't put too much stock in public opinion," he says gently. "Whatever people think doesn't bother me. I'm not someone who's easily . . . I mean, even my closest friends have the most wildly varying opinions on me or whatever, so . . . somewhere along the way, in my early twenties or something, I just figured out that it's more important to know what I thought about something than what other people think."

With that, Chilton and I say our good-byes. Later that day he'll hit the road yet again, and I ask him if he's got to pack. "No," he says with a laugh. "I've got to go back to sleep." After hanging up the phone, I slip in my tape with Big Star's "September Gurls" on it and mutter to myself, "Sleep tight, Alex." Because a patron saint needs all the rest he can get.

(June 20, 1990, City Pages)

Second to No One

MEN AND WOMEN. Rosanne Cash's records are littered with 'em. Fresh loves, failed romances. Husbands, wives. Bright promises, brighter pastures, broken vows. Mistresses, misogynists. Impetuous flings, impossible flames. Heartstrings. Hard-ons. Heartaches.

Equal parts fiction and autobiography, these characters and their never-ending quest for a mutual dialogue have been the focal point of Cash's nine-year recording career. Her songs have provided an intimate and mostly nonpartisan commentary on the battle of the sexes. But this time around—with *King's Record Shop*—she's taking sides.

Mainstream country music hasn't traditionally been a vehicle for feminism. Pioneers like Kitty Wells, Wanda Jackson, and Rose Maddox had successful careers and could therefore be considered groundbreakers in what was then a male-dominated industry. But the genre is more notorious for keeping women in a passive role—artists like Lynn Anderson and Tammy Wynette have helped deflate the movement by operating like some subservient musical coffee klatsch, typically and consistently devoting their material to the activities of their drinkin' and cheatin' men.

But Johnny Cash's oldest child is more reminiscent of a modern-day Loretta Lynn, whose self-management and songs like "You Ain't Woman Enough to Take My Man" have set her apart from the klatsch pack. Because compared to Anderson and Wynette, Rosanne Cash is an anarchist. She hasn't been as tolerant of her men, so when dessert is served and the old school's conversation on heartbreak shifts to sympathy for husbands with wandering eyes, Cash, from the new school, sings to a different tune. Lynn says, "You're My Man." Cash says, "Man Smart, Woman Smarter." Tammy says, "Stand By Your Man." Cash says, "Second to No One."

As its title suggests, *King's Record Shop*, with its sparse production (by Cash's husband of eight years, Rodney Crowell) and eclectic material, is like a leisurely browse through the new and used bins of a neighborhood record store. At least half the songs tell tales of strong women in trying relationships, but it's the anthemic opening track, "Rosie Strike Back," that sets the tone for the rest of the album.

A rallying cry for abused and battered women, "Rosie Strike Back" was written by Eliza Gilkyson, and features Patty Smyth and Steve Winwood on background vocals. To properly interpret the song, Cash drew from personal experience and the sheer power of the song itself. As a result, its authenticity is alarming; the effect is like eavesdropping on some advice doled out—in no uncertain terms—to a little sister from a big sister who's been there.

"There was a relationship I was in when I was a teenager when I felt like that," she says from the CBS Records office in Nashville, "where if I'd had the consciousness or awareness or had heard somebody say, 'You don't have to blame yourself for this, you can get out of this,' it might have made a difference then. And I'm sure that there's a lot of women who could use hearing that.

"Rodney's not the first man I've been involved with. I've known a few assholes in my time—you know, guys who have hated women or guys who used their ego to take physical advantage of women, just because they could. And that's a really ugly thing to do.

"I knew I was going to get mail about 'Rosie,'" she continues, "but what's amazing is that even before the record came out, I got a letter from a woman within the industry who had heard the record and said that she had been an abused woman in a marriage, and that 'Rosie' is gonna be her 'fight song.' It's just so moving to me to get that kind of feedback."

The video of "Rosie Strike Back" will be used as part of a national awareness campaign in October, which will attempt to bring the issue of domestic violence to the forefront and inform abused women of their rights and where to turn when in an abusive relationship. A toll-free number will be tagged on to the end of the video, letting women know that, as the song says, "There's people out there who can help you, you'll let them help you."

"I think it's real important," she says of her involvement with the campaign, "and I just hope it's part of some, you know . . . higher good. It's a really powerful song. I mean, as far as I can see, Eliza

Gilkyson got the definitive statement, musically, about talking to abused women. I might have been able to write a song like 'Rosie,' but probably not as well as her."

Only three of *King's Record Shop*'s compositions are Cash's. "If You Change Your Mind" was cowritten by Hank DeVito (who took the photograph that eventually became the *King's Record Shop* album cover) and was originally intended for the Everly Brothers. But when Crowell heard it, he insisted that Cash record it instead.

"The Real Me" is the record's centerpiece and, to date, the most intimate portrait of Cash as a survivor. She's battled cocaine and the fast lane, and, as evidenced by "The Real Me," is finally comfortable with the balance her music, marriage, and kids (seven-year-old Caitlin, five-year-old Chelsea, and Rodney's teenage daughter Hannah) bring her. It sounds like a song she's been wanting to write her entire life but held off until the time was right, until it was genuine. Until now.

"Definitely," she says of the assessment of her restraint and self-seasoning process. "It wasn't so much that I held off, but it was just that I didn't have the awareness that I needed to write it yet. That line 'I'm not a guard to hold your hand' was originally 'I'm not a nurse to hold your hand,' but I changed it. That kind of [message] about the roles women are expected to play—as caretakers and people-pleasers—and about what women are expected to do for men and how inappropriate that is, how self-denying it is. That type of song, though, is the kind of thing that the more you talk about it, the more it slips away."

Cash doesn't like talking about herself. She constantly wrestles with the inherent narcissism of her profession and usually balks when asked to decipher her songs. The bulk of her material has been loosely inspired by her relationship with Crowell—which, in song, has been a half-open, half-closed book. While her sometimes-story marriage has been well documented in her songs, she's reluctant to elaborate on the specifics. She says that what she pours out onto vinyl is sufficient, and she then draws the line, keeping the rest for herself and her family. Indeed, talking about herself and her songs are one and the same, and she's uncomfortable with discussing either subject.

"I don't, I hate it," she says, laughing at the charge. "The reason being is that it diminishes them rather than expands them. That's one of the whole problems I have with doing interviews. And after awhile, everything sounds so self-gratifying or something. The ego is very seductive, the outward part of it is. You get all this attention, and sometimes it gets out of proportion."

Ironically, the most revealing songs on *King's Record Shop* are the ones that Cash didn't write. There's the familiar all-or-nothing scenario of a relationship gone amok in John Stewart's "Runaway Train"; the intriguing double entendre, the female side of the story, in her version of Crowell's "I Don't Have to Crawl"; and the ghost of Patsy Cline nesting in John Hiatt's "The Way We Make a Broken Heart."

Unlike her own material, which she'll discuss grudgingly, other songwriters' material provides Cash with a fan's perspective first, and a singer/interpreter's slant second. She finds these songs easier to talk about, because she's got the safety net of distance. Emotionally, the trick is to choose material she feels comfortable with:

> If I've chosen correctly, then it's not hard to get into it. But if I've chosen too far outside of myself, then it's difficult, and it's an arduous process. But usually the reason I've chosen it is also the reason that I'm able to get inside it emotionally.
>
> On the new record, they all spoke to me; I didn't have to be convinced about any of 'em. Although "Tennessee Flat Top Box" [written by father Johnny] was Rodney's idea to do. I normally wouldn't have thought about doing something like that. But then the idea of doing a set piece, a period piece, really appealed to me. I was intrigued by the idea of a woman being the narrator of this song, like sitting at the side of the stage talking about the scenes that are unfolding. I tried to maintain a detached persona in it. I just really love that image, like how Rod Serling would come to the front of the screen in *Twilight Zone*.
>
> But the other stuff was more immediate, emotionally. Like "Rosie," that was just a really moving song when I first heard it, so that was instinctual, and so were the other ones. "Runaway Train" was real moving, when I first heard it, and also Benmont Tench's song "Why Don't You Quit Leaving Me Alone," and "I Don't Have to Crawl." That was natural because I'd been singing it for such a long time, and I'd always wanted to do it.

At thirty-two, she's got six LPs, two gold records, and a Grammy under her belt. She's a mother, writer of short stories, wife, reformed exercise junkie ("I hate aerobics, they're abusive"), songwriter, feminist, daughter of a country music legend; on top of it all, she has a not-so-secret ambition to be an actress. After all the accomplishments, the kids, and the acclaim, is Rosanne Cash happy?

"Yeah, I definitely am. But, you know, my concept of happiness is a lot different than it used to be. This whole thing that was written into our constitution—the pursuit of happiness—I think that tends to put it in the wrong perspective, like happiness is something outside of you that you have to pursue and attain, and once you have it, you hold on to it forever . . . rather than just accepting happiness as kind of an evolving state, one that can encompass things like grief and disappointment and sadness and anger. I think you can have all of those at the same time, and happiness is just a part of your emotional repertoire.

"I think of it as kind of a foundation, and then you have other stuff you go through that you learn from. I don't know if you *learn* that much from happiness. And I think to try and attain it as a kind of goal is kind of misdirected. I find it to be a byproduct of other things I try and achieve. But I don't know if happiness can be an everyday thing," she says with a laugh. "That would take a lot of stamina, wouldn't it?"

(September 1987, BuZZ magazine)

ELEVEN
PRINCE IN THE '90S

Emancipation

THE ARTIST FORMERLY KNOWN AS PRINCE believes in fate, which might explain the two fortune-cookie messages I got the week before I interviewed him. One read "A fool at forty is a fool indeed." The other, "Genius does what it must, and talent does what it can."

Both could be headlines for this story. Over the past three years, whenever I've requested an interview with Prince, he has said through his people—all of whom have since parted ways with him and his Chanhassen-based Paisley Park Studios—that he'd only talk when he was free from his contract with Warner Bros., his record label of the past seventeen years.

That day has finally arrived. Last month, ♀ inked a deal with the EMI–Capitol Records Group to distribute his albums on his own independent NPG label. And now that he's free at last, he's talking. In addition to last Tuesday's worldwide broadcast of the Paisley coming-out party for his three-CD set *Emancipation*, ♀ has done a handful of select interviews, for *Rolling Stone, USA Today,* and the *Oprah Winfrey Show.*

When I arrive at Paisley last Monday, a woman is laying gold carpet in the foyer, in anticipation of the following night's gala. A bodyguard who could be on loan from the Chicago Bears' front four meets me at the door and directs me to the front desk. The walls are covered with gold and platinum records, and a new paint job illustrates clouds on the stairwell leading up to the building's offices, and stars and planets on the ceiling.

The woman behind the front desk whispers to the bear, "Have you seen the Boss?" She disappears and, when she returns, tells me, "He'll be with you in a minute." A few minutes pass, and ♀ strolls into the lobby with a good-natured "Hey."

He's dressed in a sheer gray jumpsuit, draped with a black fishnet smock and several necklaces.

"The zodiac stuff was Mayte's idea," he says, referring to Mayte Garcia, the singer's wife since February 1995. "It had to be more colorful."

He leads me into a small cluttered room on the first floor, where an engineer is putting the finishing touches on "Betcha by Golly, Wow," the video for the first single from *Emancipation*. ♀ asks me if I have a tape recorder on me. I tell him that I brought one, just in case he's changed his practice of not allowing journalists to record his voice. "No way," he laughs. "Leave it in here."

The engineer cues up the clip, and ♀ is careful to let me know that it isn't finished—special effects of a rainbow and falling star will be matted in later today. And time is of the essence, for the video's world premiere on VH1, MTV, and BET is just thirty-three hours away. "I didn't have enough time," he says, "but I'm real proud of it."

We walk down a long corridor that houses several awards and is decorated with vintage Prince/♀ posters. I tell him the posters surprise me, since he has always been so tenacious about jettisoning his past.

"I never look at these," he responds. "They're just for the kids when they come in here." He takes me on a short tour of the studio, and into the huge soundstage room, where technicians and carpenters are busy putting together the set for the satellite simulcast of Tuesday's show.

He leads me into the control room of Studio B, where we settle into two swivel chairs behind the mammoth soundboard, which is decorated with two small decals of the symbol that is his new name.

"Where's that tape recorder?" he says, more teasing than accusing. I pull it out of my bag and ask him where he wants it.

"In there," he replies, and I put it in a small closet that contains some recording equipment.

"Any more?" he asks. A little insulted, I say that, no, I am not wired with a microphone and ask him if the no tape recorder rule stems from not wanting his voice out there.

"Yeah," he says. "I don't want it out there. You can call me paranoid, but . . . I mean, there's a picture disc of me back from '78 that's out there. You know, a kid tellin' stories."

The fact is, in his older age, ♀ has gotten better: there was a time when he wouldn't even allow journalists to use a pen and notepad. But when I ask him if that much is cool, he says, "Yes, yes—absolutely," and even provides me with a pencil.

Cradled on his lap is the only copy of *Emancipation* that exists in the world at this point (the set will be released Tuesday). "I carry it with me wherever I go," he says, tapping on the jewel case. "It's like my little buddy."

The rapport between us is instantly easy, which surprises me. Over the twenty years I've spent covering, listening to, and dancing to Prince/♀, I developed a theory about his reluctance toward granting interviews. I assumed he simply wasn't verbal and relied on his two main modes of communication—sex and music—to express his feelings.

Any interview, then, would likely consist of monosyllabic answers and cryptic asides. But the nearly two-hour interview proves to be exactly the contrary: he is very engaged, warm, smart, funny, deep, and extremely thoughtful.

His voice is not the slow, steady baritone of his stage banter, but an excited, animated burble. His eyes lock on mine whenever I ask him a question, and when answering he either looks directly at me, stares out into the recording room, or twirls around in his chair.

He responds to questions reflectively, confidently, curiously. The only other person I've been in a room with who exudes as much quiet energy and self-confidence is the cyclist Greg LeMond, who knew his body the way TAFKAP seems to know his muse and himself.

On the eve of what is arguably the biggest concert performance of his life, I ask him how much time we have.

"How 'bout three minutes?" he sighs, a million odds and ends obviously weighing on him. I open my notebook and hope for a little longer.

Q: Whenever the name change is ridiculed, I always tell people that there were segments of society who ridiculed Cassius Clay when he changed his name to Muhammad Ali. People change their names for religious reasons all the time, and for the most part people respect that. It seems strange, then, that people don't respect it when it happens for artistic reasons—and, in your case, religious reasons.

A: Spiritual reasons, yeah. When I changed my name, I think I may have changed it too soon, because right now I feel that my change is just complete. And it was a different reason from what everyone thinks it was.

The Warner Bros. thing had very little to do with it. When I started writing "Slave" on my face, I did it because I had become a slave to myself. We don't know how we get here.

I had to figure out my origins and where I'm headed. How did I want the story to end? And I started writing "Slave" on my face, because I felt like I was in a box spiritually, not creatively. You know, you can keep writing and writing, but that doesn't mean you're growing.

Q: Do you feel like you've grown spiritually?

A: Yeah. I don't think you ever stop growing spiritually, even if you feel like you have. But I had to do something. You know, R.E.M. can re-sign; I can re-sign; everybody can re-sign. But is that the way I want to progress? Can I take the route that I'm supposed to take? And during this time, I had to do the total recall, all the way back to '78 [when he made his first Warner Bros. record, *For You*] and before. And all these people out there started speculating: "He's upset with himself," "He's upset with life," or "He's a brat." But that's not why I used the word *Slave*. I was doing it as a reminder to myself.

It's a broad word. And by no means was I comparing myself to any people in any country—it's the concept of slavery. Look it up. And for me to write *Slave*, what does that say about my oppressor? Who became my oppressor? That's what telepathy's about—finding the truth. Warner Bros. isn't the enemy. A man is his own enemy. They couldn't stop this [*Emancipation*]. They couldn't stop anything.

I didn't know where I was going ten years ago, but now I know where I'm going to be three thousand years from now.

Q: And where is that?

A: That's a secret.

Q: You say Warner Bros. isn't the enemy. How do you feel about them now?

A: Had I not gone there, I wouldn't be here now. I love Warner Bros. now. I know everyone thinks I'm nuts when I say that, but I love everyone in my past. I love them now. They had to be there for me to get to where I am now.

You've got to love humanity. We're put here to save one another   and it's hard to swallow, sometimes.

Q: So the "Slave" thing was a way of reminding you that you had to find a way out of your spiritual box?

A: When I went through this—and everybody goes through this—I was searching. Everybody has a path to his higher self, and what I named myself was my [vision] of my higher self. You can picture a perfect self; you can see your dream. And my higher self aspired to this [*Emancipation*].

And I had to go through everything I went through to get to this. And it's hard, because you get up every morning and write *Slave* on your face . . .

Q: Was there ever a time where you thought, "All right, already. I'm over this. I'm just not going to do it today."

A: Nope! No, no, no! Because you're not free. You don't feel free.

Q: This reminds me of something I read in a meditation book once: your twenties are about experimenting with who you are, your thirties are about becoming who you want to be, and your forties are about taking that self-knowledge out into the world. I suppose it's kind of that "Life begins at forty" philosophy—that if you do the work now, the rest of your days here can be extremely fruitful and gratifying. Is *Emancipation* the first time you've been aware of that path to what you call your higher self?

A: I saw it very clearly during [the making of] *1999* [in 1983]. Everything goes by very quickly. You can see time. I'm hearing the sound of a future time, and I'm listening to it in a car.

You have to get that out of your head and onto the planet. After this [*Emancipation*], I don't feel the need [to make any more music] for a while. There won't be another record for a while. I feel like I could go to Hawaii and take a vacation.

Q: Have you ever felt that way before?

A: "When Doves Cry" and "Kiss." You go to a higher plane [of creativity] with that. They don't sound like anything else. "Kiss" doesn't sound like anything else. They aren't conscious efforts; you just have to get them out. They're gifts. Terence Trent D'Arby asked me where "Kiss" came from, and I have no idea. Nothing in it makes sense. Nothing! The hi-hat doesn't make sense.

Q: What has [pending] fatherhood meant to you, creatively?

A: I don't know if I know yet. What I do know is that it makes me conscious of, more than anything, education. The first time I saw a person of color in a book, the person was hung from a tree. That was my introduction to African American history in this country. And again, going back to doing the total recall that I did, I know that that experience set a fire in me to be free.

You know that song "Let It Be"? There's a lot of heaviness in that song. We should pay attention to that. If I was in charge of the government, I would make it mandatory that, at least once a year, we have a Chill Day—where everybody just kicked back and watched. Everybody's so caught up in [the rat race] that we never really sit back and watch.

Q: You, of all people, seem to be in need of a Chill Day. You're so prolific, it's like you're working all the time. Haven't you ever wanted to take some time off, like other artists do, to let the muse percolate a little bit?

A: I don't work that way. I am music. I feel music. When I walk around, I hear brand new things. You're almost cursed. You're not even [its maker]: you're just there to bring it forth. You know, "Can't I go to sleep?" No. You can't. But okay, now you can. And you go to sleep, and you don't hear it, and then you're lonely. No one wants to be on Earth alone.

Q: How do you feel about how you've been portrayed in the media?

A: If people would go back and read in the newspaper all the things that have been written about me that weren't true, they'd know, and they could judge things for themselves.

I don't know what happened. The media has lost control. It's got too much power. What do these people think? That they're never going to see me again? That they're not going to want to come out here and see me face to face, or want to get into one of [the gigs]? But it's all good. You see where I live. You see what it's like. There's nothing wrong—there's never been anything wrong. It's all our own destiny; we have the key to it.

Q: Which brings us back to our search for the higher self. What about people who have straight jobs, or who aren't as creative?

A: Jim, we're all creative. I'm creative with music. You're creative with your pen. The builders out there [working on the sound-stage] are creative with what they're building. Shoot, I couldn't do what they're doing. But if you go sit down with them and interview them, they'll lay some complex shit on you, and their work is very, very creative.

It takes everybody to do this. It even takes the person down the street to write the lies. It even takes *People* magazine, who said,

"We'll put you on the cover if we can have you, your wife, and your baby on it." Now. I have been a musician for twenty years. This is the best record I've ever made. You know: Kiss. My. Ass.

What time is it when people [value gossip more than art]? But again, that gives me something to talk to you about, and that gives us a joke that we can laugh about here today. It's all connected.

Q: How did the search for your higher self translate musically on *Emancipation*?

A: There's a song called "In This Bed I Scream." We laid a guitar down on the floor of the studio and just recorded it.

There was electricity in the room, and sound. It just depends on the energy coming out of the speakers and the feedback. And we just let the groove take it and built the song around the harmonics. You can hear the note, and you can watch the colors blur. And right there, rules are already broken.

You know, there was a guy, a long time ago, who figured out you can get medicine out of mold. Think about that. "I'm going to eat this ugly green and moldy thing, and it will make me well." Which is just one way of God saying, "Everything I put on Earth can take care of you." And if you turn your back on that, if you turn your back on God, you turn your back on everything.

Did you see the interview after the [Evander] Holyfield fight? They were asking him how he beat Mike Tyson. And he was sitting there with his hat on that said "Jesus Is Love." And they just kept asking [Holyfield], and he kept talking about God. That he beat Tyson because of his faith in God.

But they didn't want to hear it. They were going, "Yeah, yeah, yeah, let's get off this God stuff. How'd you beat him?" And he's saying, "I'm telling you: it was God." Now will you tell me, what's his last name?

Q: Holy. Field.

A: Thank you. We're all down here to help one another. My best friends and worst enemies have had the same last name. If someone loves you, they hate you. People think week to week. They don't think about the big expanse.

I'm aspiring to my higher self, and the name I chose for myself I wanted to represent freedom and truth and honesty.

q: Over the past few years, you've slowly retreated to Paisley, doing shows here, recording here, working here, and not venturing out for surprise gigs the way you used to, at First Avenue and Glam Slam. Even though the gigs here have usually been pretty remarkable, I sometimes got the vibe that you were a caged rat in here, with not a lot of options to play out anywhere else. Did you ever feel that way?

a: No. Not at all. Not to start something, but when people say about me that I live in a prison and don't go anywhere, it's just not true. I go to the store, I go to the video store, I go to ballets, movies, the park. I live like anybody else. But I play music every day.

Now, I ain't talking about musicians who make a record, do a tour, and then chill for eight, nine months. This is my job. This [soundboard] is my desk. If that's a prison, then everybody else going to work is in a prison, too.

If you talk to people who have money, they'll tell you that money can't buy happiness. But it does pave the way for the search.

q: What kind of advice would you give to that kid who started out doing this at [Minneapolis] Central High back in the '70s?

a: I could never give advice to myself. But I want to find out who the first person was who saw fit to sell music. Who came up with that concept? That's where the trouble started.

There's a bag of tricks [used by the music industry] that continue to work on people.

Take [R&B singer] D'Angelo. A very talented brother. Now, if I was a record executive, I'd do my best to get him to where I am now. Free. Letting it flow.

I just use D'Angelo as an example. But there's others. TLC—they're real nice people. What? When the record company gave them $75,000 and took $3 million, didn't they think TLC was gonna find out? Who's on the magazines and the Web sites and the records? Not the lawyers. Not the managers. Some artists need management. I don't. I can count.

And it all, always, comes back to God.

We are all down here to work toward one thing—love.

If I ain't got a ceiling over me, watch me fly. If I've got a ceiling over me, watch me rebel. You get enslaved to the bitterness. That's what the gangsta-rap game is all about. All those records are being sold, but they're trapped in their own bitterness.

Q: On the tip of everybody aspiring to their higher self, what do you hope for the future?

A: One day all artists will be able to be part of an alternative music-distribution setup, where there will be no limits. There will be no label president looking at his watch, saying, "Time's up! We need that record now." It's like with a painter. Would you ever say to a painter, "Oh, I'm sorry. We're running out of that color. You have to stop now."

If I was a journalist, I wouldn't write about something that wasn't positive. Like [Michael] Jordan. Phew. You can't criticize Jordan—ever. It's like Dre said [to a journalist]. You put some beats together. We'll sit here and wait. [He crosses his arms and taps his foot.] Can't do it? Okay, then take your pen and pad and get on down the road. [He bursts into laughter.] It's like with Jimmy [Jam] and Terry [Lewis]. They will never fall. They are the kings. I went to school with Jimmy. I know what he can do. He is a king. He is a king human being. And he is a good soul. Amen.

Oprah's another one. She's a queen. She was out here in the kitchen the other day. She's not like those other [talk-show hosts]. She has chosen the high road. She's all about [positivity], and where's Jenny Jones? She's on trial, isn't she? Oprah is a queen. A queen.

And it's people like that that just [inspire] me. I talked to a radio deejay recently who told me that he got into deejaying because of me. He wanted to play my music. And that just knocked me back.

It was very, very emotional. And it just made me want to go and make another whole record. I've said the words in the past, *Welcome to the dawn,* but I don't even know if I knew what they meant. Now I do.

It's the dawn of consciousness. If we all aspire to our higher selves, think of where it could go: universal knowledge. There. That's it. We'll end it on the highest note imaginable.

(November 17–18, 1996, St. Paul Pioneer Press)

Give Up the Funk

TO PROMOTE HIS JAM OF THE YEAR TOUR, which visits Target Center this week, the artist formerly known as Prince is granting interviews—via fax.

So I whipped up thirty-two questions—including a couple about the long-awaited, long-delayed, mail-order-only release of his massive new compilation, *Crystal Ball*, and its companion acoustic album *The Truth*—and faxed them off to his offices in Paisley Park in Chanhassen, where this week the Artist has been busy recording Chaka Khan and Larry Graham—two old-school funkateers who have served as opening act for many of the Jam tour dates.

What he faxed back is the following (answering twenty-one of thirty-two), verbatim, complete with computer graphic–generated eye-icons for the word *I*, numbers for words, and other cryptic characters that the pop world has come to associate with the one-and-only Artist:

1. Where are you doing this interview? What time is it?

   👁*'m in my skin. It's ten minutes 2 Armageddon.*

2. I talked to a lot of your fans who were standing in line for tickets at the Target Center the other day, and several wanted to know when *Crystal Ball* will be out. What stage is it at? When will it be available?

   It is being pressed. By Xmas, shipping will start. It is well worth the wait.

3. When you're not on the road, do you spend a lot of time on your computer? What kind of a computer do you have?

   👁 *have a Compaq given 2 me by some friends at Microsoft.*

Because of my work with Larry & Chaka, ● haven't had much time recently 4 anything other than funk.

4. Who or what inspires you these days?

   My constant source of inspiration is God.

5. The Jam of the Year tour has been getting great reviews. You come from an old school of musicians who grew up valuing live performance. Not a lot of bands bring it like you do. Do you sense that people are starved for the sort of real spontaneity and fan-musician connection that you provide?

   They're definitely starved, and ● am the chef!

6. For you, what is the biggest difference between performing live now and when you were touring nonstop in the '80s?

   Nothing. As 1999 approaches—many of my songs become more relevant.

7. Most of the time after an arena concert, you'll perform at a late-night aftershow at a club. Where do you get all the energy?

   Same answer as #4.

8. What are you reading at the moment?

   The Bible.

9. Have you ever felt like you've repeated yourself, musically?

   Of all the ?s! ●'ve written over a thousand melodies, so if ● have—no big deal! :)

10. You're always attempting to challenge yourself in different ways. You never coast; you're always pushing. Where does that drive come from?

    Same answer as #7.

11. What is the longest time away from the studio/guitar/stage you've ever spent? How did it feel?

👁've blanked out such memories. 👁've had 2 enter Studio Rehab two times in ten years. Change the subject.

12. These days, you're functioning like an independent label owner. You've expressed your admiration for people like Eddie Vedder and Ani DiFranco. Who else do you admire, business-wise?

Michael Jordan.

13. Now that you're also an independent tour promoter, do you find that being more involved with that takes time and energy away from your creativity?

Here's how U promote a concert—take out an ad in the paper, call the radio stations and give them the ticket price & the date, then just show up. How much energy is required for that? Yet another Rock 'n' Roll myth.

14. "Circle of Amour" from *The Truth* mentions four friends from your old high school, Minneapolis Central. Who are they, and what inspired you to write a song about them?

Are you trying 2 get me in2 a lawsuit? It's a fictional story!

15. I went to your high school reunion last year and talked to a couple of your old teachers. Bea Hasselmann, who was the music teacher at Central, said, "In my opinion, that '71–'81 Central was the most peacefully integrated school in the history of the state. I don't know what happened." To me, that speaks to a lot of what your music has always been about—freedom, racial harmony, positivity, and pride. Your old teachers spoke wistfully about those days, since in many ways we've gone backward as a society. Does that bother you, as well? And do your years at Central continue to inspire you to write about race?

The state of race relations affects me more than ever now that ❂ run my own affairs. Londell McMillan—my attorney—is involved in a lawsuit where a record executive made a remark that went something like this—"If we (meaning the music industry) didn't hire people with criminal records, there would be no Blacks in the music business." Hmmm.

16. Of all of the bands you've had, what has been your favorite to play with, in terms of generating live heat?

    ❂ don't set foot onstage unless it's hot. ❂'m not a judge.

17. After a long period of never playing Prince material, you're back to performing old stuff—even "Purple Rain." How does that feel now?

    Like home. These songs r like my children and ❂ love every one of them.

18. Most members of the "other side" of the Minneapolis Sound, from Soul Asylum's Dave Pirner, the Replacements' Paul Westerberg, and Trip Shakespeare/Semisonic's Dan Wilson, have acknowledged your influence on them over the years, but you've never commented on how that part of the Minneapolis Sound impacted you. Did it? Have you paid attention to that stuff over the years?

    Same answer as #10.

19. You tend to fire people, and/or people come and go pretty regularly. How does that feel, karma-wise? Does it bother you that you have a number of people out there who you were once close to, but to whom you now never speak?

    My address is the same. They just never show up. The people who pay return visits r the ones who really love me, not the pretenders.

20. Any chance that you'll perform at First Avenue anytime soon?

If they ask, ◉'d be glad 2.

21. What are five songs you wish you'd written?

> ◉ *did write them—"Sign o' the Times," "Gold," "Purple Rain," "Little Red Corvette," "The Holy River."*

(December 10, 1997, St. Paul Pioneer Press)

Everyday People

WHEN CHANHASSEN'S FOUNDING FATHERS established the Minneapolis suburb in 1852, they christened their little hamlet on the prairie with a name derived from *Chanhassan,* the Dakota Indian word for "the tree with sweet sap." Chanhassen's first settlers were farmers and railroad workers. Little did they know that some 150 years later, their great-grandchildren's neighbors would be two pioneers of funk.

Chanhassen's most famous funk father is Prince, who has based his musical and business operations out of his Paisley Park Studios there since the '80s. The newest resident is fifty-one-year-old bassist/singer Larry Graham, who, along with his wife of twenty-three years, Tina, and their fifteen-year-old daughter, Latia, moved into a modest modern bungalow near Paisley Park two weeks ago. And while Prince is now known as the Artist Formerly Known as Prince, it is no exaggeration to designate Graham as the Man Who Invented Funk.

"A lot of people have said that. All I can say is, 'Thank you,'" says Graham, a warm, gentle man who greeted his visitor with a handshake and a bear hug. The equally genial Tina sits at his side on a plush leather love seat, nodding enthusiastically at the assertion that her husband's distinctive bass playing, which first funked the world with Sly and the Family Stone in the late '60s, is the seminal ingredient that launched funk.

Even if the Man Who Invented Funk won't come out and say as much, the Grahams' lushly carpeted basement says otherwise. A pool table sits in the middle of the room, flanked by a bank of keyboards, speakers, a giant TV and stereo system, and the sort of wall decorations that would make drooling fools out of the curators of the new Hard Rock Cafe rumored to be opening on Hennepin Avenue in Minneapolis later this year.

An oil portrait of a Sly-era Graham, an awfully '70s painting of cartoon dancers doing the Freddy to his band, Graham Central

Station, adorns the wall, along with a framed concert photograph of an enraptured Graham clad in his trademark sailor suit ("I've just always loved boats," he says of his inspiration for the stage garb). And there are the gold records from his days with Sly: "Dance to the Music," "Everyday People," "Thank You (Falettinme Be Mice Elf Agin)," "Hot Fun in the Summertime," as well as the classic 1971 Sly album *There's a Riot Goin' On,* and Graham's solo smash from 1980, *One in a Million You.*

Surrounded by all this, the Man Who Invented Funk sits on a stool to have his picture taken. Tina excuses herself to go out in the backyard hothouse to pick fresh vegetables with the Artist's wife, Mayte, who has stopped by to gather greens to "make a salad for my honey." The CD player shuffles the three latest releases from the Artist's NPG Records label: Graham's *GCS2000*; former Rufus diva Chaka Khan's first album in six years, *Come to My House*; and a new album by the Artist, *New Power Soul*—all of which Graham says will be released early this summer.

As the booming, bass-heavy mix fills the room, *Pioneer Press* photographer John Doman sets up his equipment. Graham cradles his bass guitar. The fingers on his left hand probe the fret board absentmindedly, while his right hand, guided by a ring finger festooned with a band that spells out *Graham* in diamonds, tickles the strings. Instinctively, Graham's wrist pivots back and forth, and his thumb (its most prominent feature: a nail so long it could belong to a supermodel or a vampire) bends back with the elasticity of a small Slinky.

He lightly slaps the instrument's top two strings.

It happens only briefly, then Graham goes back to the business of posing. But it is a moment loaded with musical history, and so intimate: it is the equivalent of Bo Diddley giving a private lesson on the Bo Diddley beat, or having Elvis Presley explain, one on one, how he came up with his hip swivel. Graham calls it "thumpin' and pluckin'," but the most widely used term for what he does is *slap bass.* It is a style familiar to every post-Vietnam musician who has ever picked up an electric bass guitar.

It has influenced countless players, including Kool and the Gang, Bootsy Collins, and Prince, and has been sampled by a legion of hip-hop acts over the past two decades. And the man who came up with it never wanted to.

"I was a guitar player!" says Graham. "When I was fifteen, my mother, who played piano and sang, and I started playing clubs together. I was playing guitar, and we had a drummer. Then the drummer left, and I went out and rented a St. George bass.

"So it was just piano and bass. And to make up for not having the bass drum, I would thump the strings with my thumb. To make up for not having that backbeat, I'd pluck the strings with my fingers. Not thinking I was creating some new style, I was; I was just trying to do my job. Trying to get paid, you know? The good thing was, because I was not planning on staying with the bass, I did not care about playing 'correctly,' so to speak: the overhand, two-fingered style."

Graham was born in Beaumont, Texas, and moved to Oakland, California, when he was three years old. He started his career as a dancer, and played drums, clarinet, and saxophone in his high school band. He made his first record when he was thirteen with his band, the Five Riffs. In the mid-'60s, he hooked up with Sly Stone (née Sylvester Stewart), a disc jockey and producer in the Bay Area. In the late '60s and early '70s, Sly and the Family Stone served as a pop Petri dish that wed psychedelia with rock, gave birth to funk, and celebrated peace, love, black, white, and togetherness.

"Our first record was okay, but our second, 'Dance to the Music,' was when everything started to happen," says Graham. "And because I had guitar in my heart, I wasn't afraid to experiment with things like fuzztones [guitar pedals and effects], even though they weren't making things like that for bass players yet."

Along with the group's firey live shows (their performance of "I Want to Take You Higher" at Woodstock is widely regarded as the highlight of that festival), Sly gained a reputation for being unreliable and missed twenty-six of the group's scheduled eighty gigs in 1970. Drug use was widely reported, and Graham left the band in 1972 to form Graham Central Station. The same year, he met Tina, whom he married in 1975.

"She was an airline stewardess, and she used to braid everybody in the band's hair. And that takes eight hours to do! So we spent a lot of time together, and we talked about God and things," says Graham, who, at the end of the interview, gives his visitors signed copies of *Knowledge That Leads to Everlasting Life,* a Jehovah's Witness Bible-study book.

"My wife and I have been married for twenty-three years now, and I've only been away from her twice for two twenty-four-hour periods," he says. "If you see me, you see my wife and daughter. I love having my family with me, and they love me. Whenever I've traveled, I've always taken them. Even when my daughter was tiny, she was at all the recording sessions. I mean, my wife was breastfeeding and singing backup vocals. That's just the way it is. It's a blessing. Families should be together as much as they can."

The Grahams spent the past seven years in Jamaica, from where Larry worked as a session player and/or toured with the likes of the Crusaders, Carlos Santana, Aretha Franklin, Stanley Clarke, and Stanley Jordan. Last year, the Artist (whom Graham met once in 1975 when both musicians were recording for Warner Bros.) recruited Larry for one of his legendary postconcert jams in Nashville. That night led to Graham Central Station opening for several of the Artist's Jam of the Year tour dates, and to the Grahams' relocation to Chanhassen.

Ever since his "Purple Rain" days, Prince has tried to give back to his childhood heroes. He resuscitated George Clinton's career, attempted to do the same with Mavis Staples, and has now forged a similar mutual admiration society with Graham and Khan. The trio performed at the recent taping of the Essence Awards '98, which will be broadcast May 21 on the Fox network (WFTC-TV, Channel 29).

Until then, funk fans can catch the Man Who Invented Funk Friday nights–Saturday mornings at Paisley Park, where Graham Central Station and the New Power Generation have been holding regular late-night jams that often go until sun up. But like funk itself, the scheduling of such gigs is all about feeling.

"It's an interchange between hearts," says Graham. "We love what we do, and we love to share it. And it just happens. Like right now, I don't know if we're going to play this Friday or not. I don't know if anybody knows. I don't know if it matters."

These days, Chanhassen is home to several companies, including one whose marquee on Highway 5 reads "Experience is a guide post, not a hitching post." It could be the philosophy of a motivational seminar–innoculated businessperson, or a still-hungry founding father of funk. Back at his new home, as Graham hugs his visitors good-bye and raves about his wonderful, friendly neighbors in Minnesota, the voice coming out of the stereo speakers is also his.

Over an unmistakable, prototypical slapping bass line, it sings, "I don't wanna be worshipped, I don't wanna be no star. I just wanna play funky music, I just wanna play guitar."

(April 19, 1998, St. Paul Pioneer Press)

I Wish U Heaven

ON JANUARY TWENTY-FIRST, I stood at Paisley Park, watching Prince breeze through his brilliant one-night-only piano and a microphone show. Over the course of two hours, the Minneapolis-born music genius made like his hero Mozart, singing and playing his heart out, bouncing giddily up from the piano bench, dancing, strutting, and rocking—all without the power or safety net of one of his legendary funk 'n' roll bands.

"This is the first time I've done a concert alone, ever," the pink silk–clad little love god told the crowd of about a thousand. "And you're here the first night. Congrats to both of us."

To be sure, I felt lucky to be there that night, the last night I saw him live, as I did so often over the past four decades, bearing witness in small clubs and big arenas to the legend and legacy of Minneapolis's favorite son who put Uptown on the map as some utopian neighborhood where "black, white, Puerto Rican" all got along. As was often the case with Prince, the piano and microphone show felt like the beginning of yet another exciting new chapter in his storied career, another new incarnation for an artist whose changeling ways came to him as naturally as the change of seasons come to his beloved Mother Earth.

That night, just twelve short weeks ago, Prince was so spry, so ageless, he could've been that kid I first saw playing pickup basketball at Martin Luther King Jr. Park in 1975, or the first time I saw him live, with his *Dirty Mind*–era band at Sam's in 1981. At Paisley in January, with a massive Afro and a yogi's body so limber it was obviously imbued by the music that has flowed through it since birth, he looked like he'd outlive everyone in the room, and the world.

On a rainy Thursday in Minnesota, with KMOJ and the Current devoting their playlists to Prince, and as word spread around the globe that Minnesota's most beloved export had shuffled off his funky mortal coil, the main feeling I and most everyone around these parts registered was a deep gratitude for having resided in the same orbit as one Prince Rogers Nelson; for rubbing elbows with him at one time or another; for seeing him in concert or at the record store, the movie theater, at Paisley, First Avenue, or just making dinner or love to the music of His Royal Badness, as writer Martin Keller so perfectly anointed him in the '80s.

"He was ours," went Thursday's refrain on social media, over and over again, and the rest of the world will have to forgive our provincial grieving at least for the moment, because Minneapolis and Prince were joined at the hip, now and forever.

As a music fan, it was surreal and thrilling to bear witness to Prince's ascent in the '80s. My friend Chrissie Dunlap at First Avenue would always alert me to the last-minute shows he'd stage with his *Purple Rain* and *Sign o' the Times* bands, spoiling me for live music forever, and introducing me to that rare and raw electric exchange between band and audience that happens with a world-class funk band.

From then on, I was hooked, catching Prince every chance I could: in 1981 at an amazing free-form jam the night after the *Controversy* tour stopped at Met Center; in 1983 at the Minnesota Dance Theater performance at First Avenue where much of *Purple Rain* was recorded; in 1984 the week *Purple Rain* was released; in 1987 at a warm-up for the *Sign o' the Times* tour; at Glam Slam in 1990 working out material for *Graffiti Bridge,* and on and on and on . . .

As a music reporter for *City Pages* and the St. Paul *Pioneer Press,* it was thrilling to spend late nights at Erotic City, Glam Slam, and Paisley Park with him, chronicling an era that, incredibly, seemed to be happening well under the radar. In 1994, after I wrote about all these new songs he and his New Power Generation band were coming up with, he asked me to write the liner notes to his terrific 1995 album *The Gold Experience,* and what I wrote then reminds me of Prince's penchant for alternative spirituality and serves as some sort of balm on this stunningly sad day:

> Above all, Prince wants it known that this is a record about the fight for freedom—personal, artistic, political—but anyone with half an ear can suss that much out. During the making of it, he

was enamored with Betty Eadie's book *Embraced by the Light*, a first-person narrative on near-death experience, and that theme also peppers the record, most explicitly on the reincarnation dream "Dolphin." It is also implicit on several other tracks that ponder birth, death, life, and rebirth, and one man's own expectations and perceptions of himself.

More than anything, throughout my own *Gold* experience, I heard a unique, and uniquely potent, mix of purpose, celebration, and fear. There is a palpable sense of urgency here, as if Prince knows that time is running out for all of us to make connections with ourselves and the outside world. Don't believe me? Listen to the scream in the middle of "Endorphinmachine" or the guitar solo on "Gold" that concludes the album. The two things they share are desperation and liberation. Listen. Cue 'em up, back to back. Hear it? He isn't showing off; he's searching. Again. And like never before.

That was Prince, throughout his career, and that's what we mourn today—the loss of an eternal seeker, which all great artists are at heart. Over the years, I was also lucky to have had a few conversations with him, and he was regularly brilliant, funny, warm, wise, and wonderfully self-contained. His smile was mischievous and miraculous, and at the moment I'm finding it hard to believe we'll never see it flash again.

We'll also miss his worldview, and his wisdom. This is from an in-person interview I did with him for the *Pioneer Press* in November 1996, on the eve of his *Emancipation* record release:

Q: What has [pending] fatherhood meant to you, creatively?

A: I don't know if I know yet. What I do know is that it makes me conscious of, more than anything, education. The first time I saw a person of color in a book, the person was hung from a tree. That was my introduction to African American history in this country. And again, going back to doing the total recall that I did, I know that that experience set a fire in me to be free.

You know that song "Let It Be"? There's a lot of heaviness in that song. We should pay attention to that. If I was in charge of the government, I would make it mandatory that, at least once a year, we have a Chill Day—where everybody just kicked back and watched. Everybody's so caught up in [the rat race] that we never really sit back and watch.

Q: You, of all people, seem to be in need of a Chill Day. You're so prolific, it's like you're working all the time. Haven't you ever wanted to take some time off, like other artists do, to let the muse percolate a little bit?

A: I don't work that way. I am music. I feel music. When I walk around, I hear brand new things. You're almost cursed. You're not even [its maker]: you're just there to bring it forth. You know, "Can't I go to sleep?" No. You can't. But okay, now you can. And you go to sleep, and you don't hear it, and then you're lonely. No one wants to be on Earth alone. . . .

. . . And it all, always, comes back to God. We are all down here to work toward one thing—love.

Thanks, Prince, wherever you are. I was crying when I wrote this, so sue me if I went too fast.

(April 21, 2016, Minnpost.com)

My Minneapolis

Local heroes: The Belfast Cowboys bring the euphoria to the Lake Harriet Bandshell on June 24.

Lake effect

TWELVE
MIX #5
FLOAT ON

Bittersweet Symphony

FACEBOOK HAS GONE CRAZY with an exercise in which users pen twenty-five things about themselves. It's the sort of narcissism that non-Facebook users cite when dismissing Facebook, but I've learned intimate, deep, and entertaining things about friends and strangers and, thus, all of humanity. I'll take the bait:

1. I turned fifty years old on Monday.

2. I've never had a cavity, but my old band has a star on the side of First Avenue.

3. The morning of my fiftieth birthday, I watched the new Woody Allen film about a Spanish artist and the three gorgeous women who love him. By the end of the film I felt sorry for the dude and had an urge to call my boys and play Texas Hold 'Em.

4. I love Minneapolis.

5. My sister sent me a box of chocolates for my birthday, which I cracked after the movie.

6. Perhaps the truest thing I've ever sung is, "I'm a million different people from one day to the next" (The Verve).

7. I put the lid back on the box of chocolates and put it on the table.

8. I write—stories, essays, songs, books—out of something novelist Pearl S. Buck said: "The truly creative mind in any field is no more than this: A human creature born abnormally, inhumanely sensitive. To them a touch is a blow, a sound is a noise, a misfortune is a tragedy, a joy is an ecstasy, a friend is a lover, a lover is a god, and failure is death. Add to this cruelly delicate organism the overpowering necessity to create, create, create—so that without the creating of music or poetry or books or buildings or something of meaning, their very breath is cut off. They must create, must pour out creation. By some strange, unknown, inward urgency they are not really alive unless they are creating."

9. My birthday dinner was peasant's pasta, salad, and chocolate.

10. I was going to save this for the end, but when you get to be my age, you realize you might be running out of time, so just in case I don't have the chance again, I would like to say Thank you, Minneapolis. For everything.

11. After dinner, my son and I went to coach my daughter's fourth-grade basketball team, the Lynnhurst Flying Squirrels, who lived up to their name during the ninety-minute practice/freakfest. By the end, I was feeling sorry for myself and had an urge to call my boys and play Texas Hold 'Em. In Vegas.

12. When I was five, I was a Junior Commodore in the Minneapolis Aquatennial. I rode on floats and did my best to wave at the paradegoers but wasn't very good at it. Still, I'm pretty sure tooling through the lit-up streets of

downtown Minneapolis during the Torchlight Parade is why the City of Lakes has such a romantic pull on me to this day.

13. At around 10 P.M. on my fiftieth birthday, I went down to the basement—my man cave—and listened to demos of some new songs.

14. There's a reader of the *Southwest Journal* who hangs up flyers around town and writes unsigned letters to the editor complaining about the paper's "liberal bias," often citing yours truly as the main culprit. There's another reader who thinks I'm sexist because I write about women. I wonder what they do for fun?

15. Blissed out in the basement, reading Raymond Carver, hearing the dog's toenails click-clacking on the kitchen tile above me. Weird.

16. Helen Thomas gave me a journalism award once. Not for this column.

17. At two in the morning, my wife alerted me to the fact that my dog is throwing up and that all the chocolates are gone and that dogs can die from eating chocolate.

18. My grandparents came straight off the boat from Ireland and worked themselves to the bone. Sometimes I think I'm tough but not like that.

19. After I got everyone back in bed and settled down, the dog threw up a chocolate lake next to my computer.

20. I talk to strangers all the time because I love a good story and the details of the human condition in any form. Large men in bars, however, will sometimes want to kill you for doing this: "Why? Are you writing a book?"

21. I put the dog in the car and drove to the Emergency Vet clinic in Apple Valley, which at 3 A.M. in February feels like the moon.

22. I play basketball three times a week and will do so until I croak.

23. I talked to my dog during the half-hour drive, made sure he was okay, and the vet gave him fluids and activated charcoal and we were on our way.

24. My parents and all six of my siblings are still alive. And kicking.

25. As I walked out of the vet's office at four in the morning, she and the rest of the staff wished me a happy birthday, and that it was.

(February 6, 2010, Southwest Journal)

Danny Boy

"DO YOU HAVE A PLACE LIKE THIS where you're from?"

Cousin Adrien, sober as a judge as far as I could tell, was on his fifteenth pint of the day when he asked me that. His wife, cousin Marie, was at his elbow, and when they talked, the sound of their chirping sixtysomething Irish brogues was prettier than many singers I've heard.

They were standing in the heart of the Blackhill Comrades club in Blackhill, England, which last week I was lucky enough to visit and fall in love with—which happens to me a lot, in case you hadn't noticed. I went there with my mom, my sister, my brother-in-law, my three nephews, and my niece. None of us will ever be the same.

You need to hear about this place, luvs.

It is not far from New Castle, England, whose claims to fame are New Castle Brown Ale and unemployment. Blackhill is much smaller. I suppose it would be considered uncool by every ugly American standard, but at the moment I can't think of a richer town. After spending three days there, my sister, a cardiologist, said of Blackhillians, a few of whom hadn't met an American until last week, "They don't care about what you do."

She was right: they care about who you are. They don't judge; they listen. And when they do, they've got these b.s. detectors attached to their eyes that look straight into your soul and can suss out if you're all right or not.

I think we passed the test, and if they will have me, I am going back to Blackhill someday, because those people taught me something. Reminded me of something. Like, for just one example, that there may be no more beautiful sound in the world than a roomful of lost fighting souls singing, spontaneously, sadly and thoroughly unselfconsciously, along with an Irish lass named Elizabeth O'Connor to "the pipes, the pipes are calling" part of "Danny Boy."

I have never been able to hear that song and not think about what so many Irish musicians/purists I've known think about it (sentimental dreck), but after last week, I will never be able to hear it and not think of Blackhill.

That's where my grandfather, Roland Hanna, came from. His family moved from Ireland to Blackhill, where he worked fourteen-hour days in the coal mines until he was twenty-two. He moved to the Twin Cities in 1913 and never talked to his family in England again.

He married Rose Hanna (née Mullen), whose family came from Ireland and landed near Edinburgh, Scotland. She also moved to the Twin Cities in 1913 and worked at the old Nicollet Hotel, which was torn down years ago so you can't go see where my grandmother worked twelve-hour days and raised six kids with the help of her shipping clerk husband, who instead of saying "good-bye" to his loved ones always wished them "safe home."

In Blackhill, they still know something about hard work and simple pleasures and trust. They know each other's stories, secrets, and histories; they are like boyfriends and girlfriends and brothers and sisters all at once; the town itself is so enchanting it is like *Local Hero, Billy Elliot,* or *The Full Monty* come to life, but few Blackhillians I asked have seen those films because they've been too busy living them.

Most of all, they know each other's names. Names like "The Roaring Hannas," which is how my Irish-English relatives have referred to themselves for decades. Names like Uncle Peter, a font of British history and a gent with an inbred superhuman generosity and a knack for cutting to the quick of a situation with such conversational poetry as, "He's had more women than hot meals."

Names like my cousin Catherine, an angel of a woman who made this family reunion happen via telephone and e-mail and a transcontinental leap of faith. She works as a nurse three days a week; her husband, Trevor, works in a factory and as secretary of the town's soccer club. Their daughter's name is Hope. A couple of days after we returned to Minnesota, Catherine wrote to say that our departure affected the town like "a death in the family," and the funeral has been mutual.

Names like Suzie and Robert Hanna, an amazing fiddler–guitarist wife–husband team who led the ceili band that played at the Comrades club party where we drank lagers and met people like Kerry, a dark-haired Irish beauty with mischievous eyes and a devilish smile who reminded me of every Regina and Derham girl that my friends and I ever lusted after in high school. Apparently my aunts Cath and Mary picked up on this, too, because the next day Cath said, "Stay away from those brunettes in Scotland," as we left our home-away-from-home to catch the train to Edinburgh.

We didn't turn up much information on my grandmother there, but amid the magnificent chaos of the Edinburgh Fringe Fest, I visited the Writers' Museum. Outside the building, I took a picture of a brick festooned with a quote that summed up a week of family trees and newfound history: "Go back far enough and all humankind are cousins. —Naomi Mitchison (1897–1999)."

A few days earlier at the pub, cousin Adrien told me, "This part of England is renowned for its camaraderie, its friendliness. People talk to you when you walk down the road. I don't know what it's like in America, but if you came in here alone, someone would come up and say, 'Would you like a drink?'

"We may be in the backwoods as far as a lot of people are concerned, but we know what it's about."

He was standing near a sign that said, "Absolutely No Foul Language Allowed In This Club." He was flush from winning a big dominoes pot. He was smoking a pipe that smelled like sweet burning leaves and contentment. He had just finished telling me about when the steelworks closed down in 1980, and seven thousand men in Blackhill went on the dole, formed support groups, drank, bonded, survived, died.

Then he asked me his question, the one about if I had a place like this where I'm from—to which, despite the fact that I've spent most of my life searching for and occasionally finding it, I had no good answer.

(August 22, 2001, St. Paul Pioneer Press)

How to Fight Loneliness

THERE IS A RITUAL that Jeff Tweedy follows every day he is on tour. His band, Wilco, finishes a show in one town or another. After the applause dies down, the band climbs onto the bus. Hundreds of miles down the road, they pull into another town, where they check into a hotel. When Tweedy hits the sack, and when he wakes up the next day, for a few minutes he doesn't know where he is.

He climbs out of bed and finds the bathroom. He turns on the water and eases himself into the tub. There, in what may be his lone moment of peace for the day, he thinks of his wife and son back home in Chicago, and the nomadic existence his life has become. And begins to sob.

"I almost make a point of crying or something every day," says Tweedy. "Just trying not to bottle it up as much—not feeling sorry for yourself, but knowing that you're gonna feel better if you just let it out. I know that if I don't let it out, it manifests itself in a weird stage persona. But if I do, it lets me focus a little bit clearer on playing well."

To people who have never been on a stage, life on the road undoubtedly seems like one nonstop party, characterized by endless sing-alongs of Willie Nelson's "On the Road Again." But there is another—darker—side of touring that Tweedy not-so-jokingly refers to as "post-gig depression."

It comes after two hours or so of love has been showered upon the performer, only to have the plug pulled abruptly, coldly, with the artist being left alone again, unnaturally. "You can't describe that" to people who have never been through it, says Michelle Leon, the former bassist for Babes in Toyland, whose struggle with touring was one of the reasons she quit the critically acclaimed Minneapolis group.

But several musicians tried: "It's sort of like being the only person at the party without a date," says New York singer/songwriter Brenda Kahn. "You want to avoid your hotel room, because it can become a holding cell," says former Prince & the Revolution drummer Michael Bland. "It's a total loss of perspective," says Jennifer Finch, former bassist for the veteran Los Angeles punk-metal band L7.

And Dan Wilson, singer/guitarist for Minneapolis rockers Semisonic, adds, "Once in awhile, the rushing around and the loud music and the constant jostling against your band and crew and fans suddenly stop.

"I've had the worst feelings of loneliness in single hotel rooms at three or four in the morning after a show. All the hubbub and sound and praise are gone, and it feels like all the air's been sucked out of the room. It's too late to call anybody on the phone. For me, those are the really hard moments of loneliness."

Before dismissing this as yet another bunch of celebrities complaining about their lot in life, it should be noted that every musician interviewed for this story expressed a wariness about talking about the subject of loneliness on the road, for fear their comments would be construed as the gripings of spoiled brats. But the fact is, a performer's version of such solitude is more acute than that experienced by, say, traveling businessmen and businesswomen.

"I think that anyone whose career involves putting a lot of themself out on the line, ultimately there is a letdown," Finch says. "It's probably the same for people who work in an office, who've just completed a big project, too. But it complicates it when you're on a stage, and there's a very short, very intense connection with people."

Tweedy: "For the most part, I don't like to whine about it, because as hard as it can be to deal with, it's still a pretty charmed life. It's a very cool thing to get to play music for a living. But at the same time . . ."

The constant all-or-nothing tug-of-war between feelings of elation and isolation can take its toll. There have been thousands of songs written about that struggle, and over the years performers have done most anything to relieve the pain.

The cliché is that the best way to extend the warm feeling of a performance is through groupies, drugs, or drink, "anything to kill that loneliness, because it's just horrible," says Leon. "It's a killer. You're unhealthy, and hung over, and you're tired."

Tweedy has his daily cry, and he calls his wife, son, and parents every day. Bland and Kahn find refuge in their music. Wilson schedules time to read, and to write letters and songs. And Hoboken, New Jersey–based singer/songwriter Kate Jacobs writes in her journal and makes sure she has a good book on hand—solitary activities that she'd pursue at home anyway—and turns inward.

Of course, there are other ways to deal with it.

"My boyfriend isn't a musician, and it's very hard to explain what it's like to someone who hasn't been on the road," Jacobs says. "It's a different world, and I find that after ten days or two weeks, I start to be not present to the person I'm calling back home. Sometimes after a phone conversation, I feel even more isolated than before. It's amazing how quickly those ties get. . . . Nothing really happens to them, but they do get a little bit looser."

Which was the main reason Leon left Babes in Toyland, after spending five years touring the world. Some days, she'd spend eight hours in a van and ninety minutes onstage. Often, the intervals between the two experiences, when she was left to find ways to kill time, were the hardest part of her day.

"We were in Canada once, and we were staying at someone's house," she says. "It was in a residential neighborhood, so there was nothing to do but wander up and down the street, or go sit back at the bar where we were playing that night. I remember I went to a pay phone and called everyone I knew back home, and nobody was home. I kept getting answering machines. I was just miserable, and there was so much time like that."

"For me," says Finch, "the worst was when I knew there was some crisis, or a milestone with my family or friends. And I'd call, and there'd be no one around. I'd feel so helpless. At one point, my sister-in-law passed away, and we were in Finland right before Christmas. And every second, I was trying to call home, and that feeling of being detached and not able to be a part of it was awful."

In addition to feelings of disconnection, touring musicians constantly find themselves in a peculiar hurry-up-and-wait mode, racing from gig to hotel to the road to sound check to (repeat chorus). In between, there are vast amounts of downtime, and a constant blur of new places and people, which, no matter how friendly, can intensify the loneliness.

"All of these people are seeing you for the first time in months, if not the first time ever," says Wilson. "So you end up kind of struggling not to have the same conversations day in and day out with a constantly changing cast of faces. It's like being permanently stuck in that tell-your-life-story phase in the first month of the school year. I'm not saying I haven't met some pretty wonderful people on the road, but the overall effect is kind of numbing."

"When you get offstage, someone offers to let you stay at their house, and you're really tired," says Kahn. "You've already played four nights in a row, and you really don't want to be entertained. And people want to entertain you: take you out somewhere, probe you, know about you, and kind of be like you, maybe. It's really strange. You don't want to be rude, but the best thing they could do for you is say, 'Hey, man, here's the room.'"

Which is exactly what Bill Kubeczko tries to do. As director of the Cedar Cultural Center in Minneapolis, Kubeczko keeps his distance when he senses touring musicians visiting the Cedar are in need of space. He opens up the Cedar's offices for artists to make personal phone calls.

And in addition to privacy, Kubeczko attempts to personalize the backstage "riders," a sort of wish list of the performers' food and beverage needs. Because of rock stars' legendary extravagances, riders have become perhaps the most ridiculed element of the rock 'n' roll tour machinery. But according to Kubeczko, riders serve a specific purpose: capturing a small slice of something familiar for a beat-up soul far away from home.

"They're absurd, but I think that riders make artists' time on the road a little more humane," he says. "And I try to learn what people like, beyond what's just on the rider. It just makes life a little bit more sane, like, 'Oh, someone knows that bit about me that makes me welcome in this town.' Then it can be more like going to visit a friend, as opposed to 'doing a gig.'"

Be that as it may, the loneliness of the long-distance rocker can become so deeply rooted that not even a favorite food or special bottle of liquor can help. And sometimes, the one thing that most performers turn to in times of loneliness—the community of the other musicians—can make them feel like strangers in a strange band.

"You think there should be this closeness between you and your bandmates, but it's not there, because everyone is off doing their own things," Leon says.

"As I get older," says Jacobs, "I feel more isolated from the people I'm traveling with—maybe because ties at home are more important, or your family or something at home is a little more substantial, or you leave more of yourself at home. It's like you're a band of gypsies or something. Road camaraderie is what it is, but it can still leave you feeling alone."

Many of the musicians interviewed for this story actually wondered if *loneliness* is the correct word to describe their road experience. Most talked more about the change in personality that occurs, as a defense mechanism for dealing with their abrupt change in lifestyle.

And both Wilson and Tweedy put one side of their personality on hold, in order that another side could function. Indeed, over the past year, two of the hardest-touring bands in show business have been Semisonic and Wilco, both of which logged more months on the road than at home in 1996.

"When we've brought friends or family on tour in the past," says Wilson, "they'll often say afterward, 'How can you stand to sit there with each other for hundreds of miles and not say a word?' To a visitor, it sounds like *Waiting for Godot* or something, with those endless pauses between sentences. It's because on tour you learn how not to rub each other the wrong way; you turn the volume knob on your personality down to two or three."

"It's like the real you is kind of alienated," says Tweedy. "For me, I miss my dad side. You do get a lot of affection—not necessarily physical affection, but love and attention thrown at you. It's borderline adulation. But it's really a pretty empty thing. [But] you really look forward to the hour-and-a-half to two hours that you're gonna be onstage."

Which, of course, is the reason why they all endure the long trips, bad food, and crazed schedules. And after that time onstage, as many of these musicians pointed out, hitting the road after a gig—good or bad—isn't always a drag, but a quietly invigorating experience.

"I think it's a great feeling," says local guitarist Steve Tibbetts. "It's a very sharp and lucid time. It's very good for winding up cable and racking up gear."

"It's a really good feeling, sometimes," says Kahn. "It's like a melancholy loneliness that just washes over you, and it's very powerful. I kind of like it. You're alone in the world, and it's almost like no one knows where you are, so you're free."

Many musicians talk about a perpetual grass-is-always-greener mentality that touring produces. When they're home, they pine for the road, and vice versa. As a result, some simply give in to one side or the other.

Bob Dylan has been on a continuing tour for much of the past five years, to the point where now, even when he plays a concert near his home of Los Angeles, he stays in a hotel—an extreme example of what can happen when the road becomes home.

"It's so hard to decompress after a tour," Tweedy says. "If you're in the middle of a tour and you get three days off, it's almost like you might as well not come home. It's kind of like being in battle, or something. You've got this core of friends that's really insulated. You depend on each other, and you know without saying it what's going on internally.

"But it's really hard to express once you get home—all the different road stories that happened, all the people you met during the shows, somehow you forget all of it. And it takes weeks for it to come back to the surface."

Of course, once a musician comes off tour, the relationship with the road doesn't end there. It is always looming in the distance, and beckoning to be nurtured, tested, one more time.

(January 12, 1997, St. Paul Pioneer Press)

She's So Heavy

ON THE NIGHT of December 8, 1980, Yoko Ono and John Lennon were returning home to the Dakota apartment building near New York's Central Park when gunman Mark David Chapman murdered the ex-Beatle.

A couple of hours later in Minneapolis, after hearing the news, Curtiss A got up onstage with Safety Last and Slim Dunlap at the 7th St. Entry to sing a few Beatles and Lennon songs.

Since then, Ono and Curt have been keeping the Lennon flame alive in their own ways. Ono has showcased Lennon's artwork, lyrics, and recordings, while Curt has staged his Lennon tribute every year around this time.

The two artists had never spoken to each other, but to commemorate the twentieth anniversary of Lennon's death on Friday, we thought it would be a good idea to get them on the phone together.

A good idea? On one hand, we have the woman who has been myopically painted as the reason the Beatles broke up. On the other, the local legend notorious for saying exactly what's on his mind ("When I met Chuck Berry, I asked him why he always plays with such shitty bands," Curt said before the interview) and for his status as one of America's great lost soul singers.

Why not? The call happened Sunday morning, November 26. Over the course of forty-five minutes, the two discussed Lennon's legacy, Elvis impersonators, and the simple fact that all our cells are connected.

Some excerpts:

WALSH: Good morning, Yoko. I have Curtiss A with us here. Curt, can you say "Hi"?

CURT: Hi, Yoko.

YOKO: Hi, dear.

CURT: She called me "dear"!

WALSH: The reason I wanted to get you two together on the phone this morning is that in your own ways, you've both been responsible for keeping John's flame alive. Yoko, Curt has been doing his tribute to John for twenty years.

The great thing about it is that it attracts some of the best musicians in town, and it really is a celebration of John's music that has retained his spirit and irreverence and message of peace and love unlike any other live music experience that I know of. You'd be amazed by it—seeing all these people in the same room, lifted up by John's music every year.

YOKO: That's great. That's so great.

WALSH: Curt, is there anything you'd like to add to that?

CURT: Yeah. A couple of days ago, when I found out I'd be speaking to you, I was sort of amazed. And I called up some friends to ask, "What do you think I should ask Yoko?" Because there's so many things one could ask. And one thing that I wondered about . . . I'm kind of nervous.

YOKO: It's okay, go ahead.

CURT: Okay, they said they'd read an article recently where you had mentioned that you weren't really that thrilled with people celebrating any John stuff on the 8th because, you know, of what happened and that you'd prefer that it be on his birthday.

YOKO: Right. I just think that's really weird, you know, to be celebrating. I mean, what's that?

CURT: Exactly. I don't know if I would call it a celebration. It's been called a tribute, and I guess that's true, because he wrote all the music and we're singing it because it touches us. . . .

And I just wanted you to know, too, there was this other weird thing. Me talking to you . . . . Like, you've heard of Elvis impersonators?

YOKO [dubiously]: Yes . . . ?

CURT: Well, I don't want this to be like an Elvis impersonator talking to Priscilla. [Yoko chuckles.] Because I'm not an impersonator. I was a kid, and I think that when you hear music as a child, that's new, and when you hear something as mind-blowing as the Beatles were, even in the beginning . . . . You know, rock bands didn't use the chords they used.

I know you've probably read all the books, and I know John has probably told you [adopts a Liverpool accent], "I'm a fuckin' genius!" [Yoko chuckles.] But to have such a visceral feeling, or an epiphany, and you have this feeling of "Wow. I'm really alive, and I'm experiencing this, and look, the whole world is, too."

WALSH: Yoko, have you heard of any other tributes to John?

YOKO: Well, yes. I think it's a worldwide phenomenon, in a way. As you know, in tribute to John, the John Lennon Museum was set up this year in Japan and also, in Cleveland, the Rock & Roll Hall of Fame and Museum is doing a tribute exhibition that's going to go on for six months. So there's a lot of big tributes as well, but small tributes from different countries for the birthday. And on December 8, there are many tributes in every country.

WALSH: Getting back to what Curt was talking about, the birthday versus December 8. Do you personally commemorate December 8 in any way?

YOKO: Yes, well, for me it's a day of remembrance . . . and it's a very different feeling from celebrating his birthday [October 9, 1940]. So for his birthday, because it happens to be Sean's [Ono and Lennon's son's] birthday as well, we really celebrate.

December 8 is a different story. I just stay in the Dakota, quietly, a lot of meditation, etc. And many people come to Strawberry Fields [in Central Park outside the Dakota] with candles and all that, and they like to sing John's songs and everything. But it's a very different feeling.

Sean and I put out a few candles in my bedroom window, just to say, "Hey, we're with you." And if it's a cold night—I don't know if I'll do it this year—sometimes I send hot chocolate or something down to Strawberry Fields. The point is to share.

WALSH: Would you ever come to Minneapolis to see Curt's tribute? [Curt and Yoko chuckle.]

YOKO [after a long explanation about how scientists have discovered through DNA testing that we are all connected by our cells]: On December 8, we're all united in spirit. Time and distance [are a] human creation, and cells react to each other, regardless of what we're thinking. So if you're doing this thing in Minneapolis, we're all joining. I'm doing this thing in New York, and you're connected. Regardless of what you're thinking, our cells are connected, because we're just one world, one people.

CURT: . . . I loved what you were saying about the cells and all that. I think that all the time. I'm one of those people who thinks that the sun exploded and it cooled, and I guess it was Joni Mitchell who said, "We're all stardust." That's true. We're all part of the same thing.

I'm gonna ask one question . . . you know, I was worried. I didn't know what I was going to say because I don't know you.

YOKO: You do know me as much as anybody else, John Lennon included. Would you say to John, "Well, actually, I don't know you"?

CURT: This is so funny. Somebody asked me once if I thought you broke up the Beatles. And I just thought that was the stupidest thing I ever heard because, enough already. For one thing, I don't know you personally, or any of those guys, so I couldn't really have an opinion. But I've been in bands and usually, in a band, they break up because . . .

YOKO: They break up.

CURT: They've been together too long, and it's musical, and there's so many people in the world to make music with. I mean, all the time [the Beatles] would bring other guys in. That's what I do [with the Lennon tribute]. I don't just have four guys up there. We start the beginning with four, and then I start bringing up other guitar players because I want to . . .

YOKO: You want to explore, you want to experiment.

CURT: Right. I have this friend, Dave Hill, and I asked him, "What would you ask Yoko?" And he didn't want to really ask anything. He just wanted me to say that he thought that you had freed John. He said that he thought you were the best thing that could have ever happened to Beatle John, because he was depressed, and all of a sudden . . .

To me, being in love is the best thing there is. When you're in love, you don't care about how horrible things are. I mean, you do, and you want to do something about it. You want to survive. You want to make life better if you're in love. And you guys, for years there, everyone was going, "Yeah. John and Yoko. That's love." You know [laughs sardonically], more than Dick [Richard Burton] and Liz [Elizabeth Taylor].

YOKO: It manifests as love, but I really think it has a lot to do with logical direction for survival. And when I say *survival,* that includes physical survival, but also mental survival, you know?

CURT: They go hand in hand.

WALSH: People have so much invested in John's music, in their memories and in their personal experiences, but those are all experienced individually. Curt's tribute every year allows everyone to be in the same room. And many times during the night, the room actually surges and almost levitates.

YOKO: That's beautiful. You know what it is? It's a very strange thing. Whenever people gather, it's an incredible power. The thing is, that's what you're doing, Curt. When you gather people, through music or singing, you're levitating those people to the highest platform, which is great.

WALSH: One year, it was thirty below, and the television newscasters were telling everyone to stay home. I got down to First Avenue, the club where it's held, and there were a thousand people rocking to John through Curt. The streets of Minneapolis were dead, except for that club and John's music. It was really amazing.

YOKO: It's a microcosm of the world, in a way, in the big picture of the universe. I think the universe itself responds to any healing. And that's what you're doing. And I'm very, very . . .

CURT: So it doesn't bug you? [Laughs.]

YOKO [chuckling]: No, it doesn't bug me.

CURT: Do you ever feel like . . . um, okay, you're an artist. And you were an artist before you met John. And actually, the way you do things, it's like this business sense. You're supersmart about getting someone's attention.

YOKO: I don't know what you mean about "supersmart about getting someone's attention."

CURT: What I mean is, you always hear this story [when John came into a London gallery that was showing Yoko's work], and he climbed up on the ladder [that was in one of her artworks]: you got his attention. And you got it in a different way. You didn't know you were going to get his attention.

YOKO: No, of course not.

CURT: When he put the magnifying glass up there, and it said "Yes" rather than "No."

YOKO: It wasn't that I got his attention: it was that John woke up. And that's different.

CURT: It could have been anyone, though. Who knows how many other people got up there and you changed their lives with that statement? I guess what I wanted to know was . . . . You're you, and you're not him. And so people always talk to you about him. Like, I do my own stuff. I don't do John all year. I spend about a month ahead of the time every year rehearsing, but I don't spend my whole artistic existence trying to do John's songs. Like, do you still feel the need to be artistic, or isn't it as visceral?

YOKO: I really think that every time that I'm expending energy, then I should be creative in how I expend my energy.

CURT: Well, you seem very likable, I'll tell you that. You seem nice. [Laughs.] See, I was afraid of being too gauche.

YOKO: I don't like you being so patronizing of me. Why would you say that I'm likable? Is it under that assumption that maybe I shouldn't be likable? I mean, you're likable, everybody's likable, Jim Walsh is likable, we all love each other. So what is this "You're very likable," like you're surprised?

CURT: Because I'm always scared to meet new people, I'll tell you that. That's my own problem.

YOKO: No, you're saying that because most people you think don't like me, and then you're protecting me, saying "She's really likable."

CURT: I've always thought that was mean, because they don't know you.

YOKO: It's their karma, and it's their loss. If I don't like something, then that's my loss. It's sad, because people want to undermine what happened. What happened between John and me was incredible. It was just like magic. It was like a miracle. It was a miracle. It was beyond us. And the thing is, I'm very thankful about that.

And the result of all the stuff that happened, it's beautiful, but I think it would be nice if people believed that, if, from the point of view of if you believe that such a thing could have happened, it could happen in your life, too. And I would like you to know that. That miracles could happen.

CURT: Well, I'm talking to you, and I never thought that would happen. When I heard I was gonna talk to you, I was just stunned, because I never thought that would happen.

You know, I only know you guys from . . . well, like you said, we all know everybody. But you read things, and I don't like reading things, because there's always two sides to every story. But when you hear the music and see the way you act, that's a whole different thing. To me, that's more real than other people's perceptions.

YOKO: We all know each other much more than what we think. Even people who are saying something like, "I love chocolate." We use the words *love* and *hate,* and it's just words. And I think that people who don't believe in miracles, or say they don't like me, actually are totally afraid that they know me so well. It's just words.

What I really think is, whenever you were thinking of John, I was there with you, probably. And whenever you've had this concert, I probably experienced it. And I'm very thankful to you for doing so.

CURT: Wow.

WALSH: Curt, is there anything else you'd like to ask?

CURT: I'm afraid of saying something else kind of stupid.

YOKO: You're not stupid. You're wise, Curt. I don't know if you know the extent of what you're doing and how important it is. I think you're just sort of led by your love for it. That's why you're doing these concerts. I mean, you're part of the healing process of the universe.

(December 4, 2000, St. Paul Pioneer Press)

Looking for the Northern Lights

CHRISTMAS NIGHT 2014, my brother Terry and I sat in the living room of his bachelor pad apartment overlooking Lake Harriet, listening to the final mixes of *The Upside to the Downslide* and taking in the frozen splendor of the beautiful body of water that's been a spiritual touchstone to us since we were kids. It'd been a roller coaster year for the both of us, a couple of fiftysomething Irish Minneapolitans traversing music, love, life, death, and everything in between, and now we were enjoying some postholiday chill time and feeling lucky to be alive.

We'd listened to most of the record when he went out to the porch to get a breath of the unseasonably warm winter air, leaving me alone for "Looking for the Northern Lights," a personal fave that's been a staple of the Cowboys' and St. Dominic's Trio's live shows, and which the band had been struggling to capture with a recording that did justice to the song's wanderlusty magic. When he came back in, I told my bro that people in this part of the world, where the search for the northern lights is a mystical right of passage, would be listening to it a hundred years from now.

That's how I feel about the bulk of this record, a document of one of the best and hardest-working bands in the world at the height of its powers, honed over the past decade at three-hour-long sets at Lee's Liquor Lounge and Whiskey Junction, and six years of their Tuesday night marathons at Nye's Polonaise Room. The "downslide" to it all in part is the news that Nye's is doomed to soon become luxury condos. The upside? A veteran songwriter whose time has come, a band whose members have never lost the romance of balancing day jobs with the four-times-a-week grind of hauling gear, late nights, and loud bars, and who obviously take great pride in delivering heroic sets made up of so many jubilant tunes that can now, finally, be heard outside clubland.

"We're just a rock band," goes the last song here, but don't be fooled. More than anything, *The Upside to the Downslide* is the sound of a bunch of guys playing together—really, truly *playing* together—and the product of hundreds of thousands of hours spent together in a mission of spreading joy and making lives better through rock 'n' roll. May all our downslides produce such upslides, and long may these killer Cowboys ride.

(January 10, 2015, liner notes for the Belfast Cowboys'
The Upside to the Downslide)

Harriet

THE TITLE TRACK to Terry Walsh and 2 A.M.'s 1995 record *Harriet* was a pensive ballad inspired by the beautiful body of water named for Harriet Lovejoy Leavenworth, a teacher, mother, and the wife of a Minnesota army man. It was written in 1988 and sung wistfully by my brother Terry, a struggling musician and lover at the time, as a hopeful message for all dreamers and as a promise to himself:

Oh, Harriet
One day I'll look into your face
You'll be the same old place
But I'll be a different man
The kids I played with on your shore
Have all grown up now
Don't want to play anymore
They look down on me
I'm still playing
But Harriet
One day I'll look into that face
All the bad memories will be erased
'Cause I'll be a different man

That one day came to unequivocal fruition in glorious fashion last Wednesday, as my brother's ten-year-old big band the Belfast Cowboys transformed Lake Harriet and its storied if often snoozy bandshell into what had to be the happiest place on the planet. With a glorious sunset on the horizon and a couple of thousand people gathered on the benches and lawn, the Cowboys conjoined every heart there with as memorable a performance that has ever graced that stage, including Barack "Amazing Grace" Obama's visit there last June.

"Welcome to the most beautiful place in the world," said my bro at the outset, to a smattering of knowing applause, and that it is and that it has never been more so, as the Cowboys ripped through a hundred-minute set of joyful noise. Much of the material was culled from their great new CD *The Upside to the Downslide* ("Hard Working and Poor," "Looking for the Northern Lights," "Rock Band"), along with old favorites ("Bike Ride on 35W"), and Van Morrison songs and other covers ("Your Love Keeps Lifting Me Higher and Higher," "Moondance," "Call Me Up in Dreamland," "Into the Mystic," "Days Like These," "You Make Me Feel So Free").

I spent the time walking the grounds with my dog, Zero, and visiting/dancing with friends, family, neighbors, and strangers. There were my brother's sons, wandering the joint like they owned it. There was my sister Molly and her daughter Sarah, grooving to the good energy and scarfing down Harriet's famously fabulous popcorn. There were our parents, holding down a row of family and friends. There was the entire Dunlap family, with our hero Slim listening and tearing up in his wheelchair a few feet away as the band tore it up on Slim's own tune "Busted Up."

There was my cousin Ann and her family, dancing and laughing just a few months after unspeakable tragedy. There was my daughter and her boyfriend, grooving to the horns and devouring ice cream cones on their first-anniversary date. There were old schoolmates, local musicians, seagulls, sailboats, and a palpable shared feeling of one-night-only abandon. Wow.

Bill Forsyth's *Local Hero* remains one of my all-time favorite films, a 1983 slo-mo charmer about a type-A oil company man who falls in love with the simple life via a small Scottish town and its star-strewn bay front. Since I first saw it, I've dreamed of being part of a scene like the one near the end of the film, where the town gathers for an Irish-Scottish church basement dance.

The roots and history of the place and its people positively drip off the celluloid, and while I've had several live music moments that have come close to it, Wednesday was it for me—and many others. Every day since the Cowboys killed it (somebody make a commemorative brick already), I've talked to people who were happy to be there, or wished they had been. For that tribal moment we have one man-kid, who now lives in an apartment overlooking Lake Harriet and who grew up biking, walking, and running around her shore, to thank:

But oh dear God if you gave me these dreams
To tease and not be fulfilled
You know I'd rather die today
I'd rather have you take me today
And when all these dreams
When they finally come true
I'll come back here and have a laugh or two
With you
Because the love between us
Harriet will never die
Aw, Harriet
One day I'll look into your face
You'll be the same old place
But I'll be a different man

(July 1, 2015, Southwest Journal)

If You Want to Sing Out, Sing Out

SUNDAY MORNING, my two brothers, nephew, and I are climbing into a rental van and going west. I'm leaving my beloved lifelong home of Minnesota and moving to California for a year, then coming back.

I'll be studying whatever I want at Stanford University, which awarded me a fellowship, which feels weird and wonderful. But I also feel the way a friend of mine who also recently moved to California ended his going-away e-mail: I miss you guys already.

I started at the *Pioneer Press* nine years ago. All the while, I've tried my best to follow the wisest writers' advice I've heard: write about what you love. That's what every good writing coach says, but no one ever told me why. Now I know.

If you write about what you love, you might get one of the best jobs in the world: writing about music for a newspaper. They actually will pay you to listen to music, and you will find yourself at all hours of the day and night trying to give them their money's worth, trying to put into words what you think and feel about something that makes you think and feel like nothing else.

Then, those words will be made to sing by some very talented editors, and they will be printed. While the city sleeps, they will come rolling off big conveyor belts just like in the movies. Then they'll go out the door and onto trucks and into people's lives.

Some mornings, when you've written something that says exactly what you mean to say about something you love, you'll find yourself in the laps of friends, families, and complete strangers, engaged in that intimate reader–writer connection that is unique to hold-it-in-your-hands newspapers.

On those mornings, the air changes. On those mornings, your out-of-body floats over the Midway to Minneapolis, the West Side to West Bloomington. On those mornings, you can imagine bus stops and doctors' offices and lake cabins and homeless shelters and Prince's boudoir and Jessica Lange's reading room and the YMCA sauna and the Clown Lounge, and you can actually feel people—the smart ones, anyway, the hometown newspaper readers—pausing, snickering, and grousing in all the right places.

On those mornings, it can feel like you've got a hit record playing on the radio and the whole town is singing along.

If you write about what you love, one day you might find yourself at a paper like this paper, which, as your old friend Jim told you when you started, "has a great reputation as a writers' newspaper."

You didn't know what that meant at the time, but after having worked with some great newspaper writers at this great writers' newspaper, now you do. They know as well as you do that if you write about what you love, you will, from time to time, be inspired and bored and wise and wimpy. At the very least, at the end of every day, you will hit your pillow knowing you've been true to the Emily Dickinson poem a reader sent you years ago:

Lad of Athens, faithful be
To Thyself,
And Mystery —
All the rest is Perjury —

If you pay attention to that—if you write about what you love and keep the clatter of the way others do it at bay—you will find yourself with a key to a secret world where race, class, and age sparkle and fade.

You will get letters and phone calls from teachers, ministers, painters, nurses, students, cops. They will speak to you in the language of real people, and most of them will tell you they're a lot like you: they love music and words, and they don't like having their news dumbed-down or sanitized for them.

If you write about what you love, you will get correspondence that will make you feel like a bartender at closing time or a priest in a confessional. The letters will tell you about the music they're listening to, which will lead them to telling you about their lives. They will thank you for writing about their band, favorite song, dead son, daughter, husband, wife, brother, sister, or friend, and you will be welcome.

You will feel like you owe them something, and you will. You will owe them to continue writing about what you love, to do whatever it takes to stay connected with what it is that first made you want to write about what you love.

In the end, if you write about what you love, you might get the opportunity to tell your loved ones how much you love them. You might get a chance to have some heart-to-hearts and kisses and good-byes. And if you're really lucky, you might get the chance to take a road trip with your brothers, during which time you plan to discuss that kick-ass band you've been talking about forming together, or at least make up idiotic names for it.

But before you go, you might find yourself thanking everyone who has read this far and telling them that you don't take for granted this thing you've shared, this thing that goes beyond "coverage" and "content" and "customer" and telling them that it has been a pleasure beyond words, so you'll end this one with a song.

The last time you heard it was the other night at Liquor Lyle's with you and your old friend Craig. You ran into your old friend Kate and her old friend Suzanne. The four of you grabbed a table by the pool tables, and you and Kate went to the jukebox and put on some Bowie and Stones and Jane's Addiction.

Craig got out his credit card and bought Leinies and Cuervo. You talked about September 11, heroes, firemen, marriage, media, music. Then you started singing.

You'd just discovered your mutual love for *Harold and Maude,* and Cat Stevens's words started trickling out of all of you, clumsily at first, a barbershop karaoke quartet without the teleprompter: "Well, if you want to sing out, sing out, and if you want to be free, be free. 'Cause there's a million things to be, you know that there are."

You stumbled, but then Craig picked you up, as he often has; Kate inspired you, as she often does; Suzanne took a drag off her cigarette and smiled at the three of you; and in your minds you all plucked banjos and did Harold's jig on the cliff and danced Maude's nose-thumbing, hand-clapping shimmy.

You were flush in the moment, eyes locked in on each other's, but you took a second to look up to see that the pool players had stopped their games and were watching, listening.

"If you want to be me, be me," you sang, at the top of your beery lungs, drowning out the jukebox, spreading the gospel. "And if you want to be you, be you. 'Cause there's a million things to be, you know that there are . . . It's easy, ah ah ah."

For a minute or longer, you sang, volume increasing with courage. From the front bar, hard faces turned soft and beamed your way. A couple of pool players rested their chins on their sticks and grinned. An ecstatic woman from the next table joined in.

You will never forget it. Any of it.

(August 2, 2002, St. Paul Pioneer Press)

ACKNOWLEDGMENTS

First and foremost, thanks and massive respect to all the musicians and artists whose ideas about life, music, and love fill this book, and to my kids, Henry and Helen, who inspire me every hour of every day.

Thanks to my agent, Michael Croy of Northstar Literary Agency, for having the idea for this book and suggesting I put this collection together in the first place, and to my editor, Erik Anderson, for his enthusiasm, smarts, and passion for good writing and music. Thanks to Daniel Ochsner, Laura Westlund, Emily Hamilton, Heather Skinner, Kristian Tvedten, and all the good folks at the University of Minnesota Press for believing in me as a writer and in this project. Special thanks to the cover designer, Michel Vrana, for making the book look so fantastic, and to Louisa Castner for the copyediting and good words of support.

Thanks to my editors: Sarah McKenzie, Susan Albright, Terri Sutton, Judith Lewis, Don Effenberger, Sue Campbell, Pat McMorrow, Jim Tarbox, Dan Heilman, Dylan Thomas, Tim Campbell, Jon Bream, Jim DeRogatis, Andrea Swensson, Kyle Mattson, David Carr, Brad Zellar, Dylan Hicks, Steve Perry, John Leland, Ann Powers, Craig Weisbard, Michael Tortorello, Amy Nelson, Tom Surowicz, Jim Meyer, David Brauer, Randall Findlay, Jennifer Vogel, David Adams, Julie Caniglia, Joseph Rydholm, Elizabeth Larson, Jeffrey Kastner, and Erik Lundegaard—inspiring collaborators, thinkers, and writers who have been at the other end of my work at one point or another over the years, and who make up an exacting and demanding hive mind that I continue to tap into, to this day.

Thanks to all my colleagues at the *Minnesota Daily,* the *Star Tribune,* the *Florida Times-Union, City Pages,* the St. Paul *Pioneer Press, Reveille,* Minnpost.com, and the *Southwest Journal.* Thanks and "Viva Sonoma!" to the Knights of California (Stanford Fellowship class of 2003–2004). Big thanks and love to Jean Heyer, who was always there for me as a sounding board, wife, and coparent. Thanks most of all to my parents, Ann and Jerry

Walsh, two voracious readers whose love for stories, books, and each other continues to inspire.

Special thanks to you, and to all the readers, who have shared in this intimate writer-to-reader relationship, especially my brothers, Jay and Terry, and my sisters, Minnow, Peggy, and Molly, and my extended family and electronic tribe and friends near and far. Thanks to everyone who has ever reached out over the years to say that something I wrote touched them or made them think or feel, or that I had described something that they could relate to.

Putting together a book like this feels a lot like an obituary, but I know in my bones that I have much more listening, writing, and singing to do, so I will finish with my favorite phrase these days:

More to come . . .

INDEX

Jim Walsh is an award-winning author, journalist, and songwriter from Minneapolis. A columnist for the *Southwest Journal,* his writing has appeared in *Rolling Stone,* the *Village Voice,* the St. Paul *Pioneer Press, City Pages,* Minnpost.com, and many other publications. He is the author of *The Replacements: All Over but the Shouting: An Oral History* and, with Dennis Pernu, *The Replacements: Waxed-up Hair and Painted Shoes: The Photographic History.* A teacher at the Loft Literary Center, he is the former leader of bands REMs, Laughing Stock, and the Mad Ripple, and he is the ringleader behind the singer/songwriter showcase the Mad Ripple Hootenanny.